PENNY DREADFULS AND THE GOTHIC

SERIES PREFACE

Gothic Literary Studies is dedicated to publishing groundbreaking scholarship on Gothic in literature and film. The Gothic, which has been subjected to a variety of critical and theoretical approaches, is a form which plays an important role in our understanding of literary, intellectual and cultural histories. The series seeks to promote challenging and innovative approaches to Gothic which question any aspect of the Gothic tradition or perceived critical orthodoxy. Volumes in the series explore how issues such as gender, religion, nation and sexuality have shaped our view of the Gothic tradition. Both academically rigorous and informed by the latest developments in critical theory, the series provides an important focus for scholarly developments in Gothic studies, literary studies, cultural studies and critical theory. The series will be of interest to students of all levels and to scholars and teachers of the Gothic and literary and cultural histories.

SERIES EDITORS
Andrew Smith, University of Sheffield
Benjamin F. Fisher, University of Mississippi

EDITORIAL BOARD
Kent Ljungquist, Worcester Polytechnic Institute Massachusetts
Richard Fusco, St Joseph's University, Philadelphia
David Punter, University of Bristol
Chris Baldick, University of London
Angela Wright, University of Sheffield
Jerrold E. Hogle, University of Arizona

For all titles in the Gothic Literary Studies series visit *www.uwp.co.uk*

Penny Dreadfuls and the Gothic
Investigations of
Pernicious Tales of Terror

edited by

Nicole C. Dittmer and Sophie Raine

UNIVERSITY OF WALES PRESS
2023

© The Contributors, 2023

All rights reserved. No part of this book may be reproduced in any material form (including photocopying or storing it in any medium by electronic means and whether or not transiently or incidentally to some other use of this publication) without the written permission of the copyright owner except in accordance with the provisions of the Copyright, Designs and Patents Act. Applications for the copyright owner's written permission to reproduce any part of this publication should be addressed to the University of Wales Press, University Registry, King Edward VII Avenue, Cardiff CF10 3NS.

www.uwp.co.uk

British Library Cataloguing-in-Publication Data
A catalogue record for this book is available from the British Library.

ISBN 978-1-78683-970-1
eISBN 978-1-78683-971-8

The rights of The Contributors to be identified as authors of this work have been asserted in accordance with sections 77 and 79 of the Copyright, Designs and Patents Act 1988.

Typeset by Marie Doherty
Printed by CPI Antony Rowe, Melksham, United Kingdom

Contents

Acknowledgements vii
Notes on Contributors ix
List of Figures and Illustrations xiii

1 Introduction: Dreadful Beginnings
  Nicole C. Dittmer and Sophie Raine 1

Section One: The Progression of Pennys; or, Adaptations and Legacies of the Dreadful

2 Penny Pinching: Reassessing the Gothic Canon through Nineteenth-century Reprinting
  Hannah-Freya Blake and Marie Léger-St-Jean 27

3 'As long as you are industrious, you will get on very well': Adapting *The String of Pearls*'s Economies of Horror
  Brontë Schiltz 47

4 'Your lot is wretched, old man': Anxieties of Industry, Empire, and England in George Reynolds's *Wagner, the Wehr-Wolf*
  Hannah Priest 65

Section Two: Victorian Medical Sciences and Penny Fiction; or, Dreadful Discourses of the Gothic

5   'Embalmed pestilence', 'intoxicating poisons': Rhetoric of Contamination, Contagion, and the Gothic Marginalisation of Penny Dreadfuls by their Contemporary Critics
    Manon Burz-Labrande   91

6   'A Tale of the Plague': Anti-medical Sentiment and Epidemic Disease in Early Victorian Popular Gothic Fiction
    Joseph Crawford   114

7   'Mistress of the Broomstick': Biology, Ecosemiotics and Monstrous Women in Wizard's *The Wild Witch of the Heath; or The Demon of the Glen*
    Nicole C. Dittmer   137

Section Three: Mode, Genre, and Style; or, Gothic Storytelling and Ideologies

8   A Highwayman and a Ventriloquist Walk into an Inn … Early Penny Romances and the Politics of Humour in *Jack Rann* and *Valentine Vaux*
    Celine Frohn   161

9   Gothic Ideology and Religious Politics in James Malcolm Rymer's Penny Fiction
    Rebecca Nesvet   180

10 'Muddling about among the dead': Found Manuscripts and Metafictional Storytelling in James Malcolm Rymer's *Newgate: A Romance*
    Sophie Raine   200

List of Referenced Penny Titles   221
Bibliography   223
Index   247

Acknowledgements

This edited collection is a celebration of the early to mid-Victorian penny serialisations and all of the inquisitive Gothicists who seek to explore and analyse the darker side of all but forgotten literature.

We would like to thank all of the contributors to this collection whose fresh and thoughtful researches signify a revival of these serialisations.

Finally, we would like to offer a special thank you to Chloé Germaine Buckley, without whom this collection might have never spawned from imagination to publication.

Notes on Contributors

Hannah-Freya Blake is a PhD candidate at Leeds Trinity University, studying the points at which horror and gender intersect to satirise societal norms. Her contribution to the forthcoming *Speaking Picture, Silent Text* edited by A. Alyal explores voyeurism in *The Monk* and *The Devil's Elixir* in a chapter titled, 'Ekphrasis and Ecstasy: The Visual Pleasure of Portraits in Lewis and Hoffmann'. A published poet and writer, her academic studies and creative projects align in her upcoming queer-Gothic novella, *Cake Craft*.

Manon Burz-Labrande is a doctoral researcher and lecturer at the University of Vienna, Austria. Specialising in Victorian popular literature and culture, her PhD focuses on the exploration of the concept of circulation in and of the penny bloods and penny dreadfuls, through a literary and cultural analysis of their literary content, the discourses they triggered in nineteenth-century criticism, their place in the Victorian literary landscape and their diachronic circulation. She has written articles and reviews for *Victorian Popular Fictions Journal*, *Polysèmes*, *Revenant Journal* and *Wilkie Collins Journal*, as well as entries for the *Palgrave Encyclopedia of Victorian Women's Writing* (ed. Lesa Scholl). She also co-edited the *Short Fiction in Theory & Practice* special issue 'More than Meets the Ear: Sound and Short Fiction' (with Sylvia Mieszkowski and Harald Freidl), and is the editor of the collection *Spectral Sounds: Unquiet Tales of Acoustic Weird* (British Library, 2022).

Joseph Crawford is a Senior Lecturer in English Literature at the University of Exeter. His published works include *Raising Milton's Ghost* (2011), *Gothic Fiction and the Invention of Terrorism* (2013), *The Twilight of the Gothic* (2014), and *Inspiration and Insanity in British*

Poetry, 1825–55 (2019). His current research deals with medical cultures in the early Victorian period.

Nicole C. Dittmer, PhD, is a Lecturer of Victorian Gothic Studies at The College of New Jersey, Proofreader and editorial board member at the *Studies in Gothic Fiction*, and advisory board member of *Ecocritical Theory and Practice* for Rowman & Littlefield's imprint, Lexington Books. Some of her works include 'Malignancy of Goneril: Nature's Powerful Warrior', published in *Global Perspectives on Eco-Aesthetics and Eco-Ethics: A Green Critique* (2020); the monograph, *Monstrous Women and Ecofeminism in the Victorian Gothic, 1837–1871* (2022); forthcoming British Library collection *Penny Bloods: Gothic Tales of Dangerous Women* (May 2023); the contribution 'Victorianism and Ecofeminist Literature' for *The Routledge Handbook of Ecofeminism and Literature* (2022) edited by Douglas Vakoch; and a chapter, '"the terror of the rustics"; or, Witches and Werewolves: Lunar and ecoGothic Monstrosities in Catherine Crowe's "A Story of a Weir-Wolf" (1846) and *The Nightside of Nature* (1847)' for Simon Bacon and Elana Gomel's forthcoming Palgrave Macmillan collection, *Lunar Gothic* (2024). She received her PhD in Gothic Studies from Manchester Metropolitan University where she researched penny publications, medical humanities, and ecocriticism in the nineteenth-century. Website: www.nicoledittmer.com. ORCID: https://orcid.org/0000-0001-6626-2888.

Celine Frohn is a PhD candidate at the University of Sheffield. Her thesis, 'Strange laughter: early penny bloods and humour' investigates the generic dimensions of penny bloods published between 1838 and 1850. She is also the founder and general editor of Nyx Publishing, an independent publisher of queer speculative fiction.

Marie Léger-St-Jean is a freelancer, a digital humanist and a proud independent scholar working on nineteenth-century transnational transmedia mass culture. She is the founder of and mastermind behind *Price One Penny*, a bibliographical and biographical database about the countless publishers and authors involved in the production of cheap literature in London from the 1830s to the 1850s. Her single-author and co-authored work appears in collections – *Media* *and Print Culture Consumption in Nineteenth-Century Britain* (2016), edited by P. R. Rooney and A. Gasperini, *Edward Lloyd and his World* (2019), edited by R. McWilliam and S. Lill, and *Reynolds Revisited* (forthcoming) edited by M. L. Shannon and J. Conary – and in special issues of *Amerikastudien/American Studies* on digital humanities (2018) and *Victorian Popular Fictions Journal* on piracy (forthcoming).

Rebecca Nesvet has written about James Malcolm Rymer and Victorian penny fiction for *Victorians Institute Journal*, *Nineteenth Century Studies*, *Victorian Popular Fictions Journal*, *Scholarly Editing*, *Notes and Queries*, *Victorians Institute Journal*, *Victorian Network* and the *BRANCH Collective* timeline. Her edition of Rymer's *A Mystery in Scarlet* is being published by the Collaborative Organization for Virtual Education (COVE) at *www.covecollective.org*.

Hannah Priest is an Associate Lecturer in English at Manchester Metropolitan University, and the editor of *She-Wolf: A Cultural History of Female Werewolves* (Manchester University Press). She has published numerous articles and chapters on popular culture and literature, with a focus on werewolves, horror and cross-period cultural history. Under the name Hannah Kate, she is a short story writer and radio presenter, and she is the editor-in-chief at Hic Dragones.

Sophie Raine is a PhD candidate at Lancaster University researching how 'other' spaces are constructed in the penny dreadfuls. Her published articles and chapters include 'Mapping the Metropolis through Streetwalking in Parker's *The Young Ladies of London*, in *Victorian Popular Fiction Journal* (2019) and 'Subterranean Spaces in the Penny Dreadful' in the *Palgrave Handbook of Steam Age Gothic* (2021). Sophie is also the peer review editor for the online journal *Victorian Network*.

Brontë Schiltz graduated from the Manchester Centre for Gothic Studies at Manchester Metropolitan University in 2020 with a Masters in English Studies: The Gothic, and is currently working as an independent researcher. Her research interests include the televisual Gothic, the queer Gothic and Marxist horror.

List of Figures and Illustrations

Figure 1: Timeline of Gothic novels in *The Romancist*, *Novelist's Library*, and the *Novel Newspaper*.   35

Figure 2: G. Rymer. 'Guy Fawkes, or, the Fifth of November'. From Rymer's *London Scenes*. 1834.   182

Figure 3: *The Ordeal by Touch*.   186

Figure 4: 'A Clerical Weathercock'.   193

1

Introduction: Dreadful Beginnings

NICOLE C. DITTMER
AND SOPHIE RAINE

Since the early days of the Victorian period the Gothic has intertwined itself through the pages of such literature as Frederick Marryat's *The Phantom Ship* (1839), Charlotte Brontë's *Jane Eyre* (1847), and Emily Brontë's *Wuthering Heights* (1847). These celebrated texts found a place within the drawing rooms of nineteenth-century homes where the Gothic became a source of enjoyable terror. While Victorian citizens, predominantly women, indulged in their fictional tales promising 'brooding Gothic villain[s]', women in distress, monstrosities, foreboding settings and structures, or supernatural events, the literacy rate in Britain was increasing.[1] As a literary genre that was becoming more acceptable amongst the masses, the Gothic's rise in popularity began to inform lower-class publications. This resulted in marketing demands for affordable and accessible publications that replicated middle-class novels and popular discourses, yet targeted working-class readers through serialised fiction. This demand resulted in affordable penny serials which would later be known as 'penny bloods' and 'penny dreadfuls' owing to their sensationalist narratives, often violent content, but perhaps most importantly, their threat to middle-class social norms.

Penny bloods, a name that Jarlath Killeen posits was used as a 'term of attack', and the subsequent identifier, penny dreadfuls, emerged out of a necessity for accessible literature and were the embodiments of cultural crises and conditions.[2] Originally, these cheap serials were referred to as 'penny bloods'; the term 'penny dreadful' has often been used by scholars to refer to these serials from the 1860s that were targeted at a more juvenile audience, which specialised often in boys' adventure tales of highwaymen and other heroes.[3] Though the terms 'penny blood' and 'penny dreadful' have been separated based on their audiences, many of the characteristics of the bloods continued into the 1860s. John Springhall, one of the most authoritative voices on penny dreadfuls, accredited this label as a 'derogatory' categorisation of the fictional periodicals for boys in the late Victorian period.[4] While the Gothic penny dreadfuls, infused with violence and sensationalism, declined in the 1860s, the transitory serialisations that emerged during this decade, filled with tales of adventure, mimicked the same trajectory as chapbooks by becoming papers for young boys and girls.[5] Following the transition targeting adolescent readers, the new wave of pennys eventually faded into obscurity during the early 1900s. This compendium, while acknowledging the distinction between 'bloods' and 'dreadfuls', specifically uses the term 'penny dreadful' as an overarching reference to encompass the cheap literature of the Victorian period from the 1830s to the 1860s that share notable characteristics: the methods of printing and publication, the amalgatory composition of cultural discourses, the target demographic and the narrative features of melodrama and sensation.

Famed for their scandalous content and supposed pernicious influence on young readership, it is little wonder why the Victorian penny dreadful was derided by critics and, in many cases, censored or banned. The morality of working-class literature was seen as a social concern, and many of the penny's critics vehemently argued that these texts were regarded as glamorising criminality and were to be blamed for youth delinquency (Springall, '"Pernicious Reading?"'). Further exploring this assumed literary crisis, Victor Shea, in his instalment, 'Penny Dreadfuls', in the *Encyclopedia of the Victorian Era* (2004), follows the trend of criminal influence and the social fear of penny publications.[6] While revisiting the characteristics and tropes of penny literature, Shea highlights how these emulations of more notable literary works were perceived as threats to the 'decent values' of the community because the young, and easily influenced, readers would align themselves with the criminal,

Introduction: Dreadful Beginnings

or rebellious protagonists (p. 186). Although published ten years later, Stefan Dziemianowicz's *Penny Dreadfuls: Sensational Tales of Terror* (2014) revisits the same explanations previously analysed by both Springhall and Shea, amongst many other penny scholars who are discussed throughout this collection. Advertised as an anthology about penny literature, Dziemianowicz's compilation, instead, showcases Gothic short stories and novels with a short introduction specifically about penny fictions. Cataloguing how these publications were used as 'crude escapist fiction', his text also stipulates how they were read for their shocking thrills and unrefined nature.[7]

While some of these penny texts, such as George W. M. Reynolds's *The Mysteries of London* (1844–8), James Malcolm Rymer's *Varney the Vampyre* (1845–7) and *The String of Pearls* (1846–7), and the anonymously authored *Spring-heel'd Jack, The Terror of London* (1864–7), are popularised and affiliated with the Gothic genre, many dreadfuls are obscured by these more notable texts.[8] In her discussion of the lesser penny texts, Hannah Priest contends that the popularity of Reynolds's own *The Mysteries of London* overshadowed his other novels: *Faust: A Romance* (1845–6) and *Wagner, the Wehr-Wolf* (1846–7), therefore limiting 'critical attention' and denying their contextual relationship to his other 'serialised novels'.[9] Seemingly, while there is an extensive catalogue of penny publications that range from the 1830s to the late 1860s, many scholars tend to deviate their analyses to these popular, well-trodden serialisations.

These serialised texts, published between the 1830s until their eventual decline in the 1860s, were enormously popular, particularly with working-class readers. As Judith Flanders has highlighted in *The Invention of Murder* (2011), for every publisher of 'respectable fiction', there were ten for penny fiction.[10] However, despite their evidential popularity, these texts have fallen into obscurity. This could be accounted for perhaps as due to their ephemeral nature, with many titles being lost or incomplete; alternatively this could be the effects of literary criticisms from writers such as Charles Dickens and James Greenwood overspilling into contemporary scholarship.

Neglecting these texts from Gothic literary criticism creates a vacuum of working-class Gothic texts which have, in many cases, cultural, literary and socio-political significance. This compilation, then, aims to redress this imbalance and critically assess these crucial works of literature. *Penny Dreadfuls and the Gothic* incorporates essays on these traditional penny titles produced by such prolific authors as James Malcolm Rymer, Thomas Peckett Prest, and George William MacArthur Reynolds; however, the objective of this collection is to bring the less researched, and forgotten texts from neglected authors into scholarly conversation with the Gothic tradition and their mainstream relations.

The Rise and Fall of Penny Publications

Since its inception in the eighteenth century, Gothic literature has been regarded by many as a lower literary form. As Christine Berthin puts it '[t]he gothic has always been a disparaged genre, right from its early days when the critical institution classified it as 'much despised low culture.'[11] When the Gothic novel began to decline in popularity in the 1820s, a new type of Gothic fiction was to take its place and satisfy the macabre appetite of the ever-increasing literate public. The Gothic's revival in popular fiction involved the emergence of the penny dreadful which was to become as popular with readers and loathed by critics as the Gothic novel. While there have been several scholarly resurgences about penny fiction, the dreadfuls still remain the neglected and bastardised offspring of Gothic novels and eighteenth- and nineteenth-century high literature. Their impact and influence in the Gothic literary market has typically been limited to analysis of readership, market trends and their perceived pernicious influence on the juvenile reader. Influential early work on penny fiction by E. S. Turner, for example, focuses on the cultural phenomenon of popular literary culture among the working classes due to increasing literacy rates in the mid-nineteenth century.[12] Following Turner, Louis James's seminal 1963 work *Fiction for the Working Man: A Story of the Literature Produced for the Working Class in Early Victorian Urban England, 1830–1850* likens these serialisations to a 'rehandling' of Gothic stories.[13] While James does not explicitly analyse the relationship of penny publications and the Gothic, he does acknowledge that the traditional 'Gothic type of story' had disseminated into

Introduction: Dreadful Beginnings

fragmented attributes and subsumed into serials by 'hack writers' (p. 77). These boundless and disproportionate tales of the supernatural and enhanced conflicts between the virtuous heroine and dark, brooding villain, James avers, were 'indicative' that the genre 'was no longer a living one', but a divarication of tropes into these vestigial serialisations (p. 77).

More recently, scholarship has focused on these penny serials with a view to re-evaluating them and asserting their relevance as significant social and political texts which can shape our understanding of mid-Victorian culture. Ian Haywood's *The Revolution in Popular Literature: Print, Politics and the People, 1790–1860* (2004) discusses penny serials in relation to Chartist fiction, thus revealing the political ideation behind texts that were previously dismissed as purely sensationalist or derivative in nature. Mary L. Shannon, in *Dickens, Reynolds, and Mayhew on Wellington Street: The Print Culture of a Victorian Street* (2016), also attests to the radical potential of the work of the prolific writer George W. M. Reynolds by analysing his political speeches alongside his immensely popular publication *The Mysteries of London* (1844–6). Furthermore, *Edward Lloyd and his World* (2019), an assemblage of essays by Rohan McWilliam and Sarah Louise Lill, examines the impact of the prolific penny publisher Edward Lloyd on the literary market in the Victorian period by exploring his legacy and the often radical sentiments professed in the cheap fiction he published. More recently, Rob Breton's *The Penny Politics of Victorian Popular Fiction* (2021) looks at the radical discourse in early penny texts and finds that many of these texts were targeting the politicised working-class reader through the incorporation of Chartist writings.

Although there has been ongoing, and consistent, scholarship of these literary serialisations that focus on such characteristics of discourse and language, the purpose for their creation, and necessity for rapid and excessive publication, the penny immersion in Gothic scholarship is inconsistent and not yet extensively analysed; an objective that this collection seeks to achieve. As one of the first sources to consider penny titles under a Gothic lens, Montague Summers's *The Gothic Quest: A History of the Gothic Novel* (1938) examines the origin of the inexpensive serials, the publication process and their target audience.[14] However, deviating from a singular focus of consumer demand and purpose for this literature, Summers instead highlights the relationship between the role of the Gothic novel and its influence on the emergence and evolution of early nineteenth-century penny tales. Expanding upon this research of Gothic literature, Summers's subsequent compilation, *A Gothic Bibliography* (1940), functions as an index of Gothic publications that incorporates bloods and dreadfuls throughout the nineteenth century, however, as Helen R. Smith posits, much of Summers's initial information is inconsistent and filled with 'inaccuracies'.[15]

As another of the first-wave scholars to initiate a Gothic revitalisation of penny publications, Michael Anglo, in *Penny Dreadfuls and other Victorian Horrors* (1977), explores the correlation between the publishers seeking fortune in the quick productions of the genre and their exploitative plagiarising of established Gothic tales.[16] As a precursory text to subsequent scholarly analyses of the corrupted penny dreadfuls, Anglo's exposition, following the theme of Summers's earlier research, specifically sets the stage for their incorporation of the Gothic mode and the public's fascination with these aspects of intertwined sensationalism, dark romances and crime. This publication purposely offers explicit details of Gothic romances and the societal obsession with immoral individuals and dreadful vicissitudes. While Anglo's *Dreadfuls* was a much-needed full source of information about such notable publications, it unfortunately did not gain enough traction to solidify the penny's placement in the Gothic genre, and therefore, once again, the dreadfuls dissipated into obscurity.

After a long period of critical neglect and sparse publications on the subject, there was a renewed interest in penny fiction, particularly the work of the best-selling penny writer George W. M. Reynolds at the end of the twentieth century. The influence of Reynolds on both the penny writers and in bringing the penny dreadful to the attention of contemporary scholars cannot be overestimated. This research included the seminal monograph on Gothic locales – *A Geography of Victorian Gothic Fiction* (1999) by Robert Mighall. In this work, Mighall dedicates a chapter examining the influence of the work of both Charles Dickens and Reynolds on the changing Gothic landscape. Mighall contends that 'Reynolds deploys an urban sublime, transposing the moral and aesthetic meanings of the traditional Gothic landscape – thickest forests, wildest heaths – to specific parts of the metropolis.'[17] Analysis of Reynolds's work is crucial in understanding the subgenre of urban Gothic due to the widespread popularity of his work and diverse readership. This work breaks new ground in evaluating a work of penny fiction alongside so-called 'high literature'. This publication expands upon the work of Mighall by incorporating a range of penny authors and their work to show the even wider influence of penny publications on the changing landscapes and styles of Gothic literature.

In recent years, scholarship has re-evaluated the penny dreadful in relation to the Gothic genre, rather than its publication process and impact in the market. Vicki Anderson, in her relatively newer text, *The Dime Novel in Children's Literature* (2005), dedicates a chapter to the Victorian penny dreadfuls. However, similar to the works of Shea and Pope, it treads the familiar territory that focuses on the differentiation between 'bloods' and 'dreadfuls', the publications of these corruptive tales and the vast network of publishers responsible for their circulation. Utilising a different approach, some modern scholars focus on the purpose or relevance of these penny dreadfuls and the society that informed their popularity. For instance, in 2007 Robert L. Mack published a comprehensive exposition, *The Wonderful and Surprising History of Sweeney Todd: The Life and Times of an Urban Legend*, that explores the origin of this iconic Gothic character and his legacy. Similarly, Rosalind Crone, in *Violent Victorians: Popular Entertainment in Nineteenth-Century London* (2012), draws attention to the correlation of the penny texts to the 'gruesome patronage' of England's working-class citizens.[18] Looking at such penny titles as Rymer's *The String of Pearls*, Crone explores how violent themes were 'used to attract and fulfil readers' while offering a literary exposition of early Victorian culture (p. 163). While Crone's study does include the popular tale of the Sweeney Todd figuration, she deviates from a singular focus to incorporate other nineteenth-century publications to explicitly illustrate how violence was embedded in Victorian culture and discourses.

Following the trend of Victorian culture and literary integration, Anna Gasperini, in her research on violence and violations of Victorian bodies, closely examines texts of the early penny blood genre to expose the nineteenth-century medical and legal influence. In *Nineteenth Century Popular Fiction, Medicine and Anatomy: The Victorian Penny Blood and the 1832 Anatomy Act* (2019), Gasperini characterises the penny blood genre as a colossal amalgamation of disjointed information, formed from real-world facts, events, and people into a literary monstrosity.[19] Drawing attention to the concept that penny serialisations are constructed from these societal concerns, Gasperini offers an approach to these fictional works that scrutinises 'medical rhetoric and language'.[20] The resurgence of interest in the penny dreadful as a legitimate literary form, as Gasperini asserts, should be investigated through the discursive intersectionality of working-class anxieties (illegal corpse harvesting), medical developments and parliamentary Acts established to promote scientific progressions, while deterring from illegal activity.

Since the nineteenth century, penny publications have faced the intrigue of critics and scholars, being intermittently revivified and neglected. While such notable individuals, as the ones previously discussed, infused life back into these underappreciated texts, the popularity of penny titles waxed and waned without a complete resurgence in the field of Gothic academia. Our edited collection offers a unique exposition of these Victorian publications with the hope of creating and maintaining a permanent place for penny dreadfuls in Gothic studies. This essential investigation of penny publications offers essays that explore these ephemeral and obscure texts in relevance to the Gothic mode and genre. Examining such issues of marginalisation, the environment, and contemporaneous cultural discourses in these neglected nineteenth-century publications, this collection will open an unexplored, and much- needed, avenue of Gothic studies.

The Ingredients of Cheap Serials

In the 1830s, the penny press was created for England's increasingly literate working-class citizens. Initially published in Edward Lloyd's *Penny Weekly Miscellany* magazine, pennys were coupled with advertisements promoting the latest fiction. As 'descendants' of broadsides and chapbooks, penny dreadfuls, according to Anderson, displaced these former publications by revivifying Gothic novels and integrating confluent themes of horror, 'supernatural terrors' and murder.[21] These publications were formatted for serialised weekly episodic releases; therefore authors wrote in eight-page segments, sometimes resulting in unfinished stories. Tales that fell short of popularity and success, would remain undeveloped, whereas stories that achieved a large audience had the potential to maintain publications. In these situations, penny titles would run for a significant time and produce several, and sometimes excessive, chapters. This prolonged serialisation entails attaching irrelevant information and, as Dziemianowicz posits, the penny authors 'resorted to a number of tricks' to create filler for the stories (p. ix). This padding includes such material as elongated and unnecessary history and back stories for the characters; varied plot deceptions that either dissipated or resulted in dead ends; or superfluous cursory dialogue. Authors also included twists as decoy villains and additional, and garrulous dialogue, to ensure length for publication. These strategies, when employed on even the best stories, sabotaged the writing and derailed the plot (Dziemianowicz, p. ix). Descending from various traditions, penny content was considered troublesome, a lower form of literature with the potential to influence susceptible Victorian citizenry. As unique products informed by varied material, the penny publications shared a symbiotic relationship to the *Newgate Calendar* and sensation novels, thereby adopting the contextual discourses that reflected morals of the middle class through criminal admissions of guilt.

The popularity of the tales is attributed to the influences of Gothic novels and tropes of supernatural horror transposed into familiar Victorian settings. Real-world issues such as 'moral disorder' and criminality were exaggerated and transformed into works of fiction, replete with 'all the hallmarks of Gothic melodrama' to appeal to the working-class imagination, while offering an 'imaginative escape' from everyday 'drudgery'.[22] Stacey McDowell argues that these escapist serialisations achieved popularity because they 'captured the Gothic seediness of the city' and blended familiar facts with supernatural and horrific fiction (p. 489). Penny serialisations amounted to literary amalgamations of traditional celebratory folk ballads whose protagonists are outlaws (ones such as Robinson Crusoe and Robin Hood were significant sources of inspiration), broadsides, which contain factual information about crimes and executions, late eighteenth-century Gothic fiction, respected children's literature that possess elements of adventure, and, later in the century, public school stories, from authors such as Thomas Hughes and F. W. Farrar (Shea, pp. 185–6). This coalescence of fact and fiction allowed criminality and Gothic monstrosities to be perceived as heroic and glamorous, thus adding to the already tumultuous discourses in Victorian society.

Penny publications shifted focus during the mid- to late Victorian period. Upon their appearance in the 1830s and through the 1850s, these popular publications were known as 'penny bloods' due to their often bloody and lurid subject matter. Later in the century, somewhere around the 1860s, these tales were rebranded to be marketed to a juvenile audience with different content, containing adventurous exploits and heroic male protagonists. This new form of fiction that became popular in England is suggested as the 'penny dreadful'.[23] These types of boys' adventure stories appeared alongside the traditional 'bloods' rather than entirely displacing them – hence our umbrella term of 'penny dreadfuls' throughout the collection. These new penny dreadfuls, like those of the bloods, possess sensational writing, adventurous themes, violent events, capricious characters, and situational morals. Their content is typically known for being 'sensationalistic, featuring detective stories, westerns, outlaws, bandits, villains, lost loves, damsels in distress, femme fatales and melodramatic plots, with many written in instalments with suspenseful ending chapters' (Anderson, p. 76).

Although offering stories of adventure and fantasy, they were harshly criticised for the display of perverse and immoral subject matter. This cheap 'penny' literature unsettled Victorian society. The change in these episodic tales, although still maintaining popularity with adult readers, targeted younger readers. Middle-class citizens, who perceived literature as a method of social improvement, saw these publications as a threat to morality and values (McDowell, p. 490). They argued that the 'hero' protagonists who presented rebelliousness and violence would promote criminality and delinquency in working-class children. While falling decades short of what Robert Fraser calls Victorian quest romances, these penny tales, likened to Fraser's romances, are 'products of the mid-Victorian age'.[24] Similar to the quest narrative, penny serials indulge in the decadent masculine experience, while incorporating the varied anxieties of British society. Offering 'monstrous' figurations to scare the masses, this cheap material unsettled Victorian society. While not explicitly quest romances, nor fully Gothic, these texts offer patchwork characteristics which incorporate such tropes and stereotypes as the madwoman, the vampire, the werewolf and the dark romantic villain. Likening their content to that of high literature, 'penny' serialisations joined the social conversation through exploitations of Gothic tropes.

The Gothic Inspiration for 'Penny Packets of Poison'

The declining popularity of the Gothic novel in the 1820s gave rise to what Franz J. Potter refers to as 'trade' Gothic, where popular hackwriters produced Gothic texts due to its marketability, rather than for the sake of art (p. 5). While not explicitly focused on the mid-century penny bloods and dreadfuls, Potter's recent publication, *Gothic Chapbooks, Bluebooks and Shilling Shockers, 1797–1830* (2021), explores the chapbook, its origins, authors and publishers to offer a new correlation between these pamphlets and the Gothic. As 'cheap' productions, chapbooks were the bastardised eighteenth-century publications of the Gothic genre and preludes to the penny dreadfuls of the nineteenth century. This criticism and separation of canonical Gothic and trade Gothic is one which persisted throughout the mid-Victorian period as Gothic flourished and took on new forms through bluebooks, chapbooks and, later, the penny dreadful. David Punter in *The Literature of Terror* (1996) states:

> popular writers in the genre appear to have become increasingly able to turn out a formulaic product in a matter of weeks, and the eventual decline in Gothic's popularity was clearly at least partially to do with a flooding of the market, and also with the way in which the hold of the early Gothic masters tended to stultify originality.[25]

It is perhaps due to this market saturation that penny serials needed to ensure they were keeping up with the latest literary trends and ensuring their tales were invigorating and sensational enough to keep the attention of their readership. This is evident in the way that penny titles were abandoned mid-narrative if they proved to be unpopular. One of the ways the penny publishers and writers tried to ensure this popularity was by harking back to the 'Gothic masters' of the eighteenth century such as Matthew Lewis and Ann Radcliffe. These penny titles explored archaic, historic Europe, set in remote castles, monasteries and convents, and include texts such as *The Black Monk; or, The Secret of the Grey Turret* (1844) by James Malcolm Rymer or the anonymously authored *The Heiress, or, The Mysteries of Brandon Abbey* (1842). Rather than repackaging the same texts for a nineteenth-century readership, the penny serials were often modified, adapted and rewritten to encompass a range of social, political and cultural issues which had greater relevance to their readership. These texts often used the anachronistic images of historic Europe as an alternative setting to modern issues.

The penny dreadful engaged with often simultaneously different styles of the Gothic mode from various literary periods. While the Radcliffian Gothic of the eighteenth century influenced numerous penny titles, the lure of the Gothic city also proved to be popular with readers. One of the best-selling penny titles, George W. M. Reynolds's *The Mysteries of London* (1844–6) inspired by Eugène Sue's *The Mysteries of Paris* (1842–3), firmly established the urban mysteries genre within the penny dreadful. Reynolds's text reveals the darker side of London, which was home to criminal organisations, murderers and grave robbers. As Trefor Thomas suggests, the urban mysteries genre 'represents an urbanization of eighteenth-century Gothic, and a new consciousness of the city as inexplicable and impenetrable'.[26] Titles such as James Malcolm Rymer's *The String of Pearls* (1846–7) and Herbert Thornley's *A Life in London* (1846) used the city as a setting inspired by fear and uncertainty by creating disturbing and gruesome scenes and localising them to their readership.

While in the 1860s the market for penny dreadfuls became aimed at a more juvenile, male audience with boys' adventure narratives experiencing their heyday, it is crucial to note that this new market and new style did not replace the penny dreadfuls that had come before, but ran alongside them. The penny writers, acknowledging

Introduction: Dreadful Beginnings

this emerging new market, began to incorporate Gothic elements into these boys' adventure stories. The anonymously authored *The Wild Boys of London* (1866), for example, centred around a group of poor juvenile criminals who often would help in the solving of more serious crimes in the city. The text involved macabre scenes of grave-robbing and autopsy, and took place often in the subterranean den of the wild boys. These plucky heroes encountered the more sinister criminals in the city and often brought them to justice, thus combining the successful literary ingredients of the past and present penny serials. The adaptable nature of the penny dreadful and its ability to conform to the market's needs was part of its model for success. The ever-changing demands of the market and the interests of the reader could alter entire storylines depending on the social and political climate as well as literary trends. The penny dreadfuls' ability to revive and adapt seemingly played-out Gothic narratives shows their crucial importance in sustaining Gothic traditions throughout the nineteenth century.

Authorial Ambiguity and the Conflation of Authorship

The 'get rich quick' perspectives of nineteenth-century publishers allowed for an excess of hasty penny serialisations to flood the literary market, causing 'confusions of authorship' (Smith, p. 2). Due to haphazard productivity, surges of serialisations, republications and publishing houses' misconduct of author recognition, many penny tales were remiss in their assignment of authorship. While many penny titles do not have an author attributed, ground-breaking work has been carried out in attempting to discover the likely authors of these texts. Techniques to attribute authors have included connections with previous serials. For example, though *Newgate: A Romance* is anonymously authored, it does state in the title pages that it was written by the same author as *The Night Adventurer* (1846) which is attributed to James Malcolm Rymer (Smith, p. 9). Other methods of attribution involve identifying patterns in the style of penny writers, as has been done by John Adcock.[27]

It is not only anonymously authored texts which present issues for penny dreadful scholars, but the conflation of authorship. Often multiple writers would work on a serial, and it can be difficult to determine which author takes primacy. The confusion of authorship is particularly present with the work of two authors, James Malcolm Rymer and Thomas Peckett Prest, who have had several texts attributed to either or both of them, including *Newgate* (1846–7), and *The String of Pearls* (1846–7). Rebecca Nesvet has further addressed the origins of this confusion noting that George Augustus Sala was the first to claim Prest as the author, primarily to counter rumours that he himself was the author,[28] and other cataloguing references include both John Medcraft's bibliography about the Edward Lloyd publications, and Elizabeth James and Helen R. Smith's researches on the Barry Ono collection work to identify the selective authorship of penny titles.[29]

In Helen R. Smith's *New Light on Sweeney Todd, Thomas Peckett Prest, James Malcolm Rymer and Elizabeth Caroline Grey* (2002), she clarifies the centuries-old debate of 'Is it Prest or Rymer?' Offering an in-depth examination of these undetermined publications and their rightful creators, Smith provides evidence that assuages the persistent conflict of penny authorship. One such popular penny, *The String of Pearls* was, until Smith's study, apportioned to both Thomas Peckett Prest and James Malcolm Rymer. In a cross-examination of the disjointed working-class literature, Smith analyses literary characteristics such as style, content, and 'imagination' that determines a reassignment of authorship to James Malcolm Rymer (pp. 11–12). While there are those that still address the conflict of *The String of Pearls* and offer dual authorship, this collection, and the chapters herein, acknowledge Smith's research and refer to Rymer as the established proprietor of the serialisation.

Revivification of Penny Publications

In juxtaposing both forgotten and popular penny dreadfuls under the broader mode of the Gothic, we are able to bring together a much-needed compendium of scholarship that revivifies these significant Victorian texts. The first section of the book, 'The Progression of Pennys; or, Adaptations and Legacies of the Dreadful', involves three chapters that centre on the tradition and eventual adaptations

Introduction: Dreadful Beginnings

of penny narratives. The chapters herein attest to the long-standing significance of the penny serial and its impact on later Gothic texts and media, and analyse how the penny dreadfuls progressed through the 1840s until their eventual decline in the 1860s. The enduring literary and cultural significance of the dreadful is demonstrated through numerous adaptations of these texts in both the Victorian period and into the twentieth century.

Hannah-Freya Blake and Marie Léger-St-Jean, the authors of the first chapter of this section, 'Penny Pinching: Reassessing the Gothic Canon through Nineteenth-century Reprinting', consider how reprints of first-wave Gothic texts emerged alongside the production of new penny fiction. Blake and Léger-St-Jean investigate how this reproduction of original Gothic texts, in conjunction with the publications of new titles, offered a new generation of readers access to the first wave. Utilising the database *Price One Penny*, as founded by Léger-St-Jean, this chapter explores the reprinting patterns of publishers identifying a need to revisit the Gothic canon in light of these penny republications. Examining the reprints of penny fiction, Blake and Léger-St-Jean argue that the analysis of the practice allows for a more in-depth understanding of the popular 'mass market fiction' publications and how the 'first-wave' of Gothic literature continued to proliferate in Victorian society (p. 32).

Having explored the commercial reasons for the marketing and publishing of the penny dreadful, the next chapter in this section continues to look at the legacy of the penny dreadful but, instead of focusing on reactions to popular culture, examines adaptations in the light of developing economic trends in the twenty-first century. By focusing on the narratives of the penny dreadful, in regard to adaptation and legacy, it becomes clear that the penny dreadful's significance is not only due to its cultural impact, but its literary content. Brontë Schiltz, author of the chapter, '"As long as you are industrious, you will get on very well": Adapting *The String of Pearls*'s Economies of Horror', examines the penny dreadful through the essentialism of capitalism and cannibalism. Analysing later adaptations such as Stephen Sondheim's musical, *Sweeney Todd: The Demon Barber of Fleet Street* (1979) and Tim Burton's 2007 eponymous film, Schiltz postulates how the lack of resolution in each adaptation reflects Lenin's conceptualisation of capitalism.

Thereby this chapter explores commonly unobserved conversations about class and capitalism initiated by Rymer's original *The String of Pearls* (1846–7).

Subsequent to Schiltz's discussion of classism and capitalism, this section finalises the discussion of dreadfuls and their legacies by interposing Victorian imperialism into the appraisal of Reynolds's literature. The fourth and final chapter, '"Your lot is wretched, old man": Anxieties of Industry, Empire and England in George Reynolds's *Wagner, the Wehr-Wolf*' by Hannah Priest, concludes this section by discussing Reynolds's titular character Wagner in conjunction with his earlier publication, *Faust: A Romance of the Secret Tribunals* (1847). Drawing upon the reimagination of the werewolf as derivative of the Faustian legend, Priest reads *Wagner* (1846–7) alongside Reynolds's penny *Mysteries of London* (1844) to examine how man's self-determined damnation presents societal fears of Victorian capitalism and imperialism. Beyond the exploration of self-sacrifice for authority and wealth, Priest posits how Wagner's lycanthropic figure is the foundation for later texts of imperialism. It is specifically through this comparative analysis of *Wagner* and *Mysteries*, Priest contends, that the intricate complexities of these penny narratives are developed.

Moving away from adaptations, progressions and legacies of the dreadfuls' tradition, the following chapters transition to focus on the influence of institutional Aesculapian literature and the elements of language in mid-nineteenth-century penny serialisations. The second section, 'Victorian Medicine and Sciences; or, Dreadful Discourses of the Gothic', contains three chapters that examine how penny fiction engaged with crucial discourses of medicine and the sciences. These essays explore such rhetoric presented in Jean-Baptiste Lamarck's (1809) theory of evolution, the Anatomy Act of 1832, Thomas Laycock's (1840) study of neurology, and the Public Health Act of 1848, to intertwine and create a conversation that reflects the feedback loop of social concerns through institutional discourses and penny narratives, emboldened by the Gothic mode. This section begins with a chapter that examines the implications of the penny dreadfuls as literary contaminants as discussed by Manon Burz-Labrande, followed by Joseph Crawford's chapter, which investigates the influential

Introduction: Dreadful Beginnings

relationship between medical discourses and popular fiction, and concludes with Nicole C. Dittmer's chapter that offers an exposition of bio- and eco-semiotic representations of monstrous figurations of feral femininity in Victorian hysteria, witchcraft and women's correlation to nature.

The inceptive chapter of this section, Manon Burz-Labrande's '"Embalmed pestilence", "intoxicating poisons": Rhetoric of Contamination, Contagion, and the Gothic Marginalisation of Penny Dreadfuls by their Contemporary Critics', analyses the Gothicised discourse used in the criticism of penny dreadfuls. Burz-Labrande argues that by comparing the penny dreadfuls to disease and contamination, critics suggested that these forms were immoral and had a pernicious influence on their readership. Therefore, this chapter explores how contemporaneous critics utilised the circulation of penny dreadful material as a method for marginalisation and argues that this repudiation is formatted as a threat within the Gothic discourse. Burz-Labrande's investigation unfolds the menacing criticism embedded within the content of the penny circulations which ultimately discloses the social rejection of their content, audience and overall form. Examining such characteristics as 'rhetoric of contagion and contamination', Burz-Labrande posits how this content was 'weaponised' by critics of the dreadfuls as a means for upper-class society to control the populace and 'assert their dominance' (p. 92).

Moving away from metaphorical discourses surrounding disease and the literary marketplace, the next chapter explores the ways in which penny serials engaged with medical science and the Gothic representations of this profession. Joseph Crawford, the author of '"A Tale of the Plague": Anti-medical Sentiment and Epidemic Disease in Early Victorian Popular Gothic Fiction', draws directly from this relationship between medical discourses and literature of the period. Crawford examines the depictions of medical professionalism and disease epidemics in popular fiction during the cholera outbreak between 1832 and 1848. Examining texts by William Harrison Ainsworth, George W. M. Reynolds, and James Malcolm Rymer, Crawford investigates the extent to which the penny press reflected the suspicion of the medical profession that contemporary observers noted among its original target audience. Drawing from prior investigations of the Anatomy Act, body-snatching, Burkers, and resurrection men, such as those by Gasperini and James, Crawford explores how these concerns were only a small part of the dissolution of trust in orthodox medicine. The final chapter of this section, '"Mistress of the broomstick": Biology, Ecosemiotics, and Monstrous Women in Wizard's *The Wild Witch of the Heath; or The Demon of the Glen*' by Nicole C. Dittmer, continues with Crawford's discussion of medical discourse and literary influences embodied within the semiotic figure of the wild witch. Drawing from scientific texts such as Jean-Baptiste Lamarck's (1809) early theories of evolution and Thomas Laycock's *Treatise of the Nervous Diseases of Women* (1840) that correlate the biology of womanhood to the primitivity of nature, Dittmer posits that this fomentation of ferality finds purchase in the pages of penny dreadfuls. This chapter, then, specifically analyses these stipulations of women through the examination of an obscure and anonymously written penny text, *The Wild Witch of the Heath; or The Demon of the Glen* (1841), in conjunction with an eco-Gothic approach to demonstrate how penny dreadfuls of the early Victorian period draw on the pervasive sentiments of ecophobia and gynophobia to form semiotic figurations of monstrous women. Juxtaposing tropes of the sixteenth-century witch and the nineteenth-century hysteric, Dittmer speculates how the contemporary Victorian figuration of the Wild Witch is an anachronistic representation of society's historical fears of female nature embodied within the penny publication.

While the previous chapters highlight the feedback loop of cultural and medical Victorian discourses and the perpetuation of the Gothic mode in penny publications, the final section segues into intricate analyses of the intertextual styles and genres. One of the characteristics of the penny dreadful that makes it unique is its fluidity in terms of genre and style. This section, 'Mode, Genre, and Style; or, Gothic Storytelling and Ideologies', will assess how the penny dreadful explored different types of genre to appeal to its readership, at times being both horrifying and comedic. In addition, the authors of this final segment will further look at how Gothic ideologies were disseminated through varied styles of storytelling often through metanarratives, framing devices and the use of

Introduction: Dreadful Beginnings

non-fiction embedded into the narratives. The concluding portion, then, joins chapters that specifically posit such Gothic elements as narrative devices, tropes and discovered manuscripts within the pages of penny publications. Beginning with Celine Frohn's explication of humour and politics as essential to penny publications, the section then shifts to the critical discussion of Catholicism and Gothic ideologies by Rebecca Nesvet, finally resolving with Sophie Raine's dissection of narrative and metanarrative devices, and discovered manuscripts.

Celine Frohn, in 'A Highwayman and a Ventriloquist Walk into an Inn…: Early Penny Romances and the Politics of Humour in *Jack Rann* and *Valentine Vaux*', analyses how the picaresque story structure demonstrates one of the many storytelling and narrative devices employed by penny writers to appeal to a wide readership. Offering a more 'holistic approach' to the traditional violence and sensation of Gothic literature, Frohn's chapter speculates how humour is 'couched' in penny fiction, a method that essentially abates the Gothic presence of these nineteenth-century serialisations (p. 161). Frohn suggests that the humour in these stories allows for a range of political ideas to be embedded in the text, such as anti-socialist conservatism with Thomas Peckett Prest's *Valentine Vaux* (1839–40), and subversive readings of class with James Lindridge's *Jack Rann, Alias Sixteen-string Jack* (1840). This chapter argues that the episodic, comedic plot is essential in determining the appeal of earlier penny dreadfuls and thus offers a better means of analysis of the sometimes repetitive and extraneous content.

The varied use of Gothic tropes in the penny dreadful demonstrates how these texts were not only derivative from the Gothic literature that had come before but were consciously engaging with and subverting conventions of the genre. The conflicting ideologies in penny serials revealed how these texts were in dialogue not only with other supposedly higher forms of literature, but with each other. This is demonstrated in the next chapter of this section, 'Gothic Ideology and Religious Politics in James Malcolm Rymer's Penny Fiction', which illustrates the tension between competing religious ideologies in the works of one author. In this chapter, Rebecca Nesvet examines the life of the prolific penny author, James Malcolm Rymer (1814–84) and the 'representation of Catholicism' in his literary works.[30] Nesvet's chapter argues that James Malcolm Rymer, in a number of his penny titles, deploys Gothic anticlericalism whilst simultaneously critiquing and subverting this ideology. Utilising the late great scholar, Diane Long Hoeveler's (1949–2016) investigations of Gothic ideologies and Catholicism, Nesvet answers the open-ended question of how penny publications both informed and were informed by theological politics. This chapter, then, draws upon a wide range of Rymer's fiction including *The Ordeal By Touch* (1846), *The Lady in Black* (1847), *The String of Pearls* (1846–7), *The Sepoys, or, Highland Jessie* (1858) and *A Mystery in Scarlet* (1866). Nesvet suggests that the works of Rymer, and penny fiction in general, challenge the use of popular Gothic tropes, encouraging their readers to think critically about the presentation of Catholicism in literature.

While Nesvet's analysis highlights the purpose of theology in penny literature through the use of Gothic characteristics and ideological subversions, the final chapter of this collection segues into these relatively undisclosed elements by way of discovered narratives. Sophie Raine's chapter, '"Muddling about among the dead": Found Manuscripts and Metafictional Storytelling in James Malcolm Rymer's *Newgate: A Romance*', places the penny dreadful within the wider Gothic tradition of Newgate narratives centring on criminal biographies. Raine suggests that Prest's serial incorporates this tradition whilst combining multiple forms of storytelling through framing devices and metanarratives. The history of Newgate is told through found manuscripts, oral storytelling, and polyphonic narration; it is discovered in hidden locations, and uncovered through the narrator's detecting and eavesdropping. The text is a work of metafiction, referring back to not only the historic past of Newgate, but also the literary past of working-class storytelling. The narrator and the reader become Gothic tourists, uncovering the haunted history of the prison. This chapter reveals how the penny dreadful experimented with various forms and employed complex narrative devices. It is through this narrative that the reader is able to see the process through which the penny dreadful itself is created – through combining biography and fiction, and interweaving complex social and political issues with melodrama and sensation. In self-consciously reflecting on its own status as literature, *Newgate*

Introduction: Dreadful Beginnings

anticipates the demise of working-class fiction and engages in a discourse as to how the penny legacy can be preserved.

Research into the penny dreadful has come a long way in recent years, with numerous scholars challenging previous misconceptions. This compilation contributes to this reassessment of the penny dreadful and establishes how these texts can further our understanding of Gothic literary culture as well as Victorian reading habits. *Penny Dreadfuls and the Gothic* draws upon a myriad of penny titles, many of them from lesser-known authors, to create a holistic picture of the penny publishing industry, its readers and popular fiction trends. The wide scope covered by these chapters reveals how these texts were not homogeneous plagiarisms which were purely imitative, but had unique characteristics and reacted to the social milieu in a conscious and considered way. The chapters in this collection demonstrate the adaptability, complexity, and overall importance of the penny dreadful, making a strong case for its continued revival in Gothic literary studies. This edited compilation, then, is a celebration of the early to mid-Victorian serialisations and all of the Gothicists who seek to explore and analyse the darker side of the all but forgotten literature of the penny dreadfuls.

Notes

1. David Punter and Glennis Byron, *The Gothic* (Carlton, Victoria: Blackwell Publishing, 2004), p. 30.
2. Jarlath Killeen, 'Victorian Gothic Pulp Fiction', in Andrew Smith and William Hughes (eds), *Victorian Gothic: An Edinburgh Companion* (Edinburgh: Edinburgh University Press, 2012), pp. 43–56 (p. 46).
3. John Springhall, '"A Life Story for the People"? Edwin J. Brett and the London "Low-Life" Penny Dreadfuls of the 1860s', *Victorian Studies*, 33/2 (1990), 223–46 (226–7).
4. John Springhall, '"Pernicious Reading"? The Penny Dreadful as Scapegoat for Late-Victorian Juvenile Crime', *Victorian Periodicals Review*, 27/4 (Winter 1994), 326–49 (326).
5. For more details on the publishing history, marketing and content of chapbooks, refer to Franz J. Potter's informative *Gothic Chapbooks, Bluebooks and Shilling Shockers, 1797–1830* (Cardiff: University of Wales Press, 2021).

6. Victor Shea, 'Penny Dreadfuls', in James Eli Adams, Tom Pendergast and Sara Pendergast (eds), *Encyclopedia of the Victorian Era* (Danbury, CT: Grolier Academic Reference, 2004), pp. 185–6.
7. Stefan Dziemianowicz, *Penny Dreadfuls: Sensational Tales of Terror* (New York: Fall River Press, 2014), p. ix; Grolier Academic Reference.
8. Spring-heeled Jack was a cultural phenomenon during the entire nineteenth century. In 1808, he was first reported by a letter submitted to the *Sheffield Times* and identified as a malicious ghost in the park. Later, John Thomas Haines in 1840, cast the character of Spring-heeled Jack in a play as a criminal malefactor. Following this appearance, Alfred Burrage's *fin de siècle* penny dreadful recast Jack as a vengeful nobleman.
9. See Hannah Priest, '"Your lot is wretched, old man": Anxieties of Industry, Empire and England in George Reynolds's *Wagner, the Wehr-Wolf*', p. 66.
10. Judith Flanders, *The Invention of Murder: How the Victorians Revelled in Death and Detection and Invented Modern Crime* (New York: St. Martin's Press, 2011), p. 59.
11. Christine Berthin, *Gothic Hauntings, Melancholy Crypts and Textual Ghosts* (London: Palgrave Macmillan), p. 64.
12. E. S. Turner, *Boys will be Boys: The Story of Sweeney Todd, Deadwood Dick, Sexton Blake, Billy Bunter, Dick Barton, et al.* (London: Michael Joseph, 1948).
13. Louis James, *Fiction for the Working Man: A Story of the Literature Produced for the Working Class in Early Victorian Urban England, 1830–1850* (London: Oxford University Press, 1963), p. 77.
14. Montague Summers, *The Gothic Quest: A History of the Gothic Novel* (London: Fortune Press, 1938).
15. Montague Summers, *A Gothic Bibliography* (London: Fortune Press, 1940); Helen R. Smith, *New Light on Sweeney Todd, Thomas Peckett Prest, James Malcolm Rymer and Elizabeth Caroline Grey* (London: Jarndyce, 2002), p. 1.
16. Michael Anglo, *Penny Dreadfuls and other Victorian Horrors* (London: Jupiter Books, 1977), p. 11.
17. Robert Mighall, *A Geography of Victorian Gothic Fiction: Mapping History's Nightmares* (Oxford and New York: Oxford University Press, 1999), p. 48.
18. Rosalind Crone, *Violent Victorians: Popular Entertainment in Nineteenth-century London* (New York: Palgrave Macmillan, 2021), p. 89.

[19] Anna Gasperini, *Nineteenth Century Popular Fiction, Medicine and Anatomy: The Victorian Penny Blood and the 1832 Anatomy Act* (Lancaster, Glasgow, and Chicago: Palgrave Macmillan, 2019).

[20] Nicole C. Dittmer, 'Review: Nineteenth Century Popular Fiction, Medicine and Anatomy: The Victorian Penny Blood and the 1832 Anatomy Act by Anna Gasperini', *Gothic Studies* 23/1 (2020), 123–5 (123).

[21] Vicki Anderson, *The Dime Novel in Children's Literature* (Jefferson: McFarland & Company, Inc., 2005), pp. 54–7.

[22] Stacey McDowell, 'Penny Dreadfuls', in William Hughes, David Punter and Andrew Smith (eds), *The Encyclopedia of the Gothic* (Chichester and Hoboken: Wiley-Blackwell, 2016), pp. 489–90.

[23] Anne-Marie Pope, 'American Dime Novels, 1860–1915', *Historical Association: The Voice for History* (2020).

[24] Robert Fraser, *Victorian Quest Romance: Stevenson, Haggard, Kipling and Conan Doyle*, Writers and Their Work (Liverpool: Liverpool University Press, 1998), p. 1.

[25] David Punter, *The Literature of Terror: A History of Gothic Fictions from 1765 to the Present Day, Volume 1: The Gothic Tradition* (Abingdon and New York: Routledge, 1996), p. 114.

[26] Trefer Thomas, 'Introduction', in G. W. M. Reynolds, *The Mysteries of London* (Keele: Keele University, 1998), p. ix.

[27] John Adcock, 'Yesterday's Papers' (2008), http://john-adcock.blogspot.com/.

[28] See Rebecca Nesvet, 'The Mystery of *Sweeney Todd*: G. A. Sala's Desperate Solution'. *Victorian Institute Journal*, 47 (2019–20), n. p.

[29] Elizabeth James and Helen R. Smith, *Penny Dreadfuls and Boys' Adventures: The Barry Ono Collection of Victorian Popular Literature in the British Library* (London: British Library, 1998); John Medcraft, *Bibliography of the Penny Bloods of Edward Lloyd* (London: J. A. Birkbeck, 1945).

[30] See Rebecca Nesvet, 'Gothic Ideology and Religious Politics in James Malcolm Rymer's Penny Fiction', p. 220.

Section I
The Progression of Pennys; or, Adaptations and Legacies of the Dreadful

2

Penny Pinching: Reassessing the Gothic Canon through Nineteenth-century Reprinting

HANNAH-FREYA BLAKE
AND MARIE LÉGER-ST-JEAN

The so-called first wave of the Gothic, inaugurated by Horace Walpole's *The Castle of Otranto* in 1764, is typically regarded to have ended with Charles Robert Maturin's *Melmoth the Wanderer* in 1821 but, as we shall show, the first-wave Gothic continues to haunt the popular fiction market throughout the nineteenth century. While interest in penny bloods is usually limited to the original few of lasting popularity, such as James Malcolm Rymer's *The String of Pearls* (1846–7) and *Varney the Vampire* (1845–7), alongside George W. M. Reynolds's *The Mysteries of London* (1844–6) and *Wagner the Wehr-Wolf* (1846–7), our interest is in the Gothic novels from the first wave that came to be reprinted as penny bloods. Marie Léger-St-Jean's extensive online database *Price One Penny* currently lists over 1,000 penny blood titles, more than half of which are reprints, adaptations or translations – a sizeable amount worth closer scrutiny. The reprinting practices of penny blood publishers enables us to better understand the development of mass-market fiction and the ways in which the legacy of first-wave Gothic continued to capture the imagination of Victorian readers.

The Gothic, of course, is not the only literary root of the penny blood; scholars typically look to the *Newgate Calendar*, broadsides and melodrama as well. Arguably this cross-contamination is the nature of popular fiction. Across the nineteenth century, the most popular aspects of literature came to be recycled and repackaged, presented as new; we need only consider the penny blood's close cousin, the 1860s sensation school of fiction, to see how genres converge and permeate across boundaries. The Gothic is especially notorious for eschewing the confines of genre, as the first-wave manifestation and early nineteenth-century mutations of the Gothic converged with melodrama, historical novels and sentimental romance. In the nineteenth century, as Jarlath Killeen explains, the Gothic 'fragmented and took up ghostly inhabitants elsewhere, indeed everywhere, in nineteenth-century culture'.[1] Further, novels that we now consider to be exemplary of the first wave of the Gothic were known by various titles at the time, including the 'tale of terror', 'terrorist novels', 'the German school', and 'modern romance': 'Gothic' as a descriptor was seldom used. Howsoever it was named at the time, the Gothic never died — and the reprints, including those in penny weekly numbers, kept some of the original texts alive.

Given the variety of terms used to classify Gothic novels during the first wave of its popularity and its generic openness, we cross-referenced the penny bloods we discovered were reprints of novels from the period 1764–1821 with numerous modern Gothic bibliographies. Some novels from this time, such as Elizabeth Helme's *St Clair of the Isles* (1803), remain ambiguous and have fallen into obscurity but, as we will discuss, were frequently reprinted in penny weekly numbers as well as in earlier and later cheap formats. According to the data in *Price One Penny*, reprinted texts represent 3 per cent of all fiction published in penny weekly numbers between 1837 and 1860, the majority of which came from the United States. First-wave Gothic novels make up 10 per cent of all reprints in penny weekly numbers and represent close to a quarter of the pre-Victorian British texts reprinted. To contextualise these serialisations and assess their impact on the development of the Gothic canon, we sought out other nineteenth-century reprints of these same texts.[2] The dataset on which this research is based has been published online.[3] Some of the twenty-three novels it contains are unsurprising, especially regarding Ann Radcliffe's oeuvre, yet there are also some surprising inclusions, such as the presence of titles published by James Fletcher Hughes, who was 'never respectable'.[4] The examples of Hughes's texts demonstrate the persistence not only of the canonical few Gothic novels that dominate scholarship, but also of cheap, lesser-known Gothic texts. Our chapter looks at both the expected and unexpected reprinting patterns of publishers to assess the validity of the current Gothic canon, ultimately arguing that there is a need to expand Gothic scholarship to include texts which are now barely remembered but which remained popular across the nineteenth century.

Reprinting the Gothic, c. 1810–1820: Establishing a Canon

This section reviews the groundwork of early cheap serial fiction publishers and canon-forming reprint series in the first decades of the nineteenth century, demonstrating how their selections influenced future penny blood reprints. While the reprinting patterns in the early decades of the nineteenth century illustrate that the works of Radcliffe remained a favourite, publishers also established a trend for reprinting Walpole's *The Castle of Otranto* alongside Clara Reeve's *The Old English Baron* (1778). Yet other, now obscure books prove their popularity at this time in cheap serial reprints: Elizabeth Helme's *The Farmer of Inglewood Forest* (1796) and *St Clair of the Isles* (1803), and the anonymous *Fatherless Fanny* (1811).

Chapbooks in particular ensured the endurance of the Gothic. Although published since the sixteenth century, there was a notable surge in interest and output of chapbooks at the end of the eighteenth century and into the first decades of the nineteenth, driven principally by the popularity of Gothic texts.[5] One such salient example is Simon Fisher's abridgement of Matthew Lewis's *The Monk* in 1798, titled *The Castle of Lindenberg; or, The History of Raymond and Agnes. A Romance*, which was such a commercial success that Fisher was encouraged to produce sixteen more Gothic chapbooks before turning to reprinting novels in sixpenny weekly numbers in 1823 (Potter, p. 18). His 'Fisher's Library of Modern Amusement' is a notable precursor to the penny bloods in the field of Gothic reprinting (Potter, p. 34). Fisher's advertisement on the last page of the 1823 reprint of Radcliffe's first novel, *The Castles of Athlin and Dunbayne* (1789), states that he intends to print novels with a variety of interests accompanied by 'handsome Engravings ... at a trifling charge' of less than '*one-third* of the price of the most common unembellished editions'.[6] The prices of entire novels in his library varied according to their length, from 1s. for *The Castles of Athlin and Dunbayne* complete in two numbers to 6s. 6d for *The Mysteries of Udolpho* in thirteen numbers.

Radcliffe's first novel was also reprinted by John Limbird in his 'British Novelist' series, and sold for half of Fisher's price, issued in sixteen-page illustrated weekly twopenny numbers. Both series cost roughly the same amount per page but, by using double columns and larger sheets, Limbird could fit much more text into a page than Fisher. Jon Topham compares Limbird's price with other competitors, showing that even though the 'British Novelist' was among the cheapest, it 'included quality fiction in a form that could be bound for a respectable library'.[7] While critics had been concerned with the commerciality of novels throughout the eighteenth century, ensuring respectability while targeting the market remained a concern for some publishers in the early nineteenth century. Publishing Radcliffe was a sure way to ensure respectability, as she was among the most respectable writers of Gothic fiction in the first wave and remained a well-established favourite across the nineteenth century. Anna Lætitia Barbauld's *The British Novelists* (1810), to which the title of Limbird's series was certainly a nod, sold as a complete collection in fifty volumes for £12 12s. It included Radcliffe's *The Romance of the Forest* (1791; volumes 43–4) and *The Mysteries of Udolpho* (volumes 45–7), as well as Charlotte Smith's *The Old Manor House* (1793; volumes 36–7) and Fanny Burney's *Evelina* (1778) and *Cecilia* (1782) in between.[8] Homer Obed Brown sees in Barbauld's editorial and publishing enterprise a seminal moment for what he calls 'the institution of the English novel', as 'subsequent novelists now had an established, solid body of tradition, a genre, and a genealogy'.[9] Sir Walter Scott, who edited Ballantyne's Novelist's Library (1821–4), combined all of Radcliffe's novels in the tenth (and last) volume of the series. In the introduction, he describes Radcliffe as 'one of the favoured few' to found a class of literature, and goes on to praise her for leading the way 'in a peculiar style of composition, affecting powerfully the mind of the reader, which has since been attempted by many, but in which no one has attained or approached the excellencies of the original inventor'.[10] Radcliffe was an early staple of both cheap and expensive serial reprinting.

Scott and Barbauld are leading figures in what Claudia L. Johnson calls a 'surge in the business of canon-making' in the first decades of the nineteenth century.[11] Ballantyne's Novelist's Library, under Scott's steerage, reprinted very particular texts and excluded others, most notably Lewis's *The Monk*. Michael Gamer explains that though Scott had worked with Lewis on *Tales of Wonder* (1801), he was invested in transforming his reputation 'from translator of the German and disciple of Lewis to antiquarian scholar and national bard'.[12] Further, while Johnson argues that Scott uses Barbauld's *The British Novelists* as a 'template', he also 'supplement[ed] some of her selections so as to make the canon of the British novel the treasury of specific novelists' careers' (p. 174). These 'specific novelists' are mostly male; 'Mrs Radcliffe' is the only woman to appear in the six volumes dedicated to the works of a single author, while Reeve's *The Old English Baron* appears alongside eight novels by Laurence Sterne, Oliver Goldsmith, Samuel Johnson, Henry Mackenzie and Walpole in volume 5. Scott had also planned to dedicate a volume of Ballantyne's Novelist's Library to Charlotte Smith, but the series was discontinued before he had the chance.[13] The high praise he affords Radcliffe arguably demonstrates his intention to cultivate a canon largely founded on male authors, as Anne Ledoux suggests that he 'creates a critical precedent, where exceptions to a male-dominated canon can be made for extraordinary women authors', leaving other popular women writers like Fanny Burney, Elizabeth Helme and Regina Maria Roche overlooked.[14]

Barbauld and Scott thus both began a pattern of reprinting Radcliffe in particular. But this is not the only trend they established: they also partnered Reeve's *The Old English Baron* and Walpole's *The Castle of Otranto* in the same volume (volume 22 in *The British Novelists* and volume five in Ballantyne's Novelist's Library). The imprint 'J. Walker, J. Johnson …' first paired these two novels in 1808, a year after Reeve's death, a coupling that was also repeated by Limbird in the 1820s. Though there is more than a decade between the two novels' original publication date, Reeve's preface to the second edition, at which point she acknowledged authorship and changed the title from *The Champion of Virtue* to what it is most commonly known by today, directly addressed Walpole's novel. Recognising that her novel is the 'offspring' of *Otranto*, Reeve criticises Walpole's use of the marvellous and intention to excite readers, complaining that 'the machinery is so violent, that it destroys the effect it is intended to excite'.[15] Reeve suggests that her novel aims to show how true romance should be written, keeping the story 'within the utmost verge of probability … without losing the least circumstance that excites or detains the attention' (p. 3). Pairing the two novels together, then, invites a direct comparison and shows new readers how the genre developed by dialogic exchange, establishing a literary genealogy from Walpole to Reeve.

Radcliffe, Smith and the founding pair were not the only authors to have Gothic novels reprinted in the early nineteenth century. Fisher reprinted Sophia Lee's *The Recess, or, A Tale of Other Times* (1783) and Regina Maria Roche's *The Children of the Abbey* (1796). The former is set in the Elizabethan era and features fictional twin daughters of Mary, Queen of Scots, and is sometimes included in discussions of early Gothic novels, but is also viewed as a historical romance. Roche's novel was first published by William Lane's Minerva Press and mentioned alongside *The Romance of the Forest* in Jane Austen's *Emma* – Austen's Gothic parody.[16] Limbird also builds on Scott's selection for Ballantyne's and adds two novels written by Elizabeth Helme: *The Farmer of Inglewood Forest*, first published by Minerva Press in 1796, and *St Clair of the Isles*, which was first published by the Longman firm in 1803. Both novels were reprinted by Anthony King Newman, William Lane's successor, in the 1810s. In fact, Newman reprinted nearly 60 per cent of Minerva Press titles in a bid to target new audiences carried by the reputation of the press. Newman also reprinted novels initially issued by other publishers, therefore leaving under his imprint, according to the aggregated catalogue WorldCat, nearly three-quarters of the titles we have studied. A further four titles have been located by Jacqueline Belanger and her colleagues in his circulating library's catalogue held at the Bodleian.[17] They found that it includes over nine out of ten of all the new novels published between 1800 and 1816, including nearly all of those issued by Hughes and by the Longman firm.

Helme's *The Farmer of Inglewood Forest* was also reprinted in the 1820s by Sheffield-based Charles and William Thompson in their sixpenny numbers with a surprising by-line, which presents the novel as 'By the Author of Fatherless Fanny, Old English Baron, Mysteries of Udolpho, Edwin and Lucy, &c. &c.' Of course, the novel was neither Reeve's nor Radcliffe's, though the error – most likely a deliberate marketing ploy – places the group of novels listed, including Helme's, in the same category. The last novel in their list, *Edwin and Lucy*, is an obscure picaresque novel about two happy orphans, and was often reprinted as well. Throughout the 1810s, *Fatherless Fanny* was reprinted in sixpenny numbers by the Thompsons in Sheffield, by Joseph Gleave in Manchester and by Thomas Kelly, William Emans and George Virtue in London, all independently from one another, or at least with a newly set type.[18] The Thompsons' edition of 1816 provided the influential (mis)attribution to 'the author of The Old English Baron' which Emans and Kelly continued, while Gleave added an epigraph to Walpole instead.[19] The true authorship of the novel remains uncertain; its first edition, published in 1811, was attributed to 'Mrs Edgeworth', author of the Gothic-inflected *Castle Rackrent* (1800), though her father denied the attribution the following year. Regardless of the authorship, these reprints and associations with other titles indisputably connect *Fatherless Fanny* and Helme's novels to the Gothic.

While the first wave of the Gothic declined in popularity in the 1820s, collections and series in the 1810s and 1820s maintained interest in some of the most notable Gothic texts. *The British Novelists* and Ballantyne's Novelist's Library developed a canon, reprinting Radcliffe and pairing Walpole and Reeve together, while other series by Fisher and Limbird introduced novels by Roche and Helme into curated lists of reprints. These publishing patterns influenced the reprinting practices of publishers in the 1830s and 1840s. The next section will show that Roche's *The Children of the Abbey* and Helme's *The Farmer of Inglewood Forest* and *St Clair of the Isles* came to be reprinted more than Radcliffe in the second half of the nineteenth century, and penny bloods would play a pivotal role.

Victorian Gothic Reprints: The Pivotal Role of Penny Bloods

Now that the most reprinted first-wave Gothic novels of the nineteenth century have been introduced, we will sketch their relative importance in middle-class and cheap reprint series throughout the Victorian era. Moving from Bentley's Standard Novels to Milner's 'Red Library' and 'Red and Blue Library', we will highlight the innovative selection choices of penny weekly reprinters. Bentley's Standard Novels, launched in 1831 at 6s. per volume, embraced different first-wave Gothic novels and offered an alternative take on literature worth collecting, from Barbauld's and Ballantyne's. The volumes, which were issued roughly monthly, nearly all contained a complete novel. Furthermore, it was not a nationalistic project: it opened with American novelist James Fenimore Cooper's *The Pilot*.[20] However, in its first year, Bentley's Standard Novels included seven British novels from the Romantic era, including William Godwin's *Caleb Williams* (volume 2) and *St. Leon* (volume 5) and Mary Shelley's *Frankenstein* (volume 9).[21] The only overlap with the previous selections is *The Castle of Otranto*, which Bentley decoupled from Reeve's *The Old English Baron* to present it with William Beckford's *Vathek* (1786) and Lewis's translation *The Bravo of Venice* (1804) in volume 41, issued in 1834. Bentley did not include any novels by Radcliffe – a striking absence, though it may be argued that Bentley deemed yet more reprints of her novels were unlikely to turn a profit.

Other publishers from the beginning of the Victorian era reprinted their fair share of first-wave Gothic novels, but in cheap weekly numbers. Two unillustrated periodicals, *The Novel Newspaper* and *The Romancist, and Novelist's Library*, drew mainly from Limbird's selection, but also included titles previously reprinted by Newman and Bentley. Like Bentley's, neither was a nationalist project, incorporating French, German and American works in their contents. *The Romancist, and Novelist's Library* appeared in two consecutive series, both published by John Clements. The first ran in sixteen-page numbers for twopence, like Limbird's series, but presents as a typical cheap periodical with a masthead. Its reprints were probably abridged, much like a chapbook; Lewis's *Bravo of Venice*, even when printing in three columns, does not fit into twelve pages. Michael Sadleir argues that the four volumes of the first series 'merit careful

The Gothic Canon and Reprinting

study', as the selection of texts is 'of great value as evidence of the survival [of the Gothic Romance] and otherwise of individual reputations'.[22] The list of contents of the *Novel Newspaper*, which Sadleir did not have, is even more innovative in its choices. Sold for a single penny each week, the *Novel Newspaper* presented unabridged texts in two columns and incorporated half-title pages in its sixty-four-page numbers, which could be bound into a volume. Figure 1 shows the novels *The Romancist, and Novelist's Library* and *Novel Newspaper* reprinted on a timeline.

Both periodicals reprinted all the same titles as Limbird, except for some Radcliffe novels, but they did so in a different order. The two periodicals also lifted a title each from Bentley's selection (represented by triangles): *The Bravo of Venice*, which opens *The Romancist, and Novelist's Library*, and *Caleb Williams* for the *Novel Newspaper*. As we saw in the previous section, Limbird offered up a mix of the texts canonised by Barbauld in *The British Novelists* and Scott in Ballantyne's (squares), and the Helme and Roche novels that would become bestsellers in Milner's series (full circles).

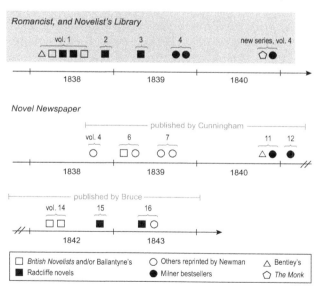

Figure 1 Timeline of Gothic novels in *The Romancist, and Novelist's Library* and the *Novel Newspaper*.

While *The Romancist, and Novelist's Library* reprints six novels that appeared in Ballantyne's in its first three volumes (1838–9), the *Novel Newspaper* did not reprint a single Radcliffe novel (full square) until volume 15 in 1842. In its preface, the unknown editor of the *Novel Newspaper* justified this return to Radcliffe by explaining that *The Italian* 'belongs to a school which is now well-nigh exploded; but its long-continued and undiminished popularity sufficiently proves that it is not unworthy of a place in our collection'.[23] Crucially, this return to the classics coincides with a change of publisher following John Cunningham's death in 1842. *The Romancist, and Novelist's Library* may have taken a similar view that the genre's popularity remained 'undiminished', as it expanded Limbird's Gothic selection with *The Children of the Abbey*, previously reprinted by Fisher, and *Raymond and Agnes; or, The Bleeding Nun*, a portion of *The Monk* (represented by a pentagon in Figure 1). The editor, William Hazlitt, was surprised to discover that Roche was still alive and so had to be paid – in his words, she 'had to be squared'.[24] The incident highlights that cheap reprinters restricted themselves to out-of-copyright novels, as the *Novel Newspaper* prefaces also make abundantly clear.

With the continued interest in Radcliffe, Walpole and Reeve, and the resurgence of Lewis's *The Monk*, which was previously confined to the chapbooks, the picture, so far from these twopence and penny weekly reprint series, matches our modern conception of what was most well received and in demand. However, especially while Cunningham was publisher, the *Novel Newspaper* reprinted five other lesser-known Gothic texts from Newman's lists (represented by the empty circles in Figure 1). Perhaps the most unexpected reprints that challenge our idea of the Gothic canon come from the reprints of books originally published in the first decade of the nineteenth century by James Fletcher Hughes, such as *Manfroné; or, The One-Handed Monk* (1809), attributed to 'Mary Anne Radcliffe', the very first Gothic novel reprinted in the *Novel Newspaper*. From 1802 to 1811, almost one hundred novels were published under Hughes's name, and they accounted for nearly 10 per cent of the market for fiction at the time. His years of active trade roughly parallel the years that the Minerva Press began to decline in domination of the publishing industry (1803–11), according to Elizabeth Neiman's analysis of records and statistics on

Lane's press. Although he fell bankrupt in 1808, Hughes resurrected his trade for a few years before his unexpected death in 1810. He was, by all accounts, a savvy salesman – or, as Lucy Cogan puts it, a 'rackety figure who specialised in popular fiction aimed squarely at feeding the public's voracious appetite for novels'.[25]

Lewis's *The Bravo of Venice* was published by Hughes in 1804, and it not only made its way into Bentley's Standard Novels and Clement's *Romancist, and Novelist's Library*, but was also reprinted by newsagent George Berger in 1839. *Donalda; or, The Witches of Glenshiel* (1805), written by Mary Julia Young, was reprinted by Benjamin Davy Cousins in his weekly miscellany *The Penny Satirist* as well as in his collection of stories *Tales of My Landlady* (1843), a nod to Scott's *Tales of a Grandfather*. *The Friar Hildargo* (1807), which Hughes falsely advertised as written by Matthew Lewis but was published with the name Edward Mortimer, was reprinted by Thomas Paine Carlile under the new title *Love and Crime* in 1841. Finally, *The Demon of Sicily* (1807) by Edward Montague was reprinted by William Dugdale in 1839 alongside *The Monk*. Like Hughes, Dugdale was a publisher with a reputation, largely known as a publisher of pornography. Although it is difficult to track Dugdale's entire output, as he published under numerous pseudonyms, *The Monk* and *The Demon of Sicily* seem to be the only Gothic novels Dugdale reprinted as penny bloods.[26] The prolific penny blood publisher Edward Lloyd would later reprint Dugdale's 190-page edition of *The Monk*, presumably from remainders. George Purkess Senior, who sometimes partnered with Lloyd, also published a 281-page edition entitled *The Monk. A Tale of the Inquisition!* both on its first page (drop-head title) and on its engraved title page. It was reissued by his sons Alfred Joseph Towers Hemmens and Henry Hemmens Purkess under the imprint J. & H. Purkess.[27] Using the original title for Lewis's novel (*The Monk*) marks a departure from the practice developed in chapbooks and followed in *The Romancist, and Novelist's Library* and signals an important innovation of the penny bloods. Penny publishers George Vickers, William Caffyn and William Job White each reprinted one first-wave Gothic novel that had previously only been reprinted by Newman. In contrast, John Lofts reprinted titles more in line with the *Novel Newspaper* contents.

Returning to Hughes, *The Friar Hildargo*, now neglected among scholars, was in fact reprinted by both Thomas Paine Carlile in 1841 under the imprint T. Paine during his short-lived career in penny-issue fiction, and again by George Peirce in thirty penny weekly numbers over 1845 and 1846. Peirce did not restore the original title, choosing instead to retain Carlile's *Love and Crime*. Carlile advertised four of the eight novels he printed as 'new', but we have found at least another, apart from *The Friar Hildargo*, which was actually a reprint of an earlier first-wave Gothic novel.[28] This second text is *The Italian Marauders*, first published in 1810 by George Hughes (who was probably J. F. Hughes's son) and reprinted by Carlile as *Angela, the Orphan; or, The Bandit Monk of Italy* (Potter, *Gothic Chapbooks*). Given this emerging pattern, it is likely that Carlile's *The Black Forest; or, The Solitary of the Hut* is also a reprint, but we have not been able to identify its source text. The persistence of *The Friar Hildargo* and a handful of other titles published by Hughes in penny weekly numbers should prompt Gothic scholars to re-examine the role of supposedly less respectable publishers in the industry.

Also reprinted more than we might expect were Roche's *The Children of the Abbey* and Helme's *The Farmer of Inglewood Forest* and *St Clair of the Isles*. They all appeared in *The Romancist, and Novelist's Library*, though split between volume 4 of the initial weekly magazine in 1840 and volume 4 of the new series in 1842 (see the full circles in Figure 1). Both of Helme's romances were also published in the *Novel Newspaper* (volumes 11 and 12), while her earlier *Louisa; or, The Cottage on the Moor* (1787) was reprinted in volume 7. The popularity of these novels persisted throughout the rest of the nineteenth century in the cheap fiction reprinting coming out of the north of England. An under-studied primary source regarding this literature is a collection of cheap literature printed in the north amassed in the 1970s and 1980s by a Yorkshire collector.[29] With a combined total of fourteen copies of their three best-selling novels issued by Milner & Co. (Halifax and London), Nicholson and Sons (Halifax, Wakefield and London), John Slater Pratt (Stokesley) and Thomas Richardson and Son (Derby), Roche and Helme feature more prominently than Radcliffe.

Other sources focused on Milner & Co. confirm their three novels were the most reprinted in the last quarter of the century.

The firm was founded by William Milner and taken over by his stepsons Francis Robert and John Edwin Sowerby after his death in 1850; they are the ones who created the cheap reprint series for which Milner & Co. is known today. Its catalogues, two of which are digitised, are especially helpful indicators of the relative popularity of each title. Between the two, new series were added, and titles were added or removed from series, in stark contrast with *The British Novelists*, Ballantyne's Novelist's Library, and Bentley's Standard Novels, whose numbered volumes confer a sense of stability. Both digitised catalogues are undated, but the firm's changing imprint helps narrow down when they were issued. *Cheap Books Published by Milner & Sowerby, Paternoster Row, London* must have been issued after 1866, when the stepsons opened their metropolitan branch, and before 1874, when the imprint became Milner & Co. *A Retail Catalogue of Books* was published after 1883, when the firm was turned into a company limited by shares, and probably in 1893 or 1894, since it was bound with other publishers' lists issued in those two years, at least for those that are dated.[30] The Milner catalogues list different series, respectively four and seven of which contained at least one Gothic novel. More research must be done into Milner & Co. to understand their publishing history.

The series containing the largest number of Gothic novels is the 1s. Cottage Library, which in the later catalogue had become the Cottage Library (Pocket Editions) to make way for a new sixpenny Cottage Library, though what made it cheaper is unclear, since both were bound in cloth and printed in the small royal 32mo format. The earlier catalogue included three Radcliffe titles (*The Mysteries of Udolpho*, *The Romance of the Forest* and *The Italian*), while the later one dropped *The Italian*. The same title could appear in more than one series, which was the case of *The Mysteries of Udolpho* in the earlier catalogue. All three of the aforementioned Milner bestsellers were issued in its Cottage Library, but their presence exploded in the later catalogue: all three appear in no less than four series: Cottage Library (Pocket Editions), Wide World Library, Red and Blue Library, and Red Library. The second series also appeared as The Wide, Wide World Library in the earlier Milner & Sowerby catalogue, a reference to an American novel. The series contained only Helme's novels and *Fatherless Fanny* (which was dropped in the later catalogue and replaced by Roche's *The Children of the Abbey*). Montague Summers recalls in his *Gothic Quest* the larger foolscap-octavo size series, the 2s. Red Library and 1s. Red and Blue Library.[31] They appeared sometime between 1874 and 1883, since they only feature in the later *A Retail Catalogue of Books*. Alongside the Helme and Roche novels, the Red and Blue Library also included Charlotte Smith's *The Old Manor House*, which Barbauld had reprinted decades earlier in *The British Novelists*. *Fatherless Fanny* appeared in both later, larger series.

The cheap penny weekly numbers did not only contribute reprints to the reception history of *Fatherless Fanny*, but also what others call a 'penny plagiarism'. Indeed, beginning in spring 1840, Thomas Peckett Prest adapted the novel for publisher Edward Lloyd under the title *Fatherless Fanny; or, The Mysterious Orphan*. In the summer, perhaps prompted by Lloyd's romance, Carlile first advertised his own edition of *Fatherless Fanny* before moving on to the banner Paine's Popular Reprints of Novels with Roche's and Helme's books. The four novels were thus first marketed as a unit in penny weekly numbers, as far as we know.[32] Sixpenny publishers Gleave and Virtue both had also reprinted *The Children of the Abbey*, *The Farmer of Inglewood Forest* and *St Clair of the Isles* in the mid-1820s after reprinting *Fatherless Fanny* a few years earlier, but they had no further engagement of note with the Gothic, which contrasts with Carlile, who reprinted Hughes's novels under new titles.[33] Pratt, who printed at least one title for Newman, also published numerous cheap editions of all four romances in the 1840s and 1850s, bound in cloth and sold for 1s.[34] His expansive catalogue incorporated much of what had been heavily reprinted in the first half of the nineteenth century. Perhaps the clearest demonstration of the enduring popularity of *Fatherless Fanny* is in William Makepeace Thackeray's *Vanity Fair* (1848), as the novel is sixteen-year-old Polly Clapp's favourite, along with Jane Porter's historical romance *The Scottish Chiefs* (1809).[35]

The four novels that found most success in Milner & Co.'s cheap reprints were also major exports, immensely popular in Spain and Brazil.[36] Xavier Aldana Reyes, reviewing reprinting patterns in Spain between the 1780s and the 1830s, identifies roughly forty-five Gothic novels of British or French origin, with several editions across the fifty years. Reyes also claims that 'writers such as Regina Maria Roche or Elizabeth Helme, who are not as well-remembered today, saw a substantial number of editions of their works published in Spain'.[37] As the final section discusses, by remaining favourites later in the nineteenth century, these texts challenge our modern conception of the Gothic canon.

Enduring Favourites: Reconsidering the Canon

In 1897, Herbert E. Wroot reviewed the Milner & Co. stock book and found that Roche's *Children of the Abbey* sold over 75,000 copies, of which 'more than 30,000' were sold after 1869.[38] This impressive number, he suggests, is 'characteristic of its class' – and yet Helme's *Farmer of Inglewood Forest*, Wroot claims, was 'even more popular' (p. 174). Sadly, Wroot does not relay how much more popular. Note, however, that these are the only two Gothic novels for which he quotes sales figures. Even Summers, in the introduction to *Gothic Quest*, recalls a 6d edition of Roche's novel in 1890, describing *The Children of the Abbey* as 'immensely popular', having been issued 'time after time', while Helme's romances 'maintained their place in a sixpenny series' as well (p. 9). These three texts were first selected for reprinting alongside one another by Thomas Paine Carlile in Paine's Popular Reprints of Novels in the 1840s. Since then, they remained a popular choice for publishers to reprint, indicating that there was a sustained, intergenerational interest in Roche's and Helme's novels. They even overtook Radcliffe's as the most reprinted novels in the second half of the nineteenth century.

Reprints of first-wave Gothic novels across the nineteenth century, including in penny weekly numbers, provide unique insight into the reception of the Gothic. While early expensive collections like Barbauld's *The British Novelists* and Scott's Ballantyne's Novelist's Library aimed to cultivate a respectable canon, with Radcliffe's work in pride of place and the pairing of Walpole's *The Castle of Otranto* and Reeve's *The Old English Baron*, later cheap press publishers reprinted more unusual choices. Novels like *The Demon of Sicily*, *The Friar Hildargo* and *Donalda, or The Witches of Glenshiel*, all originally by the 'rackety' publisher J. F. Hughes, came to be reprinted in penny weekly numbers, though some under new titles. While it might be supposed that such novels circulated among publishers as remainders or cheap copyright-free stock, which reduced financial risk, the presence of reprints in and of itself signals a longer reception history than that of the vast majority of novels, Gothic or otherwise. Even *Fatherless Fanny*, now almost entirely forgotten, was regularly reprinted, and was even adapted by prolific penny blood hack writer Prest in 1840 for Lloyd.

Although Summers described the Roche and Helme late nineteenth-century bestsellers as 'Gothic flotsam' (Summers, p. 9), by which Sharon Watson worried he unjustly meant 'the debris of literature',[39] Summers's nostalgic fondness for the Gothic suggests otherwise. We believe that by 'Gothic flotsam' Summers rather meant to distinguish between the privileged few Gothic novels that remain at the surface in twentieth-century scholarship and the many other Gothic novels which had been sunk under their weight. Some of these lesser-known texts clearly remained in circulation throughout the nineteenth century, which raises questions about how we configure what constitutes the Gothic canon. The staying power of these novels certainly warrants more discussion within Gothic scholarship and demonstrates the importance of establishing more comprehensive databases tracing the reprinting practices, not just in canon-forming series, but also of cheap publishers. As Malcolm Chase explains, 'cheap books do not survive well: they were used heavily, loosely constructed from low-cost materials, and historically have had little appeal to collectors.'[40] Only when we have recovered all the titles cheaply reprinted will we be able to overcome our class- and geography-based biases and do justice to the full breadth of Gothic reception.

Notes

1. Jarlath Killeen, *Gothic Literature, 1825–1914* (Cardiff: University of Wales Press, 2009), p. 3.
2. We consulted several bibliographies, including: Gary Kelly, *Varieties of Female Gothic: Historical Gothic*, 6 vols (London: Pickering & Chatto, 2002); Alice M. Killeen, *Le roman terrifiant ou roman noir: de Walpole*

à *Anne Radcliffe et son influence sur la littérature française jusqu'en 1840*, Bibliothèque de la Revue de littérature comparée, 4 (Paris: Champion, 1923); William St Clair, *The Reading Nation in the Romantic Period* (Cambridge: Cambridge University Press, 2004); Deborah D. Rogers, 'Primary Bibliography: Editions and Translations', in *Ann Radcliffe: A Bio-Bibliography* (London: Greenwood Press, 1996), pp. 23–34; and Montague Summers, *The Gothic Quest: A History of the Gothic Novel* (New York: Russel & Russel, 1964).

3 Marie Léger-St-Jean, 'Reprinting of first-wave Gothic novels in the 19th century: method and dataset and methodology', *Price One Penny*, new series, 27 September 2021, https://popnewseries.hypotheses.org/574.

4 Peter Garside, 'J. F. Hughes and the Publication of Popular Fiction, 1803–1810', *The Volume*, 6-IX/3 (September 1987), 240–58.

5 Franz Potter, *Gothic Chapbooks, Bluebooks and Shilling Shockers, 1797–1830* (Cardiff: Wales University Press, 2021), p. 26. The term chapbook did not come into use until 1825.

6 Ann Radcliffe, *The Castles of Athlin and Dunbayne* (London: Simon Fisher, 1823).

7 Jonathan R. Topham, 'John Limbird, Thomas Byerley, and the Production of Cheap Periodicals in the 1820s', *Book History*, 8/1 (2005), 75–106 (95).

8 Though these last two works are not Gothic per se, their inclusion illustrates the generic openness of the romance category in the late 1700s.

9 Homer Obed Brown, *Institutions of the English Novel: From Defoe to Scott* (Philadelphia: University of Pennsylvania Press, 1998), p. 183.

10 Walter Scott, 'Prefatory Memoir to Mrs Ann Radcliffe', in *The Novels of Mrs Ann Radcliffe* (London: Hurst, Robinson, and Co., 1824), pp. i–xxxix.

11 Claudia L. Johnson, '"Let Me Make the Novels of a Country": Barbauld's *The British Novelists* (1810/1820)', *NOVEL: A Forum on Fiction*, 34/2 (2001), 163–79 (166).

12 Michael Gamer, *Romanticism and the Gothic: Genre, Reception, and Canon Formation* (Cambridge: Cambridge University Press, 2004), p. 166.

13 Walter Scott, 'Charlotte Smith', in *Miscellaneous Prose Works: Biographical Memoirs*, 6 vols (Edinburgh: Cadell and Co., 1827), IV, 3–63.

14 Ellen Ledoux, 'Was there ever a "Female Gothic"?', *Palgrave Communications*, 3 (2017), 5.

15 Clara Reeve, *The Old English Baron* (Oxford: Oxford University Press, 2003), pp. 2–3.

16 Emma Hodinott, 'The Early Gothic Romances of Regina Maria Roche and the Jane Austen Connection', *The Corvey Project at Sheffield Hallam University*.
17 Jacqueline Belanger, Peter Garside and Anthony Mandal, *British Fiction, 1800–1829: A Database of Production and Reception – Phase II Report (Feb.–Nov. 2000) & Circulating-Library Checklist*; Cardiff Corvey, *Reading the Romantic Text* (Cardiff: Centre for Editorial and Intertextual Research, 2000), p. 2.
18 Gleave's third edition is dated 1820 and his sixth was published in 1827 under the imprint J. Gleave and Sons. Thanks to Robert Kirkpatrick for his genealogical research on William Emans. The earliest extant Emans title page date is 1820, while that for Kelly is 1821. All of Virtue's title pages are undated. It seems reasonable to assume that the new text came from London, since printer, publisher, bookseller and bookbinder Gleave 'published a smaller version of Thomas Kelly's list', according to Gary Kelly; see 'Sixpenny State? Cheap Print and Cultural-Political Citizenship in the Onset of Modernity', *Lumen*, 36 (2017), 37–61 (59).
19 John K. Reeves, 'The Mother of *Fatherless Fanny*', *ELH*, 9/3 (1942), 224–33 (224); Maria Edgeworth, *Tales of Fashionable Life: Vivian*, 6 vols (London: J. Johnson and Co., 1812), IV, p. vi.
20 Joseph Rezek, 'Bentley's Standard Novelist: James Fenimore Cooper', in *Transatlantic Literature and Author Love in the Nineteenth Century*, ed. Paul Westover and Ann Wierda Rowland (Cham: Springer International Publishing, 2016), pp. 49–74
21 The other texts include the Porter sisters' *Thaddeus of Warsaw* (p. 4), *The Scottish Chiefs* (pp. 7–8) and *The Hungarian Brothers* (p. 11); and the Lee sisters' *Canterbury Tales* (pp. 12–13).
22 Michael Sadleir, *XIX Century Fiction: A Bibliographical Record Based on His Own Collection*, vol. 2 of 2 (London: Constable, 1951), p. 164.
23 Preface to vol. XV, *Novel Newspaper*.
24 William Carew Hazlitt, *The Hazlitts: An Account of Their Origin and Descent: with Autobiographical Particulars of William Hazlitt (1778–1830), Notices of His Relatives and Immediate Posterity, and a Series of Illustrative Letters (1772–1865)* (Edinburgh: Ballantyne, Hanson & Co., 1911), p. 254.
25 Lucy Cogan, 'Introduction', in Charlotte Dacre, *Confessions of the Nun of St Omer* (Oxford: Routledge, 2016), p. vii.
26 Our thanks to Sarah Bull for discussing her research into William Dugdale's publishing practices with us. See also Sheryl Straight, 'The

Erotica Bibliophile' (2006), https://www.eroticabibliophile.com/publishers_dugdale_title.php. Straight's bibliography is however missing most of Dugdale's penny-number publications, which can be found in *Price One Penny*.

[27] Robert Kirkpatrick dated George Senior's edition to 1851 on the basis of advertisements. See 'The Purkess Family of Dean Street', *Pennies, Profits and Poverty: A Biographical Directory of Wealth and Want in Bohemian Fleet Street* (London: CreateSpace Independent Publishing, 2016), pp. 66–75.

[28] We are quite certain *The Black Forest, or The Solitary of the Hut* (1841) is also a reprint under a new title. *William Tell, the Hero of Switzerland* (1841) was a very popular figure at the time. We have not yet been able to identify a source and are less certain it is a reprint.

[29] Peter Miller and T. Fothergill, *William Milner of Halifax, Printer and Publisher: Checklist of a Collection of Books Printed by William Milner and His Successors and Imitators.* (York: Ken Spelman, 1991). Thanks to Claude J. Pelletier for sharing his digitisation of the St Andrews copy of this bookseller's catalogue.

[30] *Cheap Books Published by Milner & Sowerby, Paternoster Row, London, and Sold by All Booksellers* (London: Milner & Sowerby, 1866, digitised by the British Library; *A Retail Catalogue of Books* (London: Milner & Co., n.d.); 'Printing and Other Companies', *The Printing Times and Lithographer* (London: Wyman & Sons, 15 March 1883), p. 80.

[31] *A Retail Catalogue of Books*, pp. 3, 11.

[32] However, the series name did not appear in the copies of the reprints that we have seen; it seems to have only been used in advertising.

[33] Gleave did reprint both *The Old English Baron* and *The Castle of Otranto*.

[34] See University of Bristol library catalogue: https://bris.on.worldcat.org/oclc/931266932. Thanks to Kathryn Ross from Northallerton Library who kindly sent pictures of copies in the Pratt Collection.

[35] William Makepeace Thackery, *Vanity Fair* (Oxford: Oxford University Press, 2008).

[36] Sandra Guardini T. Vasconcelos, 'From the French or Not: Transatlantic Contributions to the Making of the Brazilian Novel', in Leslie Howsam and James Raven (eds), *Books Between Europe and the Americas: Connections and Communities, 1620–1860* (Basingstoke: Palgrave Macmillan, 2011), pp. 212–32 (p. 218).

[37] Xavier Aldana Reyes, *Spanish Gothic: National Identity, Collaboration and Cultural Adaptation* (London: Palgrave Macmillan, 2017), p. 42.

[38] Herbert E. Wroot, 'A Pioneer in Cheap Literature, William Milner of Halifax', *The Bookman* (London: Hodder and Stoughton, March 1897), 169–75 (174).

[39] Sharon Watson, 'Elizabeth Helme', Corvey Project, 1998, *https://extra.shu.ac.uk/corvey/aahelme/aahelmessa.htm*.

[40] Malcolm Chase, '"Stokesley Books": John Slater Pratt and Early Victorian Publishing', *International Journal of Regional and Local History*, 13/1 (2018), 32–46 (37).

3

'*As long as you are industrious, you will get on very well*': Adapting The String of Pearls's *Economies of Horror*

BRONTË SCHILTZ

Capitalism and horror are, for Karl Marx and his followers, closely intertwined. Mark Steven identifies 'a potentially meaningful relationship between cinematic gore and economic crises. Between spectacles of mutilation on the one hand, and the determinations of a failing economy on the other'.[1] However, '[w]hile Marx frequently draws on the patently gothic imagery of vampires, werewolves and spectres ... his accounts of capital also acquire a taste for human viscera, with sentences chewing their way through bodily gristle' (Steven, p. 44). Capitalism, Marx suggests, is a process of ceaseless, monstrous consumption. Aptly, then, money is the inciting force of all of the horrors in *The String of Pearls* (Rymer, 1846–7), the tale of an avaricious barber, Sweeney Todd, and his accomplice, pie shop owner Mrs Lovett. The centrality of commerce to this narrative is illustrated nowhere so clearly as during the grisly revelation that Todd murders his clients '*to cut them up for Mrs Lovett's pies!* after robbing them of all the money and valuables they might have about them'.[2]

This chapter examines how this essential aspect of the penny dreadful has bled into subsequent adaptations, focusing particularly on Stephen Sondheim's *Sweeney Todd: The Demon Barber of Fleet Street* and its direct source of inspiration, C. G. Bond's play of the same name, but also on various lesser-known adaptations. It thereby aims to expand considerations of adaptations of the text, and to examine the prevalence of economics as a central theme within them.

It is impossible to write the history of the penny dreadful without reference to class and economics. Peter Haining characterises the form as an alternative to Gothic novels, then enjoying the height of their popularity, for those without the financial means to purchase them. During the early nineteenth century, he notes, 'the vast majority of the population of Britain ... were illiterate', and among the working class, 'those who could read could hardly have afforded the price of these books ... from their pitiable wages'.[3] At this time, however, Britain was undergoing significant changes:

> Although it is generally accepted that Forster's Education Act of 1870 brought education to the masses in England ... there was a growing international movement of organizations ... providing simple schooling in the early years of the century. It was these groups ... coupled with the invention of the paper-making machine ... and the introduction of the rotary steam printing press, which created a whole new dimension for literature. (Haining, p. 23)

The dimension in question was a new and 'immense market of working-class people', who, if they 'had not actually read the Gothic novels ... were at least aware of their existence', creating an audience and demand for horrific and fantastical narratives at an affordable price (Haining, pp. 23–4).

Haining describes the work of writers of penny dreadfuls, in a fascinating parallel with Mrs Lovett's provision of delicious yet affordable pies, as 'serv[ing] an enormous public that probably that for them would have been starved of reading matter' (p. 18). While the form may be said to have benefited workers in this way, however, the industry itself was built on the exploitation of labour. As Haining notes, publishers of penny dreadfuls – most notably Edward Lloyd, who published *The String of Pearls* and employed its probable author, James Malcolm Rymer – made their fortunes by 'paying their authors a pittance (rarely more than fifty pence for an entire issue – if they could not actually get away with no payment at all) [and] employing "sweated labour" to set up the type' (p. 14).

Working conditions for typesetters were so poor at this time that one of the earliest trade unions formed following their legalisation in the United Kingdom in 1824 was the Northern Typographical Union, founded in 1830. For writers, the situation was not much better. So it was that 'in December 1846 [at which time *The String of Pearls* was proving highly lucrative] Rymer was declared bankrupt'.[4] Lloyd, meanwhile, died in 1890 as 'a millionaire' – a sum that, today, equates to over £130 million (Haining, p. 8). The history of the penny dreadful, then, follows a narrative of those in possession of the means of production profiting from the labour of a proletarian workforce. It is, in and of itself, a tale of Marxist horror. It is no wonder, then, that '[s]ome of the writers of "penny dreadfuls" had axes to grind [and] used every opportunity to play up the violent contrast between Wealth and Poverty'.[5]

Haining characterises the basis of the penny dreadful industry as the fact that workers 'needed excitement and thrills told in the simplest style to relieve the tedium of their day-to-day lives' (p. 24). This view appears somewhat blinkered, however, alongside the fact that many penny dreadfuls explicitly address the plight of the working class under the burgeoning capitalist system – and perhaps none so clearly as *The String of Pearls*. The penny dreadful opens with an introduction to Todd in his shop, where we are informed that he does 'a most thriving business' as he takes on his new apprentice, Tobias Ragg (p. 3). He is thus immediately characterised in terms of economics. Intriguingly, though, despite the negativity with which his first appearance is imbued, he is not presented as antithetical to the ordinary principles of capitalism. On the contrary, we learn that 'he rented a large house, of which he occupied nothing but the shop and parlour, leaving the upper part entirely useless, and obstinately refusing to let it on any terms whatever' (p. 3). This aversion to letting is, of course, a product of his need to keep his criminal activities concealed, yet it also marks him out as adhering to what Adam Smith considered the ethics of capitalism. In *An Inquiry into the Nature and Causes of the Wealth of Nations*, first published in 1776, Smith wrote, scathingly that 'landlords ... love to reap where they never sowed'.[6] Todd is thereby established from the very beginning of the narrative as someone who, though extracting his income by deeply immoral means, does so through his own labour. This is a tale as much about work as it is about murder.

When George Dibdin Pitt adapted the penny dreadful for the stage in 1847 as *Sweeney Todd, the Demon Barber of Fleet Street*, he relocated the first scene to the exterior of the shop, and placed Todd in conversation with 'Mr. Smith, a mechanic', responsible for crafting his now infamous chair.[7] Todd attempts to reduce the cost of Smith's work by haggling, accusing him, as an aside, of 'grabbing money', and appealing to his professional pride by insisting that '[a] mere one and sixpence will scarcely embarrass an individual in such a prosperous way of business as yourself' (Pitt, p. 19). The majority of subsequent stage plays based on *The String of Pearls* take inspiration from Pitt's, and Brian J. Burton's *Sweeney Todd the Barber*, written in 1962, is no exception. His version opens with a scene lifted almost entirely directly from Pitt's, but with the addition of far more explicit discussion of labour and capital – Todd urges Smith to '[j]ust state the amount of money you are attempting to rob me of', to which Smith replies: 'No robbery, Mr Todd, only the reward for my labour.'[8] In *Boys will be Boys*, first published in 1948, E. S. Turner identifies the penny dreadful as 'boys' fiction' that, being of a largely conservative strain, sharpens 'class prejudices', adding that Orwell's disapproval of the form clashed with a sense that 'the idea of a left-wing boys' paper makes one slightly sick; no normal boy would look at it' (p. 11). This perception appears misguided when held against accounts such as one dating from 1878, in which a man recalled that he first encountered *The String of Pearls* when 'female domestic servants used to "take in" a serial novel bearing that very title' (Haining, p. 10). The emphasis on the valuation of labour and of class struggle in the opening lines of this adaptation produced just fourteen years after the time of writing, however, further serves to contradict the assumption that left-wing themes are antithetical to the enjoyment of penny dreadfuls. On the contrary, the concerns with capital that flow through the pages of *The String of Pearls* are frequently brought to the fore in adaptations for the stage and screen – and nowhere more blatantly than in C. G. Bond's *Sweeney Todd: The Demon Barber of Fleet Street*, written in 1973, or Stephen Sondheim's famed musical of the same name, written in 1979 and borrowing heavily from Bond's alterations to the narrative.

The String of Pearls and its subsequent adaptations are firmly located in central London – then, as now, one of the world's major trading centres. Robert Mighall argues that

> The term 'urban Gothic' should have been a contradiction in terms. For the first generation of Gothic novels it would have been. The Gothic depicted what the city (civilisation) banished or refused to acknowledge, except in the form of thrilling fictions. [...] However [...] [b]y the early Victorian period, ideas of centre and margin were (ostensibly) overturned, as London, the very epicentre of the civilised world, became also, and in time pre-eminently, one of the dark places of the earth.[9]

This ambivalence is explicitly explored at the opening of these narratives. The first words of Bond's script are spoken by Anthony, who, based on Mark Ingestrie in *The String of Pearls*, is here a young sailor who has rescued Todd from the sea after he escaped unjust imprisonment presided over by a corrupt judge. He declares: 'I have sailed the world, beheld its fairest cities, seen the pyramids, the wonders of the east. Yet it is true – there *is* no place like home.'[10] Todd, however, takes a dimmer view:

> I, too, have sailed across the world, but I have seen no wonders – unless the angry noonday sun, shrivelling a man's shadow to a smudge beneath his feet, be a wonder. Or the greed and cruelty that forces a man to fight his own brother to death for a crust of bread. (Bond, pp. 1–2)

While the wealthy Anthony looks upon the world as a source of wonder, for Todd, it is a place where the human spirit is crushed by the torturous extraction of workers' labour by those in positions of power and the harsh necessities of survival in unforgiving capitalist societies. In Sondheim's adaptation of this scene, Todd describes London as 'a hole in the world [l]ike a great black pit' that is 'filled with people who are filled with shit', and at the top of which '[s]it the privileged few ... [t]urning beauty into filth and greed'.[11] It is not London's criminal underbelly that disgusts him, but its bourgeois institutions, with their capacity to wreak destruction on those of a lower socio-economic standing. In this sense, the reference to shit is particularly potent — faeces, which almost universally provokes some degree of disgust, is of course a product of consumption. William Ian Miller posits that, as soon as food has been placed in the mouth, 'it is magically transformed into the disgusting'.[12] This is the horror of Todd's London: as what Jessica Brown calls a 'character of gross appetite', the city incessantly transforms the beautiful into the repulsive.[13] In such a space,

> [t]he threat of being eaten up by the ever-sprawling urban monster is an extremity of urban angst based on appetitive dangers. Images of devouring, swallowing, drowning, and engulfing result in a sense of a cannibalistic city inhabited either by cannibals or the cannibalized. (p. 155)

Long before Todd and Mrs Lovett begin their monstrous venture, London is already a devouring space.

Given the space that London occupies in the American popular imagination, the musical's historical setting is particularly notable. In adapting *The String of Pearls*, Bond and Sondheim chose to relocate the narrative from the Georgian to the Victorian era, and thereby, as Sharon Weltman argues, 'reinsert[ed] the kind of critique viewers associated with Dickens'.[14] A common American perception of London, she suggests, is one informed by Dickens's works, figuring as a dark space made darker by its economic inequalities. The Victorian era therefore immediately connotes class conflict to American audiences. Further, as John Bush Jones posits,

> [a]t bottom *Sweeney* is profound social commentary — an indictment of not just the inequities of classism in Victorian England but of contemporary American culture as well. Sweeney suggests that the United States today is as overindustrialized and depersonalized as Charles Dickens's London, with the result that many people, like Sweeney, feel disempowered and without access to 'the system' so that the only choices left are despair or desperate action.[15]

Brown notes that this is emphasised by Tim Burton's 2007 film adaptation: '[t]he sound of grinding wheels combines with the view of an industrial mincer and oven suggesting the processes of production' in an opening sequence that 'captures the themes of dehumanized production, and the violence inherent in mass consumerism' (pp. 164–5). The enduring power of the tale of Sweeney Todd is not that it shows us the absolute extremities of human nature, but rather that it shows us the capitalist city within which an increasing number of us in the western world live and work for what it is: a cannibalistic monster that devours us and teaches us to devour. Once Todd and Mrs Lovett begin selling their human meat pies, 'it is the London public who are the consumers of human flesh, suggesting they are cannibalistic in their consuming practices' – their actual cannibalism is merely a literalisation of the capitalist conditions in which they already lived (Brown, p. 159).

Robert Mack argues that Todd's 'real business was the cutting of human throats', yet, in *The String of Pearls*, his principal objective is the theft of money and other valuables, with the slaughter of his victims a means of avoiding detection rather than his foremost purpose.[16] Indeed, the text assures us that '[t]here can be no doubt but that the love of money was the predominant feeling in Sweeney Todd's intellectual organisation and that, by the amount it would bring him, or the amount it would deprive him of, he measured everything' (Rymer, p. 127). This is expressed in Pitt's adaptation in the form of a soliloquy:

> When a boy, the thirst of avarice was first awakened by the gift of a farthing: that farthing soon became a pound; the pound a hundred – so to a thousand, till I said to myself, I will possess a hundred thousand. This string of pearls will complete the sum. (Pitt, p. 30)

This passage is replicated, closely or exactly, in numerous subsequent adaptations, such as Burton's *Sweeney Todd the Barber* (pp. 10–11), Austin Rosser's *Sweeney Todd: The Demon Barber of Fleet Street*[17] and even *The Sweeney Todd Shock 'n' Roll Show*,[18] a little-known school musical. Adding inflation from its value at Pitt's time of writing, this financial aspiration now equates to over £10 million, with the pearls alone worth almost an eighth of that sum. The Todd of *The String of Pearls* and the majority of adaptations is a man in pursuit of excessive wealth. In Bond and Sondheim's adaptations, however, his murderous exploits are not driven by mere greed.

In Sondheim's adaptation, Todd is a significantly more sympathetic character than his penny dreadful counterpart, motivated by lost love. Alfred Mollin argues that, in the musical,

> Sweeney is bitter about his unjust imprisonment. He expresses his contempt for the society that allows such injustices to occur, and he is cynical about the ability of a good man to prosper. But these passions do not initially prompt him to plan acts of revenge. The matters of his primary concern are the circumstances of his wife and his daughter, Johanna.[19]

The abuse of his family, however, is directly related to class dynamics. Had Judge Turpin, who passed a sentence of transportation on a false charge that enabled him to rape Todd's wife, Lucy, and kidnap Johanna, and later attempt to force her into marriage, not been of such high social standing, and had Todd's family not been comparatively lowly, it would not have been possible. The revenge Todd seeks is, in this sense, as much a matter of class retribution as it is of personal retaliation, as is true of Bond's version. This is made explicit by Sondheim during 'A Little Priest', in which Todd sings that '[t]he history of the world … is those below serving those up above', and then remarks: 'How gratifying for once to know … that those above will serve those down below!' (p. 86). Yet, in his quest for vengeance, his fellow workers become collateral damage.

Having been treated as such himself, Bond and Sondheim's Todd recognises that the working class are disposable, and thus can be utilised in his preparation for avenging himself and his family by murdering Judge Turpin. After Turpin escapes Todd's first attempt to murder him, Sondheim's Todd decides to kill indiscriminately, believing, in his rage, that 'all deserve to die … [b]ecause the lives of the wicked should be … [m]ade brief', while for everyone else, 'death [w]ill be a relief' (p. 79). Significantly, he is aware that killing people whom the law demonstrably holds no interest in protecting will allow him to prepare to murder Turpin without hindrance – he swears, in a near-quotation of Bond: 'I will get him back [e]ven as he gloats. In the meantime I'll practice [o]n less honorable throats' (Sondheim, p. 80). Yet, even after coming to this decision, Todd continues to define himself as a labourer – he declares that 'the work waits' (Sondheim, p. 80). Steven argues that 'because the human carriers of labour power must also consume the commodities they have produced and valorised, capitalism also means unavoidably participating in the consumption of oneself and one's fellow workers' (p. 45). In Sondheim's adaptation, this figures literally, as the bodies of Todd's victims are utilised by Mrs Lovett to make meat pies that she sells to the London public. After all, this was already the way of the world in which they live – as Todd says to Mrs Lovett, as they hatch their plan, 'the sound of the world out there … [t]hose crunching noises pervading the air' is the sound of 'man devouring man' – and so, he asks, 'who are we to deny it in here?' (Sondheim, p. 83). Their actions are not horrific because they are abnormal, but because, in a society that values human life only for its highly embodied power to produce and consume, they are not. Piatti-Farnell argues that '[c]onsumers are … their own absent referents. They remove themselves from the production line, without realizing that they are, in some form, the "meat" of the production itself.'[20] This figures literally in Pitt's adaptation, in which Turner notes the 'curious detail … that while [a] dog turned "with loathing" from bits of pie thrown to it, a newly bereaved widow showed no instinctive dislike of a pie containing portions of her late partner in marriage' (p. 36). This appears less curious, however, under consideration of how separated consumers increasingly are from the sources of their sustenance. Sondheim's Todd and Mrs Lovett, however, are acutely aware of the value of their own flesh as members of the working class. This is, after all, the spark of inspiration that strikes Mrs Lovett: 'Seems an awful waste… Such a nice, plump frame [w]ot's 'is name has' (Sondheim, p. 82). She knows that in their incessantly devouring world, what matters is not who one is, but what one is worth.

As such, her motivation for embarking on this venture, unlike Todd's, is almost entirely economic. When she proposes it, he concedes its practicality: 'These are desperate times, Mrs. Lovett, and desperate measures are called for' (Sondheim, p. 83). The suggestion is made partially as a means of assisting Todd, for whom she harbours romantic sentiments. This incentive appears to be secondary, however, to the fact that '[b]usiness needs a lift – [d]ebts to be erased' (Sondheim, p. 82). She is not, in this adaptation, a victim of capitalist violence, but an enforcer of it. Mark Fisher argues that, in the post-Fordist economic landscape,

> [a]ntagonism is not now located externally, in the face-off between class blocs, but internally, in the psychology of the worker, who, as worker, is interested in old-style class conflict, but, as someone with a pension fund, is also interested in maximizing the yield from his or her investments.[21]

This is, in many ways, the position of Mrs Lovett. Although she is aware of her disadvantaged position as a labourer – 'times is hard' – she does not, like Todd, view the solution to this dilemma as lying in an attack on those inhabiting the upper echelons of society, but in excelling as a businesswoman in order to enter those echelons herself (Sondheim, p. 14). As Mollin argues,

> [m]urder, for Mrs. Lovett, is an act like any other, to be done upon calculation of self-interest ... The capitalist ethic – elevating profit and self-interest – is not, in Mrs. Lovett, checked by conventional morality. Her capitalism is pure. And if Sweeney Todd may be characterized as a radically moral mass murderer, Mrs. Lovett is his radically immoral polar opposite. (p. 410)

Curiously, then, one distinction between *The String of Pearls* and Bond and Sondheim's adaptations is that Mrs Lovett is reshaped from an employer to a businesswoman who performs almost all of her own labour, with the exception of Tobias's assistance in the shop.

In the original penny dreadful, and in many adaptations, Lovett's bakehouse has the trappings of a factory, furnished for 'immense manufacture' with 'various mechanical contrivances for kneading the dough, chopping up the meat, &c' (p. 84). These are manned by staff who come to Mrs. Lovett destitute and 'willing to do anything for a mere subsistence' (p. 82). While Todd bleeds the wealthy for financial gain, Mrs Lovett targets the poor and desperate for their labour. At first, her employees think themselves fortunate, provided with shelter and food in exchange for their work, but soon realise themselves to be 'condemned to ... slavery' and 'victim to Mrs. Lovetts' pies' popularity', forced to become accessories to murder or to face meeting a grisly end themselves, presumably thereafter to be used as materials for the former products of their labour (pp. 160–1). Contemporary London and the Todd–Lovett enterprise become one: 'like the mid-nineteenth century metropolis, Todd's machine both sucked in newcomers, shattering their hopes and expectations, while also voraciously devouring the local population.'[22] As Sally Powell argues, this functions as an 'articulation of the threat posed by city commercialism to the sanctity and survival of the working-class individual' at a time and place in which the body was a highly sought-after commodity, and the cadavers of impoverished workers became lucrative products for anatomists.[23] In removing this element of the class critique of the penny dreadful, however, Bond and Sondheim reveal an even more disturbing reality emerging at the dawn of neoliberalism – that there may be workers who will participate in the violent extraction of value from others willingly if it guarantees their own economic advancement. As Rebecca Nesvet argues, 'Todd's incorporation of the nation into the cannibal pies might in fact lead to the loss of personal identity, agency, and even life. As "we are what we eat", the pie shop customers, too, become monstrous corporate bodies.'[24] If the choice posed to London's citizens is between allying themselves with a monstrous corporation and starvation, however, their participation begins to look more like desperation.

Carey Millsap-Spears, however, purports that Sondheim's Lovett is monstrous 'not just because of her use of human bodies as the meat in her pies, but because she is a strong female character who acts based on her own needs and wants'.[25] She later concludes that '*Sweeney Todd* is a Gothic moral: women who act on their selfish needs for love, money, and power must be punished in order to set the fictional world right again' (p. 124). Mary Jo Lodge makes a similar argument, positing that her demise 'can be read as retribution [for her] selfishly motivated attempts to move into a forbidden higher class, and as [a] metho[d] of disciplining [her] for [her] attempted transgressions'.[26] These readings, however, ignore a central facet of the text – that the higher classes are consistently portrayed as repulsively corrupt. Mrs Lovett does not deserve to die because, as a woman, she has unforgivable financial aspirations, but because she is too quick to betray her own class in pursuit of entry into another. She is complicit to the extreme in capitalism's extraction of value from the human body, and this, not her gender, renders her unforgivable. In Sondheim's musical, the majority of Todd's murders take place during a reprise of 'Johanna', in which he dolefully mourns his separation from his daughter. The majority of Mrs Lovett's 'work', by contrast, is exhibited during 'God, That's Good!', a considerably more upbeat song in which she is seen to be doing a thriving business. While 'Sweeney's crimes … develop a kind of tragically ritual inevitability', there is nothing tragic about Mrs Lovett's crimes, which she increasingly enacts with nauseatingly gleeful greed (Weltman, p. 65). She is a Gothic monster who horrifies not by evoking, as in earlier texts, the cruelty of the past, but the cruelty of a modern world obsessed with consumption. She enthusiastically advertises her products, driving her fellow Londoners to devour one another in the most literal embodiment of the ravenous impulse that makes the city the 'great black pit' that Todd so loathes.

In both *The String of Pearls* and numerous other adaptations, however, womanhood – and girlhood – is much more closely allied to victimhood within the capitalist framework. In the penny dreadful, Mrs Lovett's ability to profit from her work is inseparable from her sexual appeal. 'There was a Mistress Lovett', the author writes, 'but possibly our readers guessed as much, for what but a female hand, and that female buxom, young and good-looking, could have ventured upon the production of those pies' (p. 26). She uses this reduction of women to their sexual value to her advantage – 'some of the young fellows [who visited the shop] thought, and thought it with wisdom too, that he who consumed the most pies would be in the most likely way to receive the greatest number of smiles from the lady' (pp. 26–7). She is aware that as a female labourer, her flesh is on the market too, and she must consent to sell it in order to succeed. It is little wonder, then, that, by the close of the text, she begins to prepare for her retirement, asking her accomplice:

> when is all this to have an end, Sweeney Todd? you have been now for these six months providing me such a division of spoil as shall enable me, with an ample independence, once again to appear in the salons of Paris. I ask you now when is this to be? (p. 239)

Adapting The String of Pearls*'s Horror Economies*

This impatience, she says, is due to the fact that she 'run[s] a frightful risk, while [Todd has] the best of the profits', and because, exhausted by her own immorality, she is plagued by nightmares (p. 239). Given the principal means of her marketing, however, it may also be assumed that she knows that her business can only succeed as long as she is considered young and beautiful, and although she herself is a largely unsympathetic character, this very real reflection of society prompts consideration of women's oppression under capitalism.

This marriage of class and gender politics is rendered perhaps most disturbingly, however, in *The Sweeney Todd Shock 'n' Roll Show*. In this version, Tobias is in fact a thirteen-year-old girl, orphaned after an 'evil landlord' made her and her mother homeless, and 'overcome by the shame of [their] situation', her mother died (Miller and Lewton, p. 5). Her male disguise, she hopes, 'will enable [her] to find a home and earn a living' and save her from 'poverty and starvation' (Miller and Lewton, pp. 5–6). Having been taken on as an apprentice by Todd, his imprisonment in an asylum (an alteration from his usual fate of hanging) at the close of the narrative is not, for her, a positive one. Although she was financially and emotionally abused by him, this employment was her only source of income, and its termination therefore prompts desperation: 'Alas what will become of me? I have no master and no money' (Miller and Lewton, p. 80). Her youth is emphasised throughout the text, not least through her recurring lament of 'I'm only little', which forms the title and refrain of her song (Miller and Lewton, p. 30). Troublingly, then, her response to her financial predicament is to take 'off her cap revealing her long hair', catching the attention of Billy – a substitute for Mark – who, on seeing her, immediately forgets Susan, the unseen substitute for Johanna, and asks her: '[c]ome to my farm, marry me and let us live happily ever after', an offer she accepts (Miller and Lewton, p. 80). While the casting of school pupils would obscure the age gap between these characters, this interaction in fact portrays a female child accepting the sexual advances of a male adult in order to avoid destitution, and, despite the textual encouragement that the audience read this scene favourably, in actuality reflects a very real, and very disquieting, aspect of Victorian society. At the time in which *The String of Pearls* was both written and set, the age of consent in England was twelve, not to be increased to thirteen until the Offences Against the Person Act of 1875 or the current age of sixteen until the Criminal Law Amendment Act ten years later. With women often reliant on men for financial security in this period, this speaks to a deeply misogynistic and predatory aspect of nineteenth-century capitalism.

What makes Bond and Sondheim's adaptations the most horrifying, however, is the fact that they simply refuse to neatly end. In the final scene of Sondheim's version, the music to which the characters sing is derived from earlier scenes, with Todd singing to the tune of 'Epiphany' and 'A Little Priest', while Mrs Lovett sings to the tune of 'Poor Thing' and 'By the Sea', in the latter of which she ruminates on her dreams of a financially comfortable married life with Todd. Mollin explores how '[t]he limits of [Todd and Mrs. Lovett's] apparent accord [is] revealed during the segments of "A Little Priest" that concern the explanations of, or justifications for, their enterprise. Here, their parts cease to complement each other' (p. 411). Between Todd's lines, Mrs Lovett muses, to a different tune, that they'll '[s]ave a lot of graves, [d]o a lot of relatives favors' and that '[e]verybody shaves, [s]o there should be plenty of flavors' (Sondheim, p. 86). In his final duet with Mrs Lovett, Todd revisits this segment, reprising his reference to class difference. It is significant that Todd's final lines sung to Mrs Lovett are delivered with musical reference to class retribution, while Mrs Lovett's responses are delivered, to the tune of 'By The Sea', with musical reference to what Weltman terms her 'bourgeois aspirations' (p. 65). When Lucy's destruction, an unfaltering symbol of socio-economic inequality and of the reduction of human beings to consumable flesh, is re-enacted by Todd himself, who slits her throat after failing to recognise her, having been deceived by Mrs Lovett into believing her to be dead, the only fate appropriate for Mrs Lovett is death. This is not, as Millsap-Spears suggests, because she is a woman, but because, harbouring, in Mollin's words, a 'devotion to the spirit of capitalism', and to satiating her own desires above all else, she is a traitor to her class (p. 408). After all, when he realises that Todd has inadvertently murdered Lucy, Tobias asks him: 'Ya harmed her too, have ya? Ya shouldn't, ya know. Ya shouldn't harm nobody' – and then kills him (Sondheim, p. 153). Had Todd only killed Turpin and the Beadle, he might have lived. It is his descent into the murder of his own people – his complicity in the figurative and literal cannibalism of the working class – that leads directly to his demise alongside Mrs Lovett's, and this is underscored both by the reappearance of Lucy and by its attendant melodic reprises.

Lenin's infamous characterisation of capitalism as 'horror without end' implies, as Steven puts it, 'ceaseless horror', but also a troubling inconclusiveness – the future is precarious, and we are left to wonder: what now, and, as the subtitle of *Capitalist Realism* asks, is there no alternative? (p. 37). Even after the destruction of Turpin and the Beadle, *Sweeney Todd* leaves us with the uncomfortable sense that real change is impossible. Weltman argues that 'Todd wreaks his own terrible vengeance on the law, with the ultimate result that the new generation will inherit a world rid of both the corrupt institutions and the vitiated avenger' (p. 69). *The String of Pearls* concludes with the reassurance that 'Johanna and Mark lived long and happily together' (p. 256). However, the final image of the young lovers in Sondheim's adaptation is of them watching 'in horror' as Tobias 'moves to the grinding machine and slowly starts to turn the handle' on what they now know to be human flesh (Sondheim, p. 153). Turpin and the Beadle may be dead, but the institutions they represent remain alive and well – all that has really been achieved is destruction and trauma. Most horrifying of all, this closing image contrasts sharply with the revelation to the public in *The String of Pearls* of the monstrous crimes that occurred in Fleet Street, suggesting the chilling possibility that Tobias, despite his horrified response to Todd's actions, will continue his and Mrs Lovett's work. Having previously heard Tobias reflect on the haunting horrors of life in the workhouse and seen Turpin sentence to death a young boy who may or may not have been guilty of an unnamed crime, the audience is left with the sense that continuing to run the pie shop may be the only choice Tobias has in the brutal world he inhabits. In a city that continually devours its citizens, participating in this consumption is seemingly the only way to survive. In Bond's version, he vocalises this predicament as he refuses to accompany officers for questioning, saying: 'No, I have work to do. I must mince this meat' (p. 46).

In the late twentieth century, horror, like capitalism, is ongoing, and the future is undetermined. This is the horrific eventuality Marx envisioned when he 'imagined capitalism as cannibalism to emphasize the irrationality of a system that devours itself [and in which the] cannibal figure represents the fear that our appetite for consumption knows no end, and indeed reminds us of our potential inhumanity' (Brown, p. 7). *The String of Pearls* is perhaps not, as Powell suggests, 'an expression of profound social anxiety [regarding] the sanctity of the corpse in the face of the demand created by the anatomist', but a reflection of capitalist citizens' horrifying willingness to trade in one another's bodies in a system that demands cooperation under threat of destruction (p. 46).

The predominant argument put forth in *Splatter Capital* (2017) is that 'without forceful intervention against the system of capitalist accumulation, humankind will be subject everlastingly to the extraction of value via industrial torture' (Steven, p. 37). This is the overarching message of *The String of Pearls* and, in particular, its inconclusive adaptations, especially the work of Bond and Sondheim, proving Haining's assertion that the tale of Sweeney Todd is 'as much about society and its mores as the horrific crimes of one man'.[27] David McNally argues that '[p]art of the genuine radicalism of Marx's critical theory resides in its insistence on tracking and naming the monsters of modernity'.[28] The same could be said of the penny dreadful and its successors, and yet, unlike Marx, their authors do not turn to spectral or vampiric imagery in order to do so – reality is terrifying enough. Their utilisation of capitalism as a source of gory horror shows us not only the extremities of human behaviour, but the brutalisation that, within such an inhumane system of governance, we are all part of.

The String of Pearls borrowed from the Gothic mode to provide working-class readers with both a thrilling tale of horror and a chilling reflection of their own circumstances, all while making its publisher excessively wealthy and leaving its author in poverty. That its narrative has subsequently been so often mined for adaptations firmly in the Gothic tradition, a mode intimately concerned with social anxieties, is therefore unsurprising. *The String of Pearls* and its numerous adaptations impart a message that makes the blood run cold: under capitalism, we are always already cannibals.

Notes

1. Mark Steven, *Splatter Capital: The Political Economy of Gore Films* (London: Repeater Books, 2017), p. 12.
2. Anonymous, *Sweeney Todd, or The String of Pearls* (London: Wordsworth Editions Ltd, 2007), p. 251.
3. Peter Haining, *The Penny Dreadful, Or, Strange, Horrid & Sensational Tales!* (London: Victor Gollancz Ltd, 1975), p. 23.
4. Dick Collins, 'Introduction', in D. Collins (ed.), *Sweeney Todd: The String of Pearls* (Ware: Wordsworth Editions, 2010), pp. v–xxx.
5. E. S. Turner, *Boys will be Boys: The Story of Sweeney Todd, Deadwood Dick, Sexton Blake, Billy Bunter, Dick Barton, et al.* (London: Michael Joseph Ltd, 1975), p. 25.
6. Adam Smith, *An Inquiry into the Nature and Causes of the Wealth of Nations* (MetaLibri, 2007), p. 43.
7. George Dibdin Pitt, *Sweeney Todd* (Cabin John, MD: Wildside Press, 2002), p. 18.
8. Brian J. Burton, *Sweeney Todd the Barber* (London: Samuel French, 1984), p. 1.
9. Robert Mighall, 'Gothic cities', in C. Spooner and E. McAvoy (eds), *The Routledge Companion to Gothic* (Abingdon: Routledge, 2007), pp. 54–62.
10. C. G. Bond, *Sweeney Todd: The Demon Barber of Fleet Street* (London: Samuel French, 1973), p. 1.
11. Stephen Sondheim, *Sweeney Todd: The Demon Barber of Fleet Street* (London: Nick Hern Books, 1980), p. 11.
12. William Ian Miller, *The Anatomy of Disgust* (Cambridge, MA : Harvard University Press, 1998), p. 96.
13. Jessica Brown, *Cannibalism in Literature and Film* (London: Palgrave Macmillan, 2013), p. 157.
14. Sharon A. Weltman, 'Boz versus Bos in Sweeney Todd: Dickens, Sondheim, and Victorianness', *Dickens Studies Annual*, 42/1 (2011), 55–76.
15. John Bush Jones, *Our Musicals, Ourselves: A Social History of the American Musical Theater* (Lebanon, NH: Brandeis University Press, 2003), p. 291.
16. Robert Mack, *The Wonderful and Surprising History of Sweeney Todd: The Life and Times of an Urban Legend* (New York: Continuum, 2007), p. xv.
17. Austin Rosser, *Sweeney Todd: The Demon Barber of Fleet Street* (London: Samuel French, 1971), p. 6.

[18] Peter Miller and Randall Lewton, *The Sweeney Todd Shock 'n' Roll Show* (London: Samuel French, 1980), p. 34.
[19] Alfred Mollin, 'Mayhem and Morality in Sweeney Todd', *American Music*, 9/4 (1991), 405–17.
[20] Lorna Piatti-Farnell, *Consuming Gothic: Food in Horror and Film* (London: Palgrave Macmillan, 2017), p. 173.
[21] Mark Fisher, *Capitalist Realism: Is there No Alternative?* (Alresford, Hants: Zero Books, 2009), pp. 34–5.
[22] Rosalind Crone, 'From Sawney Beane to Sweeney Todd: Murder machines in the mid-nineteenth century metropolis', *Culture and Social History*, 7/1 (2010), 59–85.
[23] Sally Powell, 'Black Markets and Cadaverous Pies: The Corpse, Urban Trade and Industrial Consumption in the Penny Blood', in A. Maunder and G. Moore (eds), *Victorian Crime, Madness and Sensation* (Abingdon: Routledge, 2004), p. 45.
[24] Rebecca Nesvet, 'Sweeney Todd's Indian Empire: Mapping the East India Company in *The String of Pearls*', *Victorian Popular Fictions Journal*, 1/2 (2019), 75–90.
[25] Carey Millsap-Spears, '"How about a pie?": Mrs. Lovett, "Sweeney Todd", and the Double', *Studies in Popular Culture*, 35/2 (2013), 111–27.
[26] Mary Jo Lodge, 'From Madness to Melodramas to Musicals: The Women of Lady Audley's Secret and Sweeney Todd', *Theatre Annual: A Journal of Performance Studies*, 56/1 (2003), 78–96.
[27] Peter Haining, *Sweeney Todd: The Real Story of the Demon Barber of Fleet Street* (London: Boxtree, 1993), p. xiii.
[28] David McNally, *Monsters of the Market: Zombies, Vampires and Global Capitalism* (Leiden: Brill, 2010), pp. 144.

4

'Your lot is wretched, old man': Anxieties of Industry, Empire, and England in George Reynolds's Wagner, the Wehr-Wolf

HANNAH PRIEST

In George W. M. Reynolds's serialised novel *Wagner, the Wehr-Wolf* (1846–7), an old German shepherd agrees to become a werewolf in exchange for wealth, youth and power. The novel is unusual in a number of ways, not least in its inclusion of a lycanthrope as a protagonist and its early example of a transformation scene.[1] Reynolds's depiction of both the causes and mechanisms of lycanthropic metamorphosis is idiosyncratic, and, as this chapter will argue, thoroughly bound up in an exploration of broader concerns and anxieties of national identity, societal unease and personal morality. In many ways, the intention of this chapter is relatively clear. It seeks to make the case for taking *Wagner, the Wehr-Wolf* seriously as a piece of early Victorian literature, while still appreciating the novel for what it is: a knowingly Gothic, occasionally lurid and often rambling tale of sex, violence and lycanthropy. Nevertheless, when read in the context of Reynolds's other penny dreadfuls, including the generally overlooked *Faust: A Romance* (1845–6), *Wagner* emerges as a skilfully plotted novel with concerns beyond its attention-grabbing body horror.

The author of *Wagner, the Wehr-Wolf*, George W. M. Reynolds, was a writer, publisher, journalist and sometime political activist, whose works – particularly his long-running series *The Mysteries of London* (1844–8) and *The Mysteries of the Court of London* (1848–52)

– sold in high numbers in the early decades of the Victorian period, for a penny an issue. Despite this popularity, Reynolds's penny dreadfuls received criticism during his lifetime and neglect in the years following. Although a number of scholars have sought to address this oversight, the majority of the work to date on Reynolds focuses either on the writer's career itself, or on *The Mysteries of London*. *Wagner, the Wehr-Wolf* has received relatively little critical attention and is rarely read in the context of the author's other serialised novels.

Reading Wagner in Context

George Reynolds launched his *Reynolds's Miscellany*, a weekly penny-an-issue magazine in 1846. *Wagner, the Wehr-Wolf* was serialised from the first issue. Immediately prior to the launch of his *Miscellany*, Reynolds served as editor of the *London Journal*, and in 1845–6 the *Journal* serialised Reynolds's *Faust: A Romance* in weekly instalments.[2] During his tenure as editor of the *Journal*, Reynolds published a translation of the French serial novel *Les Mystères de l'Inquisition* by Paul Féval; he also published a translation of Eugène Sue's influential *Les Mystères de Paris*. In 1844, Reynolds's own 'Mysteries' novel – *The Mysteries of London* – began its first series, published in weekly numbers. The second series of *Mysteries of London* began in October 1846, the month before Reynolds launched the first issue of his *Miscellany*, and the first instalment of *Wagner, the Wehr-Wolf*.

The reason for this brief résumé of Reynolds's output in the mid-1840s is to highlight two significant facts: *Wagner, the Wehr-Wolf* was published as an immediate follow-up to *Faust* (albeit with a move from the *Journal* to the new *Miscellany*), and was published concurrently with the second series of *Mysteries of London*. Although there is little evidence available as to the identity of the weekly readership of these respective titles, new issues of *Mysteries of London* and *Wagner, the Wehr-Wolf* were arriving at booksellers and newsstands at the same time, and it is not an unreasonable to assume that a number of readers would have been enjoying them in tandem. Indeed, in his consideration of the early years of *Reynolds's Miscellany*, Andrew

King suggests that Reynolds not only assumed a shared readership for the two novels, but actually banked on it. King argues that Reynolds's decision to use his own name in the title of his new magazine was because he 'no doubt believed in the saleability of his name after the success of *Faust* in the *London Journal* and of the *Mysteries of London*, both of which carried his signature' (p. 55).

Recent scholarly criticism on Reynolds's fiction has almost entirely – though not always intentionally – erased the concurrence of these publications, introducing an artificial gap between the urban mysteries and the Gothic romances. Of all his serial fiction, Reynolds's *Mysteries of London* has received the most critical attention; however, the majority of articles examining this work make little or no reference to *Wagner*. In the admittedly smaller body of articles that specifically focus on *Wagner*, *The Mysteries of London* receives little more than a passing mention as Reynolds's 'best remembered' work.[3] At times, this separation manifests through minor editorial discontinuity. For example, the introduction to Sophie Raine's otherwise thorough consideration of *The Mysteries of London* in *The Palgrave Handbook of Steam Age Gothic* (2021) gives the original serial publication dates of *Mysteries* (1844–8), but the later date of John Dicks's collected edition of *Wagner, the Wehr-Wolf* (1857), unintentionally introducing an almost decade-long separation between the two.[4] More dramatically, some analyses introduce more of a chasm between the two works, making it genuinely hard to conceive of them as written by the same person, let alone published at the same time. In the edited collection *The Victorian Gothic*, there are two chapters focused on Reynolds's work. Jarlath Killeen's 'Victorian Gothic Pulp Fiction' discusses *Wagner, the Wehr-Wolf* as Victorian horror fiction, decrying its lack of coherent plot, articulation of hatred, focus on the 'squalid self' and 'chauvinistic nationalist bias'.[5] Critical of penny dreadfuls generally, Killeen singles Reynolds out specifically as '[o]ne of the most prolific writers of Victorian pulp' (p. 51).[6] On the other hand, Avril Horner's chapter later in *The Victorian Gothic* (2012), 'Victorian Gothic and National Identity: Cross-Channel "Mysteries"', considers *The Mysteries of London* alongside the work of Eugène Sue and Charles Dickens, arguing that Reynolds's intricately plotted work helps to 'make vivid and sustain an important dialogue concerning the nature of freedom and equality in modern urban society'.[7] The horror in Reynolds's work, for Horner, offers 'a dialogue in which the uncanny and the abject are used to interrogate the social and political realities of the time' (p. 121).

This comparison of the chapters in *The Victorian Gothic* reveals the reason why this separation of *Wagner* and *Mysteries* has occurred. With its cosmopolitan setting, links to journalism surrounding the French Revolution and explicit contemporary social commentary, *The Mysteries of London* is categorised as urban fiction. Its Gothicism is 'domesticated' and employed in the pursuit of a direct critique of 'real-life' political corruption and societal inequities.[8] Analyses of *The Mysteries of London* frequently includes comparisons with – or references to – the work of Charles Dickens, Victor Hugo, Karl Marx and Friedrich Engels. By contrast, with its late medieval setting, supernatural monsters, and copious sex and violence, *Wagner* is a pulp Gothic romance. It is generally treated as, first and foremost, a werewolf text, being evoked as a forerunner to twentieth- and twenty-first-century werewolf fiction.[9] Where literary context is offered, it is usually the Gothic tradition, looking backwards to eighteenth-century novels such as Horace Walpole's *The Castle of Otranto* (1764) and Matthew Lewis's *The Monk* (1796), and positioning *Wagner* as 'old-fashioned' (King, p. 65) and the 'last gasp' of outdated ideological concerns.[10]

This disjunction in the critical reception of Reynolds's work has been noted, and Anne Humpherys suggests that it may be, in part, the result of conflicting characteristics and discordance in the work itself. Humpherys describes Reynolds as being 'full of contradictions', noting the 'paradoxical mixture' of concerns in both his fiction and journalism (p. 79). It is also worth pointing out the inherent difficulty in analysing Reynolds's work: given that he was '[o]ne of the most prolific writers of Victorian pulp', being fully conversant with the entirety of Reynolds's output is an onerous (if not impossible) task (Killeen, p. 51). Nevertheless, the forced separation of *Wagner, the Wehr-Wolf* and *The Mysteries of London* consistently does disservice to the former, resulting in both its neglect and, I would argue, its misinterpretation.

Moreover, not only is *Wagner* often distanced from Reynolds's other fiction, but individual chapters are also read in isolation from the rest of the novel. Again, this decontextualisation leads to misinterpretation, as particular episodes – most notably the Inquisition scene – are assumed to be representative of the text as a whole. For instance, in a consideration of anti-Catholicism in British Gothic literature, Diane Long Hoeveler examines a scene from *Wagner* in which two characters are tortured by the Inquisition. She uses this scene, as well as earlier scenes in a cruel Carmelite convent, to argue that *Wagner* is 'the final stage in the Gothic textual trajectory' that uses 'the most ominous and frighteningly real manifestation of the continued power of the Catholic Church' as propaganda to the 'lower-class Protestant imaginary' in a time of heightened anti-Catholic rhetoric (p. 155). While not disputing Hoeveler's identification of anti-Catholic tropes in the Inquisition and convent scenes in *Wagner*, the conclusion drawn relies on an unfamiliarity with Reynolds's concurrent publication.[11] Hoeveler notes that some scholars have suggested that scenes depicting Inquisitions in Gothic literature can be read as 'coded critiques of English prisons or the English legal system', but finds this argument 'less persuasive' (p. 157). Inquisition scenes, for Hoeveler, are *always* 'part and parcel of the very clear and persistent anti-European and anti-Catholic ideological agenda' (p. 157). While this assessment is, perhaps, convincing when *Wagner* is considered alongside other Gothic romances, it is less so when *Wagner* is read alongside *The Mysteries of London*, a serial that includes numerous *uncoded* 'critiques of English prisons or the English legal system' (Hoeveler, p. 157). Furthermore, when *Wagner* is read in the light of Reynolds's journalism, and his translations of Sue's work, it is hard to accept that the writer was indulging an 'anti-European' ideological agenda. Richard C. Maxwell has suggested that the 'Black Chamber of the Post Office' is presented in *Mysteries of London* as the 'modern equivalent' of the 'Spanish Inquisition of the Gothic novelist' (p. 193); Horner argues that the 'Gothicisation of government strategy' in *Mysteries* is 'no mere fantasy' but rather a direct commentary on a real-life case of the Post Office opening the letters of an Italian political exile in 1844 (p. 115). In this context, a different interpretation of the Inquisition scenes in *Wagner* becomes more persuasive.

Nonetheless, it is important to remember that, although *The Mysteries of London* evokes the Inquisition as a Gothic comparative to the secretive 'horrors' of modern life, *Wagner* undeniably presents a visceral and brutal scene of torture that is explicitly presented as a feature of the Inquisition (and, at times, unequivocally a function endorsed by the Catholic Church). This returns us to Humpherys's characterisation of the 'paradoxical mixture' in Reynolds's work, but it also highlights the significant omission in almost all of the scholarship on both *Wagner* and *The Mysteries of London*: Reynolds's serial novel *Faust*. In an examination of the relationship between Reynolds's political writing and activism and his fiction, Humpherys identifies two significant shifts that occur when the writer moves from editing the *London Journal* to editing *Reynolds's Miscellany*. She asserts that the serialised novels in the *Miscellany* 'tended to be somewhat more sensational than even those in *The London Journal*', but concomitantly 'Reynolds's politics were much more in evidence' (p. 81). There are the 'mysterious contradictions' in his work: the peculiar combination of 'politics and pornography, sentiment and sensationalism' that led to criticism from his peers and, I would further add, the curious frustrations that arise when attempting to consider his fiction output as a coherent whole (Humpherys, p. 79).

It is tempting to read *Wagner* as the 'pornography and sensationalism' to *Mysteries*'s 'politics and sentiment'; however, this undermines the complexity of both texts and elides the possibility of a shared readership. As I have argued, in order to posit a possible way of navigating the complexity and contradiction between these two better-known novels, *Wagner* must be read in context. While this certainly includes a consideration of the relationship between *Wagner* and *The Mysteries of London*, I would further suggest that it is necessary to look more closely at *Wagner*'s relationship to *Faust*, its immediate predecessor. Not only will this further illustrate the 'shift' from the *London Journal* to *Reynolds's Miscellany* identified by Humpherys, but it will also allow for further elucidation of key themes in both novels.

Reynolds's Faustian Pacts

Faust: A Romance was published in weekly instalments in *The London Journal* between October 1845 and September 1846. It differs in some highly significant respects from the more canonical versions of the Faust story by Christopher Marlowe (c. 1592) and Johann Wolfgang von Goethe (1808, 1832).[12] Both Marlowe and Goethe's Faust stories are dramas, for instance, and both use the conventions of tragedy in their plot and characterisation. Marlowe's Doctor Faustus is a man of hubris; despite humble origins, he has achieved a doctoral degree at the University of Wittenberg, but his quest for knowledge leads him to necromancy, and then to a pact with Lucifer (through his intermediary Mephistophilis). Goethe's Heinrich Faust has somewhat less agency, being the pawn in a wager between the demon Mephistopheles and God himself, but he is still a man striving for absolute mastery of all human knowledge. Falling into despondency, Faust considers suicide, but he rejects this idea in favour of a pact with the Devil. Reynolds's later take on the story undoubtedly shares some similarities in its overarching plot with these earlier versions; nevertheless, as a self-styled 'romance' written as a serialised novel, it brings more Gothic sentiments and concerns to the fore. In addition to this, Reynolds's protagonist is substantively different in characterisation and motivation from his theatrical predecessors.

The novel's prologue is set in Wittenberg in 1493. Reynolds's Wilhelm Faust is not a knowledgeable scholar of esoteric subjects, but rather a humble young student, who has been condemned to a cell in a subterranean dungeon.[13] As the reader quickly learns, Faust has been imprisoned for the 'crime' of falling in love with a woman 'betrothed to one of the imperial blood'.[14] The young man is facing the 'Tribunal', and he knows that his punishment is very likely to be death; however, a 'turnkey' offers a possibility of escape, when he repeats a story about a previous prisoner reciting an incantation to summon a demon and effect his own release. Faust is initially reluctant to attempt this feat himself, but as the time of his execution approaches, he gives in to temptation and makes a pact with the demon he conjures. He will be given wealth and power beyond his wildest dreams – and be reunited with his love Theresa – for twenty-four years, during which time the demon will serve as his slave. Once the time has elapsed, Faust's soul will belong to Satan, and he will be taken directly to Hell.

Modern readers (like, possibly, Victorian readers) will be surprised to discover that Wilhelm Faust is not always the main character of *Faust*, and his pact with the Devil is frequently side-lined in favour of other plots. In fact, the first part of the novel is far more concerned with the Tribunal and with the 'Cord and Dagger' of the *Vehmgericht*, or Vehmic courts, a historical tribunal system in operation in late medieval Germany. While Hoeveler argues that invocations of secret tribunals in Gothic fiction are simply stand-ins and condemnations of 'Inquisition-style legal proceedings' (and, thus, the anti-Catholic 'ideological agenda' that permeates the Gothic mode), I would argue that there is evidence that Reynolds here does indeed mean to invoke the Vehmic courts themselves, rather than using them as a cipher for the Inquisition (p. 157).

Despite their medieval heyday, Vehmic courts were not unknown to early nineteenth-century literati. They feature in Walter Scott's novel *Anne of Geierstein, or The Maiden of the Mist* (1829), a work inspired by Goethe's play *Götz von Berlichingen* (1773), which Scott had translated into English in 1799.[15] There is undoubtedly an association of ideas of the *Vehmgericht* and the Inquisition in Reynolds's work, but I would argue that the *Vehmgericht* in *Faust* is not intended to be read as a disguised version of the Catholic Inquisition. Reynolds's *Vehmgericht* is a secret court that exerts a sinister hold over men of all stations, and which draws its power from corruption, deception and subterfuge, rather than any claim on religious or secular legitimacy. The Vehmic court in *Faust* stands above both Church and state, and it is no coincidence that the first person we see facing the Tribunal (after Faust) turns out to be Arch-Duke Leopold, the nephew of 'Imperial Majesty Maximilian the First' (ch. 1).[16]

The invocation of the *Vehmgericht* in *Faust*, therefore, is less a commentary on religious hypocrisy and more a symbol of extra-governmental megalomania. This is underlined by developments later in the text, when Reynolds introduces a plotline involving Lucreza and Caesar Borgia. The Borgia storyline takes up a good part of the second half of the novel, and it includes two authorial interjections that insist that 'this is no romance' but 'a true and faithful description' of the activities of the notorious family.[17] The Borgia section of Reynolds's story contains some of the more grue-some violence of the novel, as well as intimations of sordid sexual practices. The power-grabbing Borgia siblings serve as a reminder that, while Faust may have acquired his megalomaniacal and murderous tendencies via a pact with Satan, history can furnish us with individuals who achieved this all by themselves.

Faust and the Borgias' despicable pursuit of power – like the corrupt and secretive *Vehmgericht* in the first half of the novel – are repeatedly condemned. Reynolds gives the most explicit commentary to the Demon, who serves at times as a sardonic narrator of Faust's short-sightedness. The most pointed speech comes in chapter 56, 'The Demon's Lecture', following the death of Pope Alexander VI, the father of Caesar and Lucreza. The Demon states of Alexander's career that 'he saw before him two paths – both departing from the same place, and, though taking different directions, still converging to the same point in the end' (*Faust* 7). Lest the reader be lulled into thinking this is a specific criticism of an individual, the Demon continues:

> You mortals have an idea that it is more easy to obtain riches, and power, and glory by foul means, than by fair; – and ye are wrong! You mortals conceive that the evil path is the shorter, the more convenient, and the more ready; – and ye are wrong! (ch. 56)

Further emphasising this point, Reynolds adds a footnote to explain that he will be illustrating it for the remainder of the novel through 'the contrast existing between Faust and Otto Pianalla' (ch. 56, 2n.).

Otto Pianalla is a young and impoverished artist who appears first as the brother of Ida and old friend of Faust. He is a consistently good and honourable young man, who rescues the true Baron von Czernin, prevents his sister from poisoning her love rival Theresa, forms a wholesome romantic relationship with Nina Mazzini, a farmer's daughter, and eventually makes his fortune through his own artistic prowess and the gratitude of Arch-Duke Leopold. As Reynolds reminds us, this character stands in contrast to Faust, representing the 'fair means' to Faust's 'foul'.

Otto Pianalla is not the only contrast to Faust. At the beginning of his story, Faust is presented with an alternative path to the one he decides to take. The turnkey of the prologue reveals to Faust that he, too, was once condemned to death by the Tribunal. He was given the option of death on the wheel or spending the rest of his life as a jailer of others; he was then made aware of a third option – the incantation left on the wall by a former prisoner. As he sits in his prison cell, Faust – though he may not know it – has a series of alter egos surrounding him: the jailer, the esoteric prisoner, and his friend Otto. In this respect, Faust is very much like Richard Markham, the protagonist of *The Mysteries of London*. When Markham is sent to Newgate Prison, he encounters a 'Republican writer' and the monstrous criminal 'Resurrection Man' Anthony Tidkins. Sara Hackenberg describes Markham's fellow prisoners as 'alternative templates for alter-egos'; I argue that this description can equally be applied to the figures that surround Faust in his cell.[18]

While *Faust* and *The Mysteries of London* share many narrative tropes associated with Gothic fiction – subterranean dungeons, terrifying courts, impostors and doubles, imperious murderers, imperilled innocents – they also have certain thematic concerns in common. For the purposes of this chapter, the most significant are the persistent dangers of non-visible power structures and the human propensity for choosing 'the evil path' when presented with a choice. Exploring *Mysteries*, Humpherys suggests that Reynolds 'seems to have a very dark view of the human potential for good'; in *Faust*, the Demon vocalises that 'dark view' in his lecture.[19]

Wagner, the Wehr-Wolf, published immediately after the conclusion of *Faust* and concurrent with the second series of *The Mysteries of London*, ostensibly seems to confirm Reynolds's 'dark view'. The novel is – in the parlance of modern television series – a spin-off of *Faust*, rather than a direct sequel, but it is clear that Reynolds imagined that readers would probably be familiar with the earlier novel (which concluded in September 1846) when embarking on the next (which began in November). The story's prologue is set in January 1516 in the Black Forest. A ninety-year-old shepherd sits alone in his hut, bemoaning his loneliness since the disappearance of his only surviving grandchild, Agnes. A stranger arrives and quickly offers him a possible remedy: Fernand Wagner can have his youth and health restored on the condition that he agrees to become a werewolf once a month and 'prey upon the human race'.[20] Wagner must act as a companion to the stranger for eighteen months, after which time he will be free to decide what he wants to do next.

When Wagner asks the stranger's name, his guest whispers something in his ear that frightens him. Notably, though, the reader is not told what this is. Later on, we see a portrait of this companion in Wagner's apartment, bearing the inscription, 'F., Count of A., terminated his career on the 1st August, 1517' (ch 6). The name 'Faust' does not actually appear until chapter 17 of *Wagner*; however, readers of Reynolds's earlier novel will understand the reference. In the final chapter of *Faust*, the Count of Aurana 'terminated his career' (i.e., died) at the very end of July 1517. This is a rather charming literary technique by Reynolds – again, reminiscent of more recent televisual crossovers – as readers familiar with *Faust* will enjoy the subtle intertextualities, but readers unfamiliar with it will gloss over them without marring their understanding of *Wagner*.

Fernand Wagner ends the prologue agreeing, not only to a monthly lycanthropic transformation, but also to be the companion and 'slave' to Wilhelm Faust. Interestingly, while both Marlowe and Goethe give their versions of Faust a servant named Wagner, the character does not appear at all in Reynolds's *Faust*. Reynolds introduces his Wagner in a separate but related story, and I would argue he does so in order to further develop some thematic concerns of the earlier work, particularly the interrogation of personal morality and societal unease. Nevertheless, there are also significant stylistic differences between the two novels that are revealing of the ways in which these thematic concerns are developed from one to the next.

As previously noted, Humpherys has argued that Reynolds's fiction became 'somewhat more sensational' when he moved from the *London Journal* to the *Miscellany* (p. 81). In truth, a comparison of *Faust* and *Wagner* makes one think this is something of an understatement. *Wagner* has been described by modern scholars as 'an attack on Christianity' (Killeen, p. 51), 'gory, lewd, and often Gothic to the point of absurdity' (Boucher, p. 23) and 'a crude, hastily written potboiler'.[21] Again, as noted, there are two elements of the narrative that have had the most critical attention: the physical transformation of Wagner into werewolf form, and the torture of Guilia Arestino and Isaachar ben Solomon in the dungeon of the Inquisition. These two episodes introduce a visceral body horror that goes beyond what was seen in *Faust*, even in that earlier novel's more sensational episodes. The writing lingers on descriptions of broken and tortured bodies – all of which have been stripped of clothing – with emphasis on both physical and mental trauma. And yet the two scenes constitute just two chapters, with nearly fifty others separating them (*Wagner*, chs 12, 61). I would not dispute that the two scenes in question are both graphic and disturbing, featuring as they do one of the first (if not the first) painful transformation scenes in English werewolf literature, and a prolonged depiction of physical torture during which an innocent Jewish man screams at the Inquisition judge that he is a 'monster'.[22] However, focusing on these two passages in *Wagner* alone, without contextualising them with reference to other plot points, can lead to misinterpretation and underestimation.

Wagner is a novel that includes a paradigm-shifting werewolf transformation and a horridly Gothic scene of Inquisition torture. It also includes (among other things) an unsettling anti-heroine who feigns being deaf and dumb while repeatedly returning to a manuscript that appears to describe someone cutting at a murdered corpse with a scalpel; the said anti-heroine getting marooned on a desert island and having an intensely physical relationship with her handsome werewolf lover while dressed only in flowers; a slow-burn cross-cultural friendship between Manuel (a Catholic), Isaachar (a Jew), and Ibrahim (a Muslim convert); and a werewolf fighting a giant anaconda.

The dramatic physical transformation of Wagner into werewolf form is a significant part of the narrative, and a significant part of the way Reynolds crafts his tale as a *horror* story. However, the reason behind Wagner's transformation is no less dramatic or unusual. While early modern witchcraft treatises and trial broadsheets associated lycanthropy with a demonic compact, this was understood as a very different sort of Satanic relationship. As with witches, werewolves were imagined as simple-minded or malicious individuals who were deceived by Satan into performing blasphemous rituals. The individuals arrested, tried and executed as werewolves by historical Inquisitions were generally poor, uneducated and disenfranchised.[23] What is presented in Reynolds's fiction is a very different type of arrangement. Wagner enters into a Faustian pact, with youth, wealth and vigour being the payment in exchange for becoming a werewolf at the end of each month.

Interestingly Wagner's demonic compact is not only paralleled by Faust's own contractual arrangement in the previous novel, but also by the fate of another character within *Wagner*. Alessandro Francatelli, the brother of the woman beloved by the brother of the woman beloved by Wagner (a network of relationships typical of Reynolds's Gothic fiction), travels to Constantinople and ends up working for the Florentine envoy to the Ottoman Empire. He briefly meets a woman in a bazaar and falls instantly in love with her. The woman – who we later learn is named Aischa – offers him a potential deal: if Alessandro converts to Islam and goes to work for the Empire, he will eventually get the chance to be with her. Aischa's temptation of Alessandro mirrors closely the Demon's temptation of Faust and the later attempted temptation of Wagner:

> [S]he gradually developed to his imagination the destinies upon which he might enter, offering herself as the eventual prize to be gained by a career certain to be pushed on successfully through the medium of a powerful, though mysterious, influence. (ch. 45)

Like Faust before him, Alessandro cannot help but yield to temptation. He converts and becomes Ibrahim, despite not actually changing his belief system.[24] He obtains a position in the government of the Ottoman Empire, rising quickly through the ranks until Alessandro/Ibrahim is second only to Solyman the Magnificent, obtaining possibly the most power of anyone in the entire novel and, eventually, able to quash the Inquisition and drive it out of Florence. He also gets the woman for whom he renounced his home, his faith and his family. And, like Faust with Theresa before him, Ibrahim immediately gets bored with Aischa and cheats on her. In this case, his infidelity is with multiple women of a dazzling array of nationalities and creeds. Faust and Ibrahim sell their souls for love, and it is instantly corrupted by a selfish libido.

Anxieties of Industry, Empire, and England

It should be clear from the previous discussion that *Wagner, the Wehr-Wolf*, like *Faust* before it, offers little direct commentary on the state of early Victorian England. While *The Mysteries of London* makes unequivocal – frequently polemic – criticisms of social and political realities, this specific engagement with the detail of 'real-life' England is, unsurprisingly, absent in the Gothic romances. Nevertheless, I would argue that, much like Reynolds's Gothicisation of the Post Office in *Mysteries*, his sensational tales of sardonic demons, megalomaniacal Borgias, arcane manuscripts, desert islands, giant anacondas, poison, mayhem and intrigue are not 'mere fantasy' (Horner, p. 115).

Both *Faust* and *Wagner* feature sinister judiciary bodies that operate beyond the jurisdiction of monarchy, government, and empire, and have the power to impose sentences of imprisonment, corporal punishment and execution. In *Faust*, this body is the *Vehmgericht*; in *Wagner*, it is the Inquisition. Both of these institutions have some basis in historical fact, though both are Gothicised by Reynolds for entertainment purposes. As previously argued, there are clear parallels between the *Vehmgericht* of *Faust*, the Inquisition of *Wagner* and certain contemporary and urban institutions in *Mysteries*. In addition to this, small details in *Wagner* encourage us to see Reynolds's Inquisition as more closely aligned to English legal systems than one might expect. As well as a 'chief judge', his Inquisition court is staffed by a 'procurator fiscal' or 'attorney-general' who, like the judge, wears scarlet robes trimmed with ermine (ch. 36). A small insight into the functionality of the Inquisition court brings this Gothic scene into closer dialogue with *Mysteries*: 'Defendants in civil cases were alone permitted in that age and country to retain counsel in their behalf; persons accused of crimes were debarred this privilege' (*Wagner*, ch. 36). This is reminiscent of the pseudo-legalities of the *Vehmgericht* in *Faust*, but also of the desperation of Richard Markham in *Mysteries*, who is forced to navigate the pitfalls of securing legal counsel after being sent to Newgate Prison.

In his article 'G. M. Reynolds, Dickens and the Mysteries of London', Maxwell explores the connections between the work of George Reynolds and Charles Dickens, suggesting that the proliferation of secretive institutions and organisations in Victorian fiction can be connected to changes in governmental structures and strategies. He argues that democratic government in nineteenth-century Europe 'established new possibilities for individual fulfilment while also prompting an extension of the public domain', resulting in 'a complex interaction between secrecy and publicity (p. 194). Maxwell goes on to assert that, in these circumstances, power can be achieved by 'shrouding, once again, public affairs in secrecy' and acting 'secretly in a society which is presumed to operate publicly' (p. 194). While the romanced world of sixteenth-century Italy (the setting for both *Faust* and *Wagner*) is several centuries away from the 'democratic government' of nineteenth-century England, Reynolds constructs worlds in which 'good' and open rulers (Emperor Maximilian I, Lorenzo de' Medici, Suleiman the Magnificent) are constantly in danger of being bamboozled by those who would shroud the mechanics of power in secrecy, just as a glimpse into Buckingham Palace in *Mysteries* reveals an impotent and naïve Victoria whose unelected special advisers run the country.

Secretive extra-governmental judicial bodies are, therefore, a thematic concern across all three of the novels. The question arises, therefore, as to why Reynolds made the choice to switch from the *Vehmgericht* of *Faust* to the Inquisition court of *Wagner*. The Inquisition is a more standard Gothic trope, redolent of the anti-Catholic ideologies discussed by a number of scholars of Gothic fiction, including by Rebecca Nesvet in her chapter for this volume. If the intention was to evoke the secretive power structures behind the social and political realities of nineteenth-century Britain, why resort to a sensationalised image best known from earlier fiction? Why move from the tribunal to the torture chamber?

Humpherys's assertion that Reynolds's fiction became 'somewhat more sensational' on his move from the *London Journal* to the *Miscellany* is evidenced here. I would argue that Reynolds replaced the *Vehmgericht* with the Inquisition precisely *because* it moved us from the tribunal to the torture chamber. The use of the Inquisition allows Reynolds to heighten the horror, introducing the possibility of broken bodies, pierced flesh and the spectacle of the *auto da fé*. In a similar way, Reynolds replaces Faust – a powerful but corporeally human creature – with a werewolf, introducing the potential for body horror beyond anything in the earlier novel. Faust commits a number of crimes and subterfuges during his twenty-four-year Satanic 'career'; the first time we see Wagner transform, he eats a child and splatters a monk's brains across a gravestone (ch. 12). Werewolves and Inquisitions go hand in hand here, allowing Reynolds to increase the levels of terror and gore, not because he had developed a virulent anti-European sentiment between September and November 1846, but because he had a new magazine to sell.

Reynolds's commercial interests cannot be entirely disregarded in a consideration of the content of his fiction. An argument that Reynolds's fiction becomes more sensational in the *Miscellany* is supported by the assertion that the author knew how to 'appeal to every taste represented by an audience of lower-middle-class and working-class readers' (Maxwell, p. 80). There is a persistent assumption in much of the criticism of penny dreadfuls that these readers would be male; however, there is evidence in Reynolds's writing that suggests an assumed a female audience as well. A fleeting image of female reading habits appears early in *Faust*: Theresa, imprisoned in Linsdorf Castle by the dastardly Count Manfred, finds a hidden manuscript apparently written by another woman, which outlines a terrible story of murder, abduction and near-immurement. Initially startled, Theresa calms herself with the thought that it is 'only a portion of a romance', which would account for the 'frightful events' described on the page.[25] The genteel and innocent Theresa seems rather familiar with the horrors of Gothic romance here. In a different way, *Wagner* appears to be attempting to appeal to both male and female readers when Wagner and his lover Nisida are shipwrecked on the apparently paradisiacal Isle of Snakes. If the scene in which Nisida takes her first naked swim in the Mediterranean – 'seem[ing] to rejoice in allowing the little wavelets to kiss her snowy bosom' – is a titillating image for male readers, then the image of Wagner, described entirely from Nisida's perspective, bursting forth in all his 'god-like' glory with his 'gleaming ... naked weapon' poised to wrestle a giant anaconda to death may well be something for the ladies (chs. 38, 43).[26]

Reynolds clearly understood the power of horror to entice and entertain both male and female readers – perhaps female more than male, as he styled his more gruesome and lascivious tales 'romances', a term associated with what we now call 'the Gothic' and, at least in the eyes of some, with young female readers.[27] For some, the turn to horror by this audience is a response to the effects of industrial capitalism. Killeen argues that 'the working classes, crowded into the rather less intellectually stimulated and salubrious quarters of city life, had to encounter such desubjectification every day of their lives', so that it is no wonder they 'turned to the penny press to supply a virtual slaughterhouse' (p. 49). Raine posits the ubiquitous subterranean spaces of penny dreadfuls as reflective of anxieties of 'working-class living conditions ... labour exploitation, the anonymity of city life and the oppressing of working-class literature' (p. 62). *The Mysteries of London* addresses this head-on, of course, and with little obfuscation. As they share a number of thematic and narrative concerns, we might also read these anxieties in *Faust* and *Wagner*, though somewhat shrouded by a veil of sensationalised late medieval ghastliness. As in *Mysteries*, 'ordinary' people are often the collateral damage of royalty and aristocracy in *Faust* and *Wagner*, whether it is the people of Vienna condemned to die of plague on the Count of Aurana's selfish whim, or *Wagner*'s tragic Calanthe, brought to Grand Vizier Ibrahim's harem to satisfy his 'voluptuous' pleasures and then brutally murdered by his mother-in-law's slaves and dumped in the Bosporus (ch. 53). The workhouse – chilling totem of industrialised England – is directly linked to the Inquisitions in *Mysteries*; the wealthy inhabitants of sixteenth-century Naples live side by side with 'miserable wretches [with] nowhere to lay their heads'; the 'grossest superstition' of the medieval Viennese proletariat is exploited during an outbreak of Black Death by self-serving hypocrites, resulting in a resistance to sensible health precautions and an explosion of conspiracy theories such as one might see in a modern urban setting during a pandemic.[28] Reading the Gothic romances alongside the urban mysteries allows us to re-evaluate the use and misuse of lower-class bodies in his fiction, reminding us that Reynolds 'knew as well as Marx did that feudalism had already been replaced by industrial capitalism' (Humpherys, p. 87).

But Not Entirely Wretched

The Mysteries of London offers a grim view of industrial England, with bodies broken in the prison and the workhouse, or by poverty and vice. Even the 'monstrous' antagonist Anthony Tidkins is given an entire chapter to himself to explain why, really, society is to blame (ch. 62). Societal inequalities lead directly to crime and sin; as the reader is told in *Wagner*, '[t]he desperate man who hovers hesitatingly between right and wrong, invariably adopts the latter course' (ch. 25). Anthony Tidkins becomes the ghoulish Resurrection Man; Alessandro Francatelli begins a life of religious hypocrisy and debauchery; Faust sells his soul to Satan.

Significantly, there is one character who, despite facing the same desperation as Tidkins, Faust and Alessandro/Ibrahim, does not yield his soul, and that is Fernand Wagner himself. Wagner's pact is a Faustian pact, in that it is a contract with Faust himself, rather than with Satan. In a rather idiosyncratic move, Reynolds shifts the idea of demonic compact away from the hubris of esoteric learning (as seen in Marlowe and Goethe's plays) and into something more akin to a multi-level marketing scheme. Faust recruits Wagner, just as he in turn was recruited by the unseen former prisoner in the Vehmic jail. Wagner buys the starter pack but is reluctant to commit himself further.

Ultimately, *Wagner* emerges as by far the most hopeful of the novels under consideration in this chapter, despite it also being the most violent and lascivious. Although it has been argued that the heightened brutality in *Wagner* takes readers to a 'virtual slaughterhouse' of desubjectification, in fact much of the body horror focuses us on suffering, trauma and redemption of the individual subject in a quite startling way. In *Faust*, Reynolds writes a description of the massacre of the Viennese Jews, with an accompanying polemic against anti-Semitic brutality; in *Wagner*, he introduces us to an individual subject, Isaachar, shows us inside his house, encourages us first to get to know him and then to identify with him as he is tortured on the rack. The Inquisition scene in *Wagner* may be excessive and semi-pornographic, but it is also the most sustained and radical endorsement of empathy the book has to offer. We 'see' the torture of Isaachar, not peeping through the keyhole like 'voyeuristic gorehounds', but from the perspective of his friend, Manuel d'Orsini.[29]

In the end, Wagner does not agree to sell his soul to Satan as Faust did. Nor does he give in to the lure of debauchery that comes with easy-gotten power. Although, as I have shown, the novel engages in an oblique way with anxieties of national governance, industrial capitalism and extra-legislative power structures, *Wagner, the Wehr-Wolf* emerges as a more intimate tale about personal morality and values. As the Demon tried to explain to us in *Faust*, 'it is as easy ... to follow the course of virtue as of vice ... Because it is more pleasant to pursue a path margined with flowers, than one environed with briars' (ch. 56). He continues:

> Ask the thief whether the luxuries purchased by the stolen coin outvalue the crust which he earned by his honest toil? Ask the adulterer and the seducer whether the pleasures of his illicit passion excel the charms of a pure and holy love? Ask the monarch whether he sits the more comfortably on a throne encrusted with the miseries of his people! ... Has vice no other punishments than those which outraged laws can inflict? Has virtue no rewards beyond those which mundane aggrandisement can give? Is domestic misery no punishment? Is domestic peace no reward? (ch. 56)

And, indeed, *Wagner* ends with a vindication of the Demon's lecture. For all its blood and gore and sex, *Wagner, the Wehr-Wolf* ends on a scene of domestic peace. Flora and Francisco, Count of Riverola, survive the revelations of the final chapters, watch Wagner and Nisida die as a result of their missteps (but go to Heaven together because their missteps were not entirely ill intentioned), and then settle into a companionable marriage and family life. Unlike Faust and Ibrahim, Francisco has put in some honest toil to secure the affections of Flora, who has had trials of her own, including imprisonment in both a Carmelite convent and the cells of the Inquisition. In the end, though, they are happy, and *Wagner* concludes with an endorsement of companionate marriage, as the reader leaves Flora and Francisco to enjoy 'the sweet solace of each other's sympathy' (ch. 64).

In conclusion, *Wagner, the Wehr-Wolf* is a more sustained piece of horror fiction than the penny dreadfuls Reynolds wrote and published concurrently. On the one hand, it is far more sensationalist with its lurid torture scenes and continual references to sex, skinny-dipping and anacondas. On the other, it uses its more visceral moments as a corrective to the 'dark view' of humanity, imbuing them paradoxically with a sense of hope and comradeship. As I have argued throughout this chapter, the critical dismissal of *Wagner* and its decontextualisation from Reynolds's other serialised novel have led to misinterpretation and undervaluation. It is only when *Wagner* is read alongside *Faust* and *The Mysteries of London* that one is able to understand the complexity of its narrative development.

Ultimately, *Wagner* is a novel written for entertainment, albeit entertainment for 'gorehounds'. As I have indicated in my exploration of some of the overlooked sections of the text, such as Wagner and Nisida's island seclusion or the idiosyncratic relationship between Isaachar, Ibrahim and Manuel, there are many pleasures to be had in *Wagner*, even for the twenty-first-century reader. Unlike *The Mysteries of London*, the novel does not foreground its engagement with contemporary societal and political issues, but that does not mean this engagement is not present. Developing both narrative and thematic concerns first explored in *Faust*, Reynolds allows concerns of the modern world – living conditions of the working class, for instance, and anxieties of imperial and national power structures – to work subtextually throughout the novel.

In a much more notable way than either *Faust* or *The Mysteries of London*, *Wagner* can be read as a precursor, not only to contemporary werewolf fiction, but to contemporary horror fiction more generally. Reynolds's exuberantly visceral narrative is dismissed by some as bad taste, but this horridness is actually the means through which the author is able to engage with more fundamental questions about humanity and society.

The novel's surprisingly hopeful denouement resolves a number of the questions that have been raised by Wagner's Gothic adventures – and also some that linger from the more downbeat ending of *Faust*. That is not to say that the concerns of the modern world that permeate the text are entirely dissipated, but *Wagner* ends with a final couple whose domestic happiness suggests that, perhaps, horrors can be survived, and anxieties soothed.

Until the next tale begins…

Notes

1. On *Wagner, the Wehr-Wolf* as an unusually early precursor to contemporary werewolf fiction, see Chantal Bourgault Du Coudray, *The Curse of the Werewolf: Fantasy, Horror and the Beast Within* (London and New York: I. B. Tauris, 2006); Hannah Priest, 'Like Father Like Son: Wolf-Men, Paternity and the Male Gothic', in Robert McKay and John Miller (eds), *Werewolves, Wolves and the Gothic* (Cardiff: University of Wales Press, 2017), pp. 19–36.
2. It is beyond the scope of this chapter to discuss the circumstances of Reynolds's departure from the *London Journal* and his possible reasons for launching his own weekly publication. For discussion of this, see Andrew King, '*Reynolds's Miscellany*, 1846–1849: Advertising Networks and Politics', in Anne Humpherys and Louis James (eds), *G. W. M. Reynolds: Nineteenth-Century Fiction, Politics, and the Press* (Aldershot and Burlington, VT: Ashgate, 2008), pp. 53–74; Anne Humpherys, 'G. W. M. Reynolds: Popular Literature and Popular Politics', *Victorian Periodicals Review*, 16/3–4 (Fall–Winter 1983), 79–89.
3. See, for example, Abigail Boucher, '"Her Princes Within Her Are Like Wolves": The Werewolf as a Catholic Force in *Wagner, the Wehr-Wolf*', *Revenant*, 2 (2016), 22–41.
4. Sophie Raine, 'Subterranean Spaces in the Penny Dreadful', in Clive Bloom (ed.), *The Palgrave Handbook of Steam Age Gothic* (London: Palgrave Macmillan, 2021), pp. 61–76 (p. 61).
5. Jarlath Killeen, 'Victorian Gothic Pulp Fiction', in Andrew Smith (ed.), *The Victorian Gothic: An Edinburgh Companion* (Edinburgh: Edinburgh University Press, 2012), pp. 43–56 (pp. 50, 51).
6. It is worth noting that 'pulp' is used in the derogatory sense throughout the chapter, implying poor quality writing with mass appeal.
7. Avril Horner, 'Victorian Gothic and National Identity: Cross-Channel "Mysteries"', in *The Victorian Gothic*, pp. 108–23 (p. 121).
8. See, for example, Horner, 'Victorian Gothic and National Identity'; Richard C. Maxwell, Jr, 'G. M. Reynolds, Dictions and the Mysteries of London', *Nineteenth-Century Fiction*, 32/2 (September 1977), 188–213.
9. See, for example, Carys Crossen, *The Nature of the Beast: Transformations of the Werewolf from the 1970s to the Twenty-first Century* (Cardiff: University of Wales Press, 2019); Bourgault Du Coudray, *The Curse of the Werewolf*. My own work has also on occasion taken this approach, comparing the transformation of Wagner to scenes in contemporary film and television. See Hannah Priest, 'Like Father Like Son'.

10. Diane Long Hoeveler, *The Gothic Ideology: Religious Hysteria and Anti-Catholicism in British Popular Fiction 1780–1880* (Cardiff: University of Wales Press, 2014), pp. 254ff.
11. Abigail Boucher has also identified elements of the narrative that can be read as direct criticism of the Catholic Church. See Boucher, '"Her Princes Within Her Are Like Wolves"'.
12. Christopher Marlowe, *Doctor Faustus*, ed. David Scott Kastan (New York and London: W. W. Norton & Company, 2005); Johann Wolfgang von Goethe, *Faust, Part I*, trans. David Constantine (London: Penguin Classics, 2005); Johann Wolfgang von Goethe, *Faust, Part II*, trans. David Constantine (London: Penguin Classics, 2009). For a discussion of the relationship between these texts, and the precursors and contexts of the story, and their later legacies, see Sara Munson Deats, *The Faust Legend: From Marlowe and Goethe to Contemporary Drama and Film* (Cambridge: Cambridge University Press, 2019); Inez Hedges, *Framing Faust: Twentieth-Century Cultural Struggles* (Carbondale: Southern Illinois University Press, 2005).
13. Subterranean spaces are a recurrent feature in Reynolds's fiction and are often places of confinement and punishment. See Raine, 'Subterranean Spaces in the Penny Dreadful'.
14. George Reynolds, *Faust*, 1 (1845; Manchester: Hic Dragones, 2016), Prologue.
15. The concept was clearly well enough known for William Makepeace Thackeray to use the term '*Vehmgericht*' in his serial novel *Vanity Fair* (1847–8) to describe a secretive 'court' of servants who pass judgement on Becky Sharp. Alternatively, Thackeray had read *Faust*.
16. Admittedly, the Arch-Duke is in disguise at this point, as a simple traveller named Charles Hamel, but the implication becomes clear when readers learn his true identity later in the story: even a member of the imperial family is not immune to the *Vehmgericht*.
17. George Reynolds, *Faust* 7 (1846; Manchester: Hic Dragones, 2016), chapters 51, 53.
18. Sara Hacklenberg, 'Vampires and Resurrection Men: The Perils and Pleasures of the Embodied Past in 1840s Sensational Fiction', *Victorian Studies*, 52/1 (Autumn 2009), 63–75 (71). It should be noted that readers of *Faust* may well have been familiar with the scenes of Markham's imprisonment in *Mysteries of London*, as this chapter was published just a few months before the first instalment of *Faust* appeared in the *London Journal*.

[19] Anne Humpherys, 'The Geometry of the Modern City: G. W. M. Reynolds and "The Mysteries of London"', *Browning Institute Studies*, 11 (1983), 69–80 (77).

[20] George Reynolds, *Wagner, the Wehr-Wolf* (1846; Manchester: Hic Dragones, 2015), Prologue.

[21] Brian J. Frost, *The Essential Guide to Werewolf Literature* (Madison: University of Wisconsin Press, 2003), p. 66.

[22] See, for example, James Sutherland Menzies, 'Hughes the Wer-Wolf' (1838) and Leitch Ritchie, 'The Man-Wolf' (1831) for instances of non-painful werewolf transformations. Both in Andrew Barger (ed.), *The Best Werewolf Short Stories 1800–1849: A Classic Werewolf Anthology* (Collierville, TN: Bottletree Books, 2010).

[23] For discussion of the inclusion of werewolves in Inquisition witch trials, see, for example, Rita Voltmer, 'The Judge's Lore? The Politico-Religious Concept of Metamorphosis in the Peripheries of Western Europe', in Willem de Blécourt (ed.), *Werewolf Histories* (Basingstoke: Palgrave Macmillan, 2015), pp. 185–204; Willem de Blécourt, 'The Werewolf, the Witch, and the Warlock: Aspects of Gender in the Early Modern Period', in Alison Rowlands (ed.), *Witchcraft and Masculinities in Early Modern Europe* (Basingstoke: Palgrave Macmillan, 2009), pp. 191–213; Rolf Schulte, '"She Transformed into a Werewolf, Devouring and Killing Two Children": Trials of She-Werewolves in Early Modern French Burgundy', in Hannah Priest (ed.), *She-Wolf: A Cultural History of Female Werewolves* (Manchester: Manchester University Press, 2015), pp. 41–58.

[24] Alessandro/Ibrahim will later refer to himself as 'a renegade to suit his worldly purposes, and not from conviction' (Reynolds, *Wagner, the Wehr-Wolf*, chapter 62). The man's behaviour is not a critique of Islam, but rather of easy-won power. At the end of the novel, we see another conversion, when Manuel d'Orsini becomes Mustapha Pasha. As Manuel/Mustapha is converting from conviction and not for his own worldly purposes, this is presented in a more positive light.

[25] George Reynolds, *Faust* 2 (1846; Manchester: Hic Dragones, 2016), chapter 10.

[26] I use some licence here, as the term 'god-like' to describe Wagner's physical appearance does not occur in this chapter. It does, however, appear in chapters 53, 56 and 63.

[27] On the development of the term 'romance' and its relationship to 'the Gothic', see Hannah Priest, 'Black Weddings and Black Mirrors: Gothic as Transgeneric Mode', in Jolene Zigarovich (ed.), *TransGothic*

    in Literature and Culture (New York and Abingdon: Routledge, 2017), pp. 199–217.
28 George Reynolds, *The Mysteries of London* (1846; Manchester: Hic Dragones, 2016), chapter 185; George Reynolds, *Faust* 3 (1846; Manchester: Hic Dragones, 2016), chapter 23; George Reynolds, *Faust* 11 (1846; Manchester: Hic Dragones, 2017), chapter 88.
29 The phrase 'voyeuristic gorehounds' is taken from Matt Hills's analysis of the *Saw* film franchise. Anachronism aside, much of what Hills says about the reception and response to the *Saw* films resonates with the critical dismissal of Reynolds's Gothic romances. See Matt Hills, 'Cutting into Concepts of "Reflectionist" Cinema: The *Saw* Franchise and Puzzles of Post-9/11 Horror', in Aviva Briefel and Sam J. Miller (eds), *Horror after 9/11: World of Fear, Cinema of Terror* (Austin: University of Texas Press, 2011), pp. 107–23 (p. 121).

Section II

Victorian Medical Sciences and Penny Fiction; or, Dreadful Discourses of the Gothic

5

'Embalmed pestilence', 'intoxicating poisons': Rhetoric of Contamination, Contagion, and the Gothic Marginalisation of Penny Dreadfuls by their Contemporary Critics

MANON BURZ-LABRANDE

'Penny packets of poison',[1] 'sickly scenes',[2] 'a contagious disease',[3] 'unhealthy',[4] 'the plague of poisonous literature'[5] – a large number of the unflattering metaphors and analogies used in the penny dreadfuls' heavily mediatised criticism draw on the circulation of diseases and of moral evil, through images of contamination and contagion. These gruesome sensational stories and their supposedly corruptive influence soon were cast as obstacles to the contemporaneous cultural hegemony, as the upper and middle classes tried to steer the newly developed cheap mass market towards literature that imparted 'useful knowledge'.[6] In their potential to spoil moral purity, the penny dreadfuls' contents echo Christopher Pittard's definition of crime and criminality as moral contaminants in late Victorian detective fiction, in a society that strives for literal and metaphorical cleanliness.[7] The activation of the contamination and contagion rhetoric thus problematises this anxiety of cleanliness, and is a direct reaction to the massive scale of distribution of penny publications, 'attaining an almost uncountable circulation' as Fanny Mayne, publisher of the Evangelical weekly magazine *The True Briton*, describes in 1852.[8] The depiction of their circulation numbers as nearly impossible to record recurs in various pieces of contemporary criticism: from 'hundreds – yes, thousands – of pernicious penny works published' (Mayne, p. 3) to exaggerated claims of 'millions' (Mayne, p. 8) of numbers and fantasies of a 'wilderness of words',[9] the vague estimations only concur in their staggeringly high quantity. Such phrases betray the feeling of threat that this scale posed. The spread of penny literature indeed far surpassed its sales numbers, since the issues, once acquired, kept circulating through communities rather than becoming a static possession, contained on a shelf. Contrary to beautifully bound novels in a middle- or upper-class household, the 'perishable penny-issue' circulated until it was either destroyed or reused; and Louis James describes how the quality of the issues 'left no encouragement to readers to preserve the weekly instalments once they had been read. There were too many uses for paper.'[10] The scale of their circulation, but also the way they were circulated, was therefore both new and against the tide. The upper classes' inability to control the phenomenon, combined with the social and political implications of the working class's growing literacy from the 1840s, led to a public war on the penny dreadfuls' successful industry, as critical newspaper articles, pamphlets and essays multiplied. The dynamic nature of their circulation, along with its scale, meant that the threat they posed was too potent – or too contagious – to simply be removed with, say, a 'penny-dreadful-ectomy' to stop its supposedly dangerous influence. The rhetoric of contagion and contamination which pervades contemporaneous criticism develops as a result of this omnipresence and in order to make sense of their very popularity.

In this chapter, I will analyse how contemporary critics weaponised the penny dreadfuls' successful material circulation to marginalise these cheap publications successfully. By decrying their content as both immoral and dangerous, accusations connect to what Fred Botting associates with the monstrous: 'works that transgressed the codes of reason and morality, presenting excessive and viciously improper scenes and characters'.[11] In rejecting these publications, I argue, many Victorian critics constructed the penny dreadful as a metaphorical monster thanks to a Gothicised discourse of circulation as a threat, which relied on a language of excess. The consistent rhetoric of contagion echoes what Botting describes as the pervasive and subversive nature of the monster: 'monstrosity', he states, 'disrupt[s] systems of classification and value' ('Monstrosity', p. 205). The pervasiveness of the penny dreadfuls can certainly be traced to their active, yet stealthy circulation. Their subversive quality, in terms of content, is at the heart of several contributions to this volume, but I believe it has its roots in their very format too, which concurs with Jack Halberstam's definition of the monster as a 'specifically deviant form'.[12] Amidst a change in consumption practices – responding to the burgeoning mass entertainment market – from those typical of the novel or poetry to that of popular reading material, the penny dreadfuls disturb the previously predominant Romantic notion of the literary work as a precious item to preserve in one's library. Stephen Colclough, in *Consuming Texts* (2007), quotes from Voltaire's *Candide* (1759) to remind the reader of the value of the novel not only as a literary story, but as an item: one 'had to have it in your library, like an ancient monument, or like those rusty medals that have no commercial value'.[13] Penny dreadfuls were consumed in a vastly different way, their ephemerality thus deviating from the norm. They challenged the respected nature of authorship, too, as they were not only published anonymously but also sometimes written by several different authors and aimed at financial profit more than at presenting a teleological plotline. These characteristics disrupt the system of value traditionally associated with literature up to the end of the eighteenth century, and I contend that the fear of the penny dreadfuls' dissemination that underlies such criticism is what led to a rejection of their form, literary content and readership. As a consequence, the penny dreadfuls were quickly cast as a literary monstrosity. Following Michel Foucault's postulate on discourse as exercising power and shaping our view of the world and its 'truth', the contemporary criticism of penny dreadfuls can thus be read as a system of exclusion, in that this discursive construction of penny dreadfuls as a negative force 'poisoning' both culture and society has dominated the definition of literature and its accepted canon for over a century.[14]

The rhetoric of contamination and contagion on which this discourse draws echoes historical, social and scientific contexts, and thereby plays on contemporary fears of social order's potential disintegration to legitimise the penny dreadfuls' marginalisation. To situate the tropes and rhetorical devices at play here, I will begin by addressing the historical context of disease outbreaks that led to the rise of modern epidemiology, and how the various public health and urban planning measures, as forms of 'biopower' as theorised by Foucault, impact the collective representation of contagion. Building on this, I will address the fashioning of penny dreadfuls as a contagious disease and analyse what this discourse revolves on and how it is linked to a broader rhetoric of health and contamination. I will then turn to the notion of a 'poisonous' literature as a threat to the Empire as a whole by shedding light on tropes of early botanical Gothic, before concluding on how casting the penny dreadfuls as a literary monster actually reveals their innovative potential as a formative experiment in the growing literary marketplace.

Contagion, Contamination, and the Rise of Modern Epidemiology

The rhetoric of contagion and contamination is best analysed in the light of the scientific understanding that prevailed throughout the 1840s and 1850s, in the heyday of penny bloods. During this period, notions of disease contamination and infection were still uninformed by bacteriology, and the idea of environmental transmission was still extremely rudimentary.[15] In 1842, Edwin Chadwick, who had been one of the main architects of the notorious 1834 Poor Law, published a *Report on the Sanitary Condition of the Labouring Population of Great Britain* after a three-year inquiry. This unprecedented study of the state of public health led, in 1848, to the passing of the first Public Health Act as well as of the Nuisance Removal and Contagious Diseases Act, both of which were aimed at improving the sanitary conditions of the lower classes. For the Public Health Act, Chadwick put forward economic arguments, hoping to save money on poor relief by improving the working class's health. Poor people's health, therefore, was more of a side effect than the Act's actual goal. Though the establishment of the Central Board of Health was a major step forward, the Act itself only had a short-term impact; and given that the framework put into place did not compel any action (such as research) in the matter, it is not surprising these laws did not lead to a better understanding of contagious diseases either.[16]

To understand the growing scientific knowledge in this domain, and the changes that subsequently occurred, one year in particular is key. Although the major cholera outbreak of 1854 was only one of many that swept through the city of London, this precise epidemic allowed Dr John Snow's research to develop, which had considerable consequences. With the help of the local clergyman, the Rev. Henry Whitehead, Snow traced the source of the outbreak to a specific water pump on Broad Street, which allowed him to further investigate the hypothesis of a water-borne disease he had already postulated in 1849 and published as *On the Mode of Communication of Cholera*. Though now considered a cornerstone of Victorian medicine, Snow's theory was overlooked for many more years, and the long-standing 'miasma theory', which maintained that diseases were transmitted via the atmosphere and that clean air would resolve the problem, prevailed until the 1880s.

In the nineteenth century, contagious diseases tended to come with a strong moral connotation, and justifications would be looked for in a family's morality, or in the constitution of the neighbourhood. Cholera, for example, was thought to be a punishment for offences against bourgeois standards – of cleanliness or other – established as 'natural', and was understood as a 'lower-class filth disease'.[17] Because of what it represented, any spreading of disease needed to be contained, both literally (to physically prevent their circulation) and figuratively, for instance by attributing them to a precise social class, so that members of the other classes could feel safer. This belief led to a socially organised London topography exemplified by the case of Regent Street, which was planned in order to act, in the words of its architect John Nash, as 'a boundary and complete separation between the streets and squares occupied by the nobility and the gentry, and the narrow streets and meaner houses occupied by mechanics and the trading part of the community'.[18] Almost fifteen years later, Nash reported to Parliament that 'in forming that street, [his] purpose was, that the new street should cross the Eastern entrance to all the streets occupied by the higher classes, and to leave out to the East all those bad streets'.[19] In short, London was being redesigned in order to include, in

Johnson's words, a 'kind of *cordon sanitaire*', which was to separate well-to-do areas from working-class ones.[20] At the same time, areas such as the East End were branded a 'locus of Victorian contagion' (Burgan, p. 46) – which lent support to measures of public health such as the creation of Victoria Park in 1839.

Johnson's choice of words above is crucial, as the image of the *cordon sanitaire* has its history in almost contemporaneous developments in epidemiology on the other side of the Channel. First introduced in the 1820s to prevent a yellow fever outbreak spreading from Spain to France across the Pyrenees, the notion was later championed by Dr Adrien Proust in 1874, when he argued that a *cordon sanitaire* was the best way to interrupt the circulation of disease outbreaks throughout Europe and protect France.[21] But it also echoes the *casier sanitaire* in Paris, a *fin de siècle* system of information-gathering and surveillance 'informed by both medical and social knowledge, backed by the authority of the state and the possibility of official intervention'.[22] In their combination of intervention and control, both the *casier sanitaire* and the *cordon sanitaire* show one of the two forms of Foucault's concept of biopower, as they are part of an apparatus of biopolitics, built with 'its major function at a given historical moment that of responding to an *urgent need*' – that of managing the population's health by preventing the spread of diseases.[23] The *cordon sanitaire* thus evolves from a tool for public health to a tool furthering the marginalisation of the lower classes. It therefore inhabits both its potential meanings: 'a guarded line between infected and uninfected districts, to prevent intercommunication and spread of a disease or pestilence'; and 'a measure designed to prevent communication or the spread of undesirable influences' (*OED*), whereby 'undesirable influences' can be read as the lower classes and their attributed link with diseases and with putting society at risk. Both literally and figuratively, the *cordon sanitaire* perfectly represents the upper-class fears of a physical and metaphorical contamination.

In spite of the major scientific advances made in the domain of epidemiology in the mid-nineteenth century, the moral dimension attached to contamination and contagion does not exactly subside. Far from it, actually, as becomes visible later in the century with the matter of sexually transmitted diseases and the Contagious

Diseases Acts that would trigger another important moralist debate in the 1860s. In interweaving public health, class and morality, the mid-nineteenth-century context of the cholera outbreaks lays the groundwork for discourses of Foucauldian 'docile bodies' that resurface and take over later social issues.[24] But in addition to this, it also provides a context from which perhaps 'fashionable' words might be borrowed to strengthen other types of admonition of the lower classes' (im)morality, as in the case of penny dreadful criticism. Drawing on the same rhetoric to lend a more solid-looking basis to a scientific-sounding discourse and to show indisputable concern for the greater good, contemporary critics undoubtedly rely on the established associations between social strata and contamination (be it literal or figurative). In the following sections of this chapter, I will analyse the foundations and mechanisms of this pseudo-scientific discourse and the part played by the rhetoric of contagion, contamination, and ill health.

Penny Dreadfuls as a Contagious Disease

The criticism launched at penny dreadfuls over the nineteenth century was often centred on analogies and metaphors that draw on contagious diseases. The following excerpt from James Greenwood's *Seven Curses of London* (1869) is a particularly striking example:

> It is a contagious disease, just as cholera and typhus and the plague are contagious, and … needs not personal contact with a body stricken to convey either of these frightful maladies to the hale and hearty. A tainted scrap of rag has been known to spread plague through an entire village, just as a stray leaf of 'Panther Bill,' or 'Tyburn Tree' may sow the seeds of immorality amongst as many boys as a town can produce. (pp. 141–3)

According to Greenwood, penny literature is a metaphorical 'plague' as well as the literal one, likened to contagious diseases with the potential to infect 'an entire village', either morally or physically. Its representation as spreading uncontrollably directly links 'contagion' with the publications' successful circulation, rhetorically rendering their dissemination pejorative. It comes as no surprise that Greenwood chose to include cholera as a point of comparison: Sabine Schülting convincingly analysed it as both 'the product of industrialisation, urbanisation, and imperialism and simultaneously their antagonist, threatening the idea of progress and civilization'.[25] This particular disease echoes the supposed danger posed to society by the penny dreadfuls, and cholera thus 'provides the metaphor that draws all of society's problems into a single conceptual cluster', as argued by Mary Poovey in her analysis of an earlier cholera outbreak in Manchester.[26]

Concern deepens as everyone is a potential target, whatever their physical health: even the 'hale and hearty' could catch these 'frightful maladies'. Greenwood's use of the pronoun 'it' ensures that the 'frightful maladies' he refers to are, grammatically, both the 'contagious disease', spread by a 'scrap of rag', *and* the literature, passed on by a 'stray leaf'. By appealing to shared personal experience in order to be more persuasive and asking, 'Which of us can say that his children are safe from the contamination?' (*Seven Curses*, p. 141), he locates both himself and his readers on the same side of the issue, i.e. the only 'right' one – surely, if his own as well as his readers' children are in danger, then this is a 'disease' that needs to be taken seriously.

Penny dreadfuls even take on a form of agency, from spreading the plague to 'sow[ing] the seeds of immorality' among boys, identified as the most likely to fall victim. This foreshadows what John Springhall has defined as the 'penny dreadful panic', with the cheap publications becoming the perfect scapegoats for (late) Victorian juvenile crime.[27] The choice to focus on children and boys in particular, rather than on a broader and more indefinite readership, reinforces the idea that a particularly fertile ground is needed for these 'seeds' to disseminate and grow. This metaphor thus acts as a perversion of the parable of the sower found in the Gospel of Matthew (the first book of the New Testament), one in which the seeds that are sowed are the opposite of God's message, and their meeting fertile ground is to be avoided, as growth and dissemination are unwanted. Of the two publications Greenwood mentions by name, *Tyburn Tree: Or, The Mysteries of the Past* (1849) is particularly noteworthy in this context, as it reinforces the connection with immorality and with the potentially dark fate awaiting readers if contaminated.[28] Indeed, the 'Tyburn Tree' is associated with centuries of public hangings, as it is the popular name for the gallows at the main site of execution for the London area from the 1400s to 1783. 'Tyburn' was synonymous with capital punishment, and the choice of this precise title foreshadows the fate of the boys who might, according to Greenwood, become criminals, should they read penny dreadfuls.

Finally, the 'stray leaf' in this quotation illustrates once more the uncontrollable circulation of these publications through communities, as it conjures up the image of a page of these stories flying from one place to the next, landing to contaminate and taking off again to be blown elsewhere and contaminate again, thereby echoing miasma theory in that the 'disease' is airborne. It 'needs not personal contact with a body stricken', Greenwood tells his readers, thereby heightening the paranoia surrounding the circulation of the penny dreadfuls as something you cannot escape, however much you strive to stay afar. Steven Johnson explains that the miasma theory remained persuasive for so long because it drew its power 'not from any single fact but rather from its location at the intersection of so many separate but compatible elements', which he lists as '[t]he weight of tradition, the evolutionary history of disgust, technological limitations in microscopy, social prejudice', and which made it 'almost impossible for the Victorians to see miasma for the red herring that it was' (pp. 134–5). By resorting to these connotations and the alliance of cultural factors behind the hegemony of miasma theory, Greenwood relies upon another context of social prejudice and of disgust to render his criticism more persuasive.

A few years later, in his essay 'A Short Way to Newgate' (1874), Greenwood wields the plague metaphor again, but this time develops it from a general threat to a more class-specific issue. The threat of contamination and contagion has been displaced in order to be localised within precise spheres of society, and the concern expressed does not relate to the personal any more. Instead, it is directly related to the circulation and 'propagation' of penny dreadfuls:

> [S]ince its baleful influence is – as is generally supposed – confined almost entirely to the vulgar ground it is indigenous to, and there is

little fear of its spreading beyond certain well-defined and ascertained limits easy to avoid; since it is not, according to the popular acceptation of the term, 'catching,' and one need labour under no alarm lest it come on the wings of the wind in at our pleasant chamber window, and street cabs are not likely to be impregnated with it ... why – why, there's an end of it.

It is, however, a plague not included in the ordinary category that is the subject of this paper – the plague of poisonous literature. (*Wilds of London*, p. 158)

Although the metaphor of the plague is consistent in both pieces of Greenwood's criticism, its characteristics are now significantly different as the potential contamination does not seem to spread quite as uncontrollably. The first paragraph of this quotation maintains the metaphor of the plague throughout, by pointing at its development as well as its means of contagion, until the author announces almost dramatically and in a new paragraph constituted only by this one-line revelation, that he intends to deal not with 'the ordinary category [of plague]', but with 'the plague of poisonous literature'. Contrary to the potential of the 'stray leaf' in his earlier text, there is now 'little fear of its spreading': it is now presented as 'confined almost entirely to the vulgar ground it is indigenous to', that is to say the lower-class areas in which penny dreadfuls circulate.

The *cordon sanitaire* developed earlier in this chapter is therefore present both physically, through the city's evolving design and the fact that the so-called plague is 'confined'; and metaphorically, as protecting the upper classes from direct contact and infection. Poor areas of the city are once again morally and geographically identified as places where diseases come into being and develop: described as 'indigenous' to these areas, diseases are painted as 'belonging naturally' to these neighbourhoods.[29] Admittedly, the 'wings of the wind' could still carry the potentially infectious stray leaf to less 'vulgar' grounds, but the physical domestic upper-class space and its 'pleasant chamber window[s]' should be enough to keep it at bay; and indeed Greenwood then proceeds to list typical upper- and middle-class urban spaces as 'not likely to be impregnated with it', thanks to the *cordon sanitaire*. Once this reassuring conclusion is reached, Greenwood nevertheless points out that this 'plague of poisonous literature' should not be ignored and left to increase, but rather identified and remedied. Ultimately, this is the purpose of his essay, in which he proceeds to describe twelve different penny publications and ascertain their supposed immorality in the hope of helping the people turn away from them. While Greenwood opens with the metaphor of the plague, the last sentence explicitly addresses the publications' attributed monstrous character: 'It is hard to credit that fathers of families would so long have endured the existence of [such publications] if they really knew the monsters each and every one of these worthies were' (*Wilds of London*, p. 172). Such a conclusion is reached after an extensive list of the publications' 'deadly pernicious ingredient[s]' (p. 172), which leads me to consider the broader rhetoric of health and contamination employed by contemporary critical voices, further than that of the precise contagious diseases of the time.

'Pernicious' Literature and the Rhetoric of Bodily Health and Contamination

Among the various ways the penny dreadfuls as reading material are described as harmful, one specific word is used repeatedly: critical voices put emphasis on their '*decidedly pernicious* character'.[30] While Springhall rightly links it to the 'moral panic scapegoating the penny dreadful', he does not investigate the term's powerful potential in its literal and direct connection to health.[31] From the Latin *perniciosus*, meaning 'destructive', the word 'pernicious' is defined by the *OED* as 'extremely severe or harmful, life-threatening, fatal' when used about a disease, and 'causing or likely to cause harm, especially in a gradual or insidious manner' when used about a thing, action or intent.[32] Interestingly enough, the term's very first listed definition is the one with a medical context: for example, 'pernicious anaemia' is an existing medical condition first identified in the nineteenth century. The term 'pernicious' can therefore easily assume both a metaphorical and a literal meaning, as it always describes something causing grave damage and is always associated with situations involving a stealthy development and a gradual process. When Alfred Harmsworth claims in 1895 that his *Halfpenny*

Marvel was 'founded to counteract the pernicious influences of the Penny and Half-penny Dreadfuls', he denounces the publications' immoral impact and their potential for destruction, caused gradually by their supposedly 'harmful' effect on society's morals at large according to his rhetoric.[33] Decades prior, Mayne already resorted to this image in her privately published work *The Perilous Nature of the Penny Periodical Press* (1852), where she denounces the 'hundreds – yes, thousands – of pernicious penny works published' (p. 3). The menacing presence of something 'pernicious', thus with a destructive potential, is further emphasised by other types of associations and images, for example when Greenwood describes the 'deadly pernicious ingredient[s]' that constitute the usual tropes of penny literature (*Wilds of London*, p. 172). This instantaneously brings to mind the idea of ingesting a potential poison, something that will, in the end, prove fatal – and Greenwood does indeed call the penny dreadfuls 'penny packets of *poison*', relying again on the same alliteration (*Wilds of London*, p. 158, emphasis added). This association, along with the penny dreadfuls' immense circulation and potentially uncontrollable dissemination, draws the image of a type of literature that endangers physical integrity as well, by slowly but surely contaminating physical bodies and minds as well as society's metaphorical body. Proliferating in spite of such critical discourses, penny dreadfuls represent a potential danger, a threat to the established order and constitution of British society. The many images involving contamination and the potential ill health of the nation as a body echo the medieval metaphor of the body politic and the problem of the 'King's two bodies' traced by Ernst Kantorowicz. As the body politic represents the state's independence from the body natural of the head of state (i.e. while the head of state or monarch dies, the body politic is 'more ample and large' and transcends the individual),[34] the idea of it becoming diseased therefore bears much larger implications than that of a potentially diseased body natural, as it raises the threat of social disintegration. The use of such images of contagion and of a broader rhetoric of ill health therefore emphasises the threat that is posed – not to the individuals, but to the whole body of the nation.

In addition to the broader image of the body of the nation, the metropolis itself – as the epicentre of penny publications and their circulation – is also presented as a sick body many times in both literary and journalistic pieces. The literacy boom and the popularity of the penny dreadfuls coincide with the decades of extremely rapid expansion of the city of London. This fast-developing urbanisation created a sense of loss of control, as the ever-growing monster 'swallowed up' previous geographical boundaries as well as any previous conception of the city and its functioning. As a result, London turns into a defamiliarised environment and becomes an entity of which every class and every community needs to make sense. This further reinforces the idea of anything that circulates fast through this newly enormous city as uncontrollable and potentially untraceable, which, in turn, implies that the periodical print culture's expansion participates in turning the city into this new entity.

In this context, London is sometimes likened to a living body, particularly in the case of contagious diseases outbreaks. The image of the city's infected or sick 'body parts' (i.e. neighbourhoods, most often poor) conceptualises topography as (healthy or unhealthy) anatomy. One of the most notable instances of the recurring use of this trope is Frederick Oldfield Ward's 1851 essay on 'Sanitary Consolidation': in it, Ward, a doctor with interests in social and sanitary reform, describes how a 'dissection' of the city's sanitary system reveals tumours, abscesses and London's dire need of a 'sanitary surgeon'.[35] Mary Burgan analyses anatomy as an 'activating trope in [the] variation on the cartography of London because it fasten[s] upon the fear of infection, of disease as threatening the entire body' (p. 43): in this case, this trope helps to enlarge the threat rhetorically, whether the potential danger is originally associated with one precise part of the city or not. The same mechanism is used in criticism of penny dreadfuls: the *Motherwell Times*, on 2 March 1895, deplored their popularity by stating that '[t]ons of this trash is vomited forth from Fleet Street every day'.[36] Here, Fleet Street, as the centre of British printing and publishing at the time (so much so that it remains a metonymy for the British press even now), is the metaphorical mouth that, as a sign of bad health, projects the city's bodily fluids, 'vomiting forth' a virtually uninterrupted flow of publications, the quality of which is likened to either 'trash' or to a chewed and partly digested version of literature. Though the symptoms are only described in one precise part of the (urban) body, they echo once again a potentially sick London or, more broadly speaking, a potentially sick society contaminated by this new version of literature that is supposedly 'pernicious' – or even poisonous.

Botanical Gothic: Poisoning the Nation, Threatening the Empire

Many of the examples analysed so far in this chapter associate contamination not only with a disease, but with poisonous material. When describing 'penny packets of poison', Greenwood makes liberal use of this subtext, but the description of the 'plague of poisonous literature' also relies on this additional layer to drive its point home:

> There is a plague that is striking its upas roots deeper and deeper into English soil – chiefly metropolitan – week by week, and flourishing broader and higher, and yielding great crops of fruit that quickly fall, rotten-ripe, strewing highway and by-way, tempting the ignorant and unwary, and breeding death and misery unspeakable. (*Wilds of London*, p. 158)

The fertility hinted at previously is once again brought into play here, and the 'seeds of immorality' now draw on colonial discourse, as they have become 'upas roots' planted deep into 'English soil' – 'chiefly metropolitan' referring to London as the epicentre of periodical publication and circulation. In terms of propagation, although the metaphor of roots is much more static than the earlier 'stray leaf' and could thus be less threatening, it also ascribes considerably more strength to the phenomenon, highlighting how anchored it is in its society. Furthermore, Greenwood is in all likelihood referring to the upas tree, known to botanists as *Antiaris toxicaria*, which is a tree in the mulberry family found in tropical regions such as Australia, tropical Asia, tropical Africa and many countries formerly part of the British Empire, such as Tonga. Although widely used for other purposes (its fruits are edible; its bark is used to dye clothing), the upas tree is most famously known for its poisonous latex. The word 'upas' itself means 'poison' in

Javanese, and *Antiaris toxicaria* is known as 'arrow poison wood' in such places as China for example, as it was deemed 'one of the most deadly vegetable products of creation'.[37] 'Upas roots', in Greenwood's opening paragraph, is therefore to be read as 'poisonous roots'. This tree first became known in Britain thanks to an account published in the *London Magazine* in December 1783, and was later popularised by the British poet and naturalist Erasmus Darwin in his set of two poems entitled *The Botanic Garden* (1791). In the latter, Darwin describes the tree as such:

> Fierce in dread silence on the blasted heath
> Fell UPAS sits, the HYDRA-TREE of death.
> Lo! from one root, the envenom'd soil below,
> A thousand vegetative serpents grow;
> In shining rays the scaly monster spreads
> O'er ten square leagues his far-diverging heads.[38]

Darwin's poem depicts the upas tree as a threatening presence, emphasised by the choice of capitalisation, and surviving even in such devastated landscape as the 'blasted heath' that echoes the three Shakespearean witches. This first intertextual hint associates the tree with evil, unnatural forces, which is further reinforced by its (once again capitalised) denomination as 'the HYDRA-TREE of death'. Like the mythological Lernean Hydra vanquished by Heracles, whose many heads would regrow twice as numerous when cut, the roots of the tree multiply unstoppably, further spreading their poison or 'venom'. Greenwood's choice of qualifying the roots as 'upas roots deeper and deeper into English soil' is thus clearly reminiscent of Darwin's poetic description; but it also develops a colonialist dimension as the poisonous tree from the confines of the Empire is described as infecting English soil, like an agent of the reverse colonisation conceptualised by Stephen Arata.[39] In this, the upas tree therefore qualifies as a killer plant, 'closer to home than ever, which feed[s] off the era's anxieties and interests', in the botanical Gothic fiction subgenre that Daisy Butcher describes in *Evil Roots: Killer Tales of the Botanical Gothic* (2019).[40] She explains that '[w]ith the rise of imperial global access, rare and exotic plant specimens became available for the rich Victorian collector', and this became linked to a form of 'ecophobia' developing from a 'deep-rooted fear of foreign environments and sense of the unknown lurking in colonial jungles' (pp. 7–9).[41] Tales of the upas tree in the Victorian period thus can be described as written in the botanical Gothic subgenre. Though a more factual account of the characteristics of *Antiaris toxicaria* was later published in 1844 in *The Student: A Magazine of Theology, Literature, and Science*, after that, 'few things have been the subject of so many fabulous stories as the upas' (Buel, p. 470). Tales circulated throughout the rest of the century of the tree exhaling deathly vapours (remaining strikingly similar to Hyginus' version of the mythological 'Fabula' of the Hydra, which was 'so poisonous that she killed men with her breath'), and of upas trees surrounded by skeletons as no one could reach its trunk alive (*Fabulae*, p. 30).[42]

The picture Greenwood paints of this 'plague [with] upas roots' is a rather paradoxical one, as the undeniable fertility is intertwined with motifs of wrongness and death. The seemingly positive aspects of 'flourishing broader and higher' and 'yielding great crops of fruit' are instantaneously counterbalanced by the fact that the fruits 'fall quickly' and are 'rotten-ripe', which hints at an inherent rottenness inseparable from their state of ripeness: however 'great' these crops are, healthy fruits are not available, as they never seem to be ripe without being rotten. They therefore come hand in hand with images of decay, 'breeding death and misery unspeakable' by way of temptation. There is of course a strong religious undertone here as well, as we are presented with a Garden of Eden-type of landscape where the fruit, which seemed encouragingly positive, is actually what brings demise. This echoes the original *London Magazine* account in 1783, which told the story of a priest in the Dutch East Indies who believed that 'God caused this tree to grow out of the earth' in order to punish a people 'addicted to the sins of Sodom and Gomorrah'.[43] The 'scaly monster' and 'thousand ... serpents' in Darwin's poem, less than a decade later, strengthen the association with temptation and the Garden of Eden ('The Botanic Garden', p. 74). James William Buel's description of the 'deadly upas tree' in 1887 is also framed within a Christian context, as he writes about seeing a picture of the tree for the first time 'in the temperance department of [his] father's library' and calls it 'a vegetable product of the devil's rearing' (p. 470). The very title of his work, *Sea and*

Land: An Illustrated History of the Wonderful and Curious Things of Nature Existing Before and Since the Deluge* (1887), already announces this backdrop. And although Greenwood does not explicitly refer to religion, his own work is interspersed with Christian references framing his argument. For example, the choice of the number seven for the title of his 1869 work *Seven Curses of London* echoes the seven cardinal sins, which mirror the seven virtues historically recognised within Christianity. In *The Wilds of London* (1874), he chooses to select for the purpose of his argumentation exactly twelve penny dreadfuls, or 'twelve penny packets of poison' – the number twelve being considered a perfect number symbolising completeness as well as God's authority and power, Greenwood positions himself as an authority on his subject matter, his study as close to perfection and completeness as can be.[44] Through the recurring use of this religious subtext, Greenwood inscribes his criticism in a long-standing moralist tradition intricately linked with the vast number of religious pamphlets that circulated at the time and intertwines the thread of contamination rhetoric with that of immorality once more.

The Penny Dreadful Monster

In conclusion, when dealing with penny dreadfuls as the 'plague' of literature, the repeated use of fashionable contamination discourses reveals a deeper fear of the growing porousness of the boundaries of class and of society. This rhetoric of contagion therefore constructs a discourse in the Foucauldian sense, in which language – here the consistent use of these contamination metaphors – together with contemporary social practices highlights the power dynamics at play. Power is indeed exercised within this discourse, as the upper classes use the rhetoric I have analysed in this chapter in order to assert their dominance and attempt to control the growing popular culture. Penny dreadful publications both allowed and embodied a new mode of consumption and an appropriation of mass culture as well as literature. Consequently, they rapidly also came to represent the broader notion of change. This infiltration of a domain previously reserved for higher spheres of society – that is, literature – is seen as a threat to a so far seemingly undisturbed cultural hegemony (at least in this precise area). As a reaction to this, critical voices construct the penny dreadful phenomenon as a Gothic monster, 'combin[ing] the markings of a plurality of differences' (Halberstam, pp. 5–6): penny dreadfuls are presented as the culmination of a number of attributes marked as 'differences' in relation to their contemporary society and what it strives for. Associated with immorality, ill health and/or the foreign, they are effectively fashioned as nothing else than a monster foreshadowing social disintegration, which therefore needs to be removed. Through this, penny dreadfuls become what Botting describes as Gothic terrors:

> Not only a way of producing excessive emotion, a celebration of transgression for its own sake, Gothic terrors activate a sense of the unknown and project an uncontrollable and overwhelming power which threatens not only the loss of sanity, honour, property or social standing but the very order which supports and is regulated by the coherence of th[e]se terms.[45]

In other words, through their overwhelming circulation, penny dreadfuls pose a threat in that they are not only unknown (as being a completely new form of popular literature and mass entertainment) but put the established characteristics of the contemporary order into question. By destabilising one or several of them, the very coherence that allows society to keep functioning unaltered is thrown out of kilter, and terror is the result of the realisation of this fragility. Discourses of contamination and contagion represent a way to try to make sense of this staggering phenomenon. Later in her critical piece, Mayne talks of penny dreadfuls as a problematic 'species of periodical literature' (p. 11). By designating them as 'the lower species of literature' and wishing for a 'purer' or 'purified species', Mayne likens works of literature to living organisms, as a way to externalise the phenomenon as something 'other' that is intruding in society rather than a direct consequence of the lower classes' access to literacy and involvement in the marketplace (pp. 12–13). At the same time, categorising penny dreadfuls as the 'lower species' could be read with hindsight as a parallel with bacteria, i.e. infectious micro-organisms circulating rather uncontrollably, the functioning of which was still largely unknown at that point and would remain so until the works of Louis Pasteur and Robert Koch soon after, in the 1870s. And when Walter Parke publishes a piece in the *Dublin University Magazine* in 1875, it somehow seems to answer Mayne's concerns, as his article proposes a 'Physiology of Penny Awfuls'. Considering that physiology is defined as the branch of biology that deals precisely with the functions of living organisms (*OED*), such choice of words partakes in a 'narrative of contagion' (Burgan, p. 44) that maintains penny literature in the role of an independent, out-of-control entity, which leaves a trail of metaphorically and literally contaminated spaces everywhere it circulates.

The use of the consistently critical rhetoric of contamination and contagion acts as a real-life illustration of the amalgamation of the penny dreadfuls and their fictional contents. It reveals a fear to see the readership become the criminals featured in some of the stories, as their characteristics 'are assumed to be the characteristics of their readers, and vice versa'.[46] The potential contamination of the lower classes' morals is consistent with a social anxiety of cleanliness and moral purity, which, as Pittard explains, becomes clearly dramatised in *fin de siècle* detective fiction, to be read as complicit with the drive for social purity as it 'aligns detection with the act of cleaning'.[47] This potential contamination picks up on the contagion already described in penny dreadful criticism, in that they, too, are represented as potentially spoiling moral purity. In late Victorian detective fiction, though, cases tend to end up solved and reasons for disturbance neutralised (either with criminals being arrested or with the source of the trouble eradicated altogether). In the case of penny dreadfuls, on the contrary, the cause of trouble is not successfully removed, as circulation numbers prove their dominance of the market over publications produced with the aim of providing the lower classes with supposedly better, or improving, literature.[48] Society's morals and purity do not emerge either unscathed or safe from these tensions in the literary marketplace. The fact that the potential moral contaminants end up contained and eradicated in *fin de siècle* detective fiction therefore could be understood as a reaction to the penny dreadfuls' refusal to comply with what was 'expected' of them, in terms of literary content and of circulation. Rather, they resist it. The penny dreadfuls seem to revel in proving the social anxiety of cleanliness and order justified, all the while establishing a new mode of literary consumption, and thereby paving the way for new genres and modes of reception.

Notes

1. James Greenwood, *The Wilds of London* (London: Chatto & Windus, 1874), p. 158.
2. William Hepworth Dixon, 'The Literature of the Lower Orders. Batch the First', *Daily News*, 440 (26 October 1847), 3.
3. James Greenwood, *Seven Curses of London* (London: S. Rivers, 1869), p. 143.
4. Anonymous, 'The Literature of Vice', *The Bookseller*, 110 (1867), 123.
5. Greenwood, *Wilds of London*, p. 158.
6. For more on the penny publications' relationship with popular education and marketplace interactions with 'useful knowledge' organisations, see Manon Burz-Labrande, '"Useful Knowledge" versus "Wastes of Print": Working-Class Education and Edward Lloyd', *Victorian Popular Fictions Journal*, 3/1 (Spring 2021), 123–39.
7. Christopher Pittard, *Purity and Contamination in Late Victorian Detective Fiction* (Farnham: Ashgate, 2011), p. 3
8. Fanny Mayne, *The Perilous Nature of the Penny Periodical Press* (London: Oxford Printing Press for Private Circulation, 1852), p. 3.
9. Margaret Oliphant, 'The Byways of Literature: Reading for the Million', *Blackwood's Edinburgh Magazine*, 84 (August 1858), 200–16.
10. Louis James, *Fiction for the Working-Man, 1830–1850* (London: Oxford University Press, 1963), pp. 8, xii–xiii.
11. Fred Botting, 'Monstrosity', in M. Mulvey-Roberts (ed.), *The Handbook of the Gothic* (Basingstoke: Palgrave Macmillan, 2009), pp. 204–5 (p. 204).
12. J. Halberstam, *Skin Shows: Gothic Horror and the Technology of Monsters* (Durham, NC and London: Duke University Press, 1995), p. 2.
13. Stephen Colclough, *Consuming Texts: Readers and Reading Communities, 1695–1870* (New York: Palgrave Macmillan, 2007), p. viii.
14. See Michel Foucault, 'The Order of Discourse', in R. Young (ed.), *Untying the Text: A Post-Structuralist Reader* (Boston, London and Henley: Routledge & Kegan Paul, 1981), pp. 48–78.
15. Mary Burgan, 'Mapping Contagion in Victorian London: Disease in the East End', in D. N. Mancoff and D. J. Trela (eds), *Victorian Urban*

Settings: Essays on the Nineteenth-Century City and Its Contexts (New York: Routledge, 2015), pp 43–56 (p. 48).

[16] See 'The 1848 Public Health Act' on the website of the UK Parliament. *https://www.parliament.uk/about/living-heritage/transformingsociety/towncountry/towns/tyne-and-wear-case-study/about-the-group/public-administration/the-1848-public-health-act/*.

[17] Pamela K. Gilbert, *Cholera and Nation: Doctoring the Social Body in Victorian England* (Albany: State University of New York Press, 2008), p. 37.

[18] Quoted in John White, *Some Account of the Proposed Improvements of the Western Part of London, by the Formation of the Regent's Park, the New Street, the New Sewer, &c. &c.* (London: W. & P. Reynolds, 1814), p. xlviii.

[19] John Nash, Esq. 22 April 1828 Report, in *Reports from Committees, Vol. IV* (ordered by the House of Commons to be printed in 1828 and to be preserved at the Bodleian Library, Oxford), 74.

[20] Steven Johnson, *The Ghost Map: A Street, an Epidemic and the Hidden Power of Urban Networks* (London: Penguin, 2008), p. 20.

[21] For more about Dr Adrien Proust and the *cordon sanitaire*, see Chloé Leprince, 'Quand le père de Marcel Proust inventait le "cordon sanitaire"', *France Culture: Histoire*, *https://www.franceculture.fr/histoire/quand-le-pere-de-marcel-proust-inventait-le-cordon-sanitaire*; and Pierre-Louis Laget, 'Les lazarets et l'émergence de nouvelles maladies pestilentielles au XIXe et au début du XXe siècle', *In Situ*, 2 (2002), DOI: *https://doi.org/10.4000/insitu.1225*.

[22] David S. Barnes, *The Making of a Social Disease: Tuberculosis in Nineteenth-Century France* (Berkeley: University of California Press, 1995), ch. 4. Online at *http://ark.cdlib.org/ark:/13030/ft8t1nb5rp*.

[23] Michel Foucault, 'The Confession of the Flesh' (interview, 1977), in C. Gordon (ed.), *Power/Knowledge: Selected Interviews and Other Writings* (New York: Pantheon Books, 1980), p. 194.

[24] See for instance Judith R. Walkowitz, *Prostitution and Victorian Society: Women, Class, and the State* (Cambridge: Cambridge University Press, 1980); and Carol Smart, *Regulating Womanhood* (London: Routledge, 2002).

[25] Sabine Schülting, *Dirt in Victorian Literature and Culture: Writing Materiality* (New York: Routledge, 2016), p. 52.

[26] Mary Poovey, *Making a Social Body: British Cultural Formation, 1830–1864* (Chicago: University of Chicago Press, 1995), p. 58. Her analysis focuses on James Phillips Kay's investigation after an outbreak in Manchester in 1831 (published in 1832 under the title *The Moral and*

Physical Condition of the Working Classes Employed in the Cotton Manufacture in Manchester).

27 John Springhall, *Youth, Popular Culture and Moral Panics: Penny Gaffs to Gansta-Rap, 1830–1996* (London: Palgrave, 1998). See in particular pp. 71–97.

28 Marie Léger-St-Jean attributes it to James Lindridge in her *Price One Penny* database, but it was indeed published under the pseudonym of Jayhohenn Deehiseekayess.

29 'Indigenous' is defined by the *Oxford English Dictionary Online* as 'Born or produced naturally in a land or region; native or belonging naturally to (the soil, region, etc.)'.

30 Charles Knight, quoted in Mayne, *Perilous Nature*, p. 8; emphasis original.

31 John Springhall, '"Pernicious Reading"? "The Penny Dreadful" as Scapegoat for Late-Victorian Juvenile Crime', *Victorian Periodicals Review*, 27/4 (Winter 1994), 326–49 (342).

32 All definitions quoted here come from the *Oxford English Dictionary Online*.

33 This statement was the tagline on the front cover of Alfred Harmsworth's *Halfpenny Marvel* (1893–1922) from October 1895 onwards. See Elizabeth James and Helen R. Smith, *Penny Dreadfuls and Boys' Adventures: The Barry Ono Collection of Victorian Popular Literature in the British Library* (London: The British Library, 1998), pp. xviii–xix.

34 Edmund Plowden quoted in Ernst H. Kantorowicz, *The King's Two Bodies: A Study in Mediaeval Political Theology* (Princeton: Princeton University Press, 1957), p. 9.

35 Frederick Oldfield Ward, 'Sanitary Consolidation', *Quarterly Review*, 88 (March 1851), 435–92.

36 Quoted in Kate Summerscale, *The Wicked Boy: The History of a Victorian Child Murderer* (New York: Penguin Press, 2016), ch. 7 (Kindle).

37 James William Buel, *Sea and Land: An Illustrated History of the Wonderful and Curious Things of Nature Existing before and since the Deluge* (Toronto: J. S. Robertson and Bros., 1887), p. 470.

38 Erasmus Darwin, 'The Botanic Garden', in A. Komisaruk and A. Dushane (eds), *The Botanic Garden by Erasmus Darwin, Volume II* (London and New York: Routledge, 2017), p. 74.

39 For a detailed exploration of reverse colonisation, see Stephen D. Arata, 'The Occidental Tourist: *Dracula* and the Anxiety of Reverse Colonization', *Victorian Studies*, 33/4 (1990), 621–45; reprinted as 'The Occidental Tourist: Stoker and Reverse Colonization' in his

monograph *Fictions of Loss in the Victorian Fin de Siècle: Identity and Empire* (Cambridge: Cambridge University Press, 1996), pp. 107–32.

[40] Daisy Butcher, 'Introduction', in D. Butcher (ed.), *Evil Roots: Killer Tales of the Botanical Gothic* (London: British Library, 2019), p. 7.

[41] Here she refers also to Cheryl Blake Price, 'Vegetable Monsters: Man-Eating Trees in *Fin-de-Siècle* Fiction', *Victorian Literature and Culture*, 41 (2013), 311–27.

[42] An English version can be read in Mary A. Grant (trans.), *The Myths of Hyginus* (Lawrence: University of Kansas Press, 1960).

[43] Quoted in 'The Vegetable Kingdom. The Upas Tree', *The Student: A Magazine of Theology, Literature, and Science, Vol. I* (London: James Gilbert, 49, Paternoster Row, 1844), p. 38.

[44] Annemarie Schimmel, *The Mystery of Numbers* (New York: Oxford University Press, 1993), p. 193.

[45] Fred Botting, *Gothic* (London and New York: Routledge, 1996), p. 7.

[46] Manon Burz-Labrande, '"Useful Knowledge" versus "Wastes of Print", Working-Class Education and Edward Lloyd', *Victorian Popular Fictions Journal*, 3/1 (Spring 2021), 123–39 (131).

[47] Christopher Pittard, *Purity and Contamination in Late Victorian Detective Fiction* (Farnham: Ashgate, 2011), p. 3.

[48] For more detail on the penny publications' relationship with popular education and how it contributes to the failure of the Society for the Diffusion of Useful Knowledge in the late 1840s, see Burz-Labrande, '"Useful Knowledge" versus "Wastes of Print"'.

6

'A Tale of the Plague': Anti-medical Sentiment and Epidemic Disease in Early Victorian Popular Gothic Fiction

JOSEPH CRAWFORD

'Burn the doctors': Anti-medical Sentiment in Britain, 1828–40

We should begin with the riots. In 1829, a crowd in Nottingham attacked a doctor, accusing him of plotting to have a child murdered so that he could dissect its body.[1] In 1831, an anatomy theatre in Aberdeen was attacked and destroyed by the townsfolk after human body parts were found buried in its back garden (Durey, pp. 175–6).[2] In 1832, a Liverpool hospital was besieged by an angry crowd, who accused the doctors within of murdering their patients (Durey, p. 162).[3] In London, another hospital was attacked, while an old man being taken for treatment by a surgeon was seized and carried home by a crowd who claimed they were saving him from being 'burked' (Morris, p. 108). In Sunderland, the people threatened to 'burn the doctors', and there were anti-medical riots in Manchester, Sheffield, Glasgow and York (Durey, p. 178; Morris, p. 46).[4] Doctors travelling in Scotland found that the people threw stones at them and threatened to pull down the houses they lodged in: in Edinburgh the townsfolk wrecked their vans and attacked their hospitals, while in Glasgow surgeons were set upon by mobs throwing mud and yelling 'medical murderer' and 'Burkers' (Morris, pp. 68, 108–9). In Paisley, the people roamed from the house of one doctor to the next, destroying their shops and smashing their windows: only when the Fourth Dragoons arrived from Glasgow was the mob finally forced to disperse (Morris, pp. 108–9; Durey, pp. 178–9). In Manchester, a hospital was attacked by a mob carrying the coffin of a decapitated four-year-old boy, whose head had been replaced with a brick by surgeons: 'To the hospital', the rioters shouted, 'pull it to the ground' (Morris, p. 110). As in Paisley, the police found themselves unable to quell the riot, which was only put down by the arrival of four troops of hussars (Morris, p. 110; Durey, pp. 179–80). In 1833 the Cambridge University anatomy theatre was attacked by the townsfolk, and in 1835 another anatomy theatre, this time in Sheffield, was destroyed by an infuriated crowd (Durey, pp. 241–5). Surveying these incidents, and the many similar events which occurred during the same years, it seems safe to describe the early 1830s as a period during which relations between the medical profession and the British public reached an all-time low.

This chapter explores the ways in which this distrust of doctors was reflected in the popular Gothic literature of the 1830s and 1840s. That such literature was preoccupied with body-snatching has been noted by scholars such as Louis James; and Anna Gasperini's recent monograph discusses how 'penny blood' fiction responded to the anxieties prompted by the 1832 Anatomy Act.[5] However, these concerns over 'Burkers' and 'resurrection men' constitute only one part of a much wider suspicion of medical professionals visible within the Gothic fiction of the era, a suspicion that must be understood in relation to the sinister reputation that orthodox doctors acquired among the urban poor during the 1830s and 1840s. This chapter will explore the reasons why the British medical profession enjoyed so little popular trust during these years, before discussing how these attitudes were manifested in the popular Gothic fiction of the period.

The collapse of popular trust in orthodox medicine was due to four interlinked events: the Burke and Hare murders of 1828, the cholera epidemic of 1831–2, the Anatomy Act of 1832 and the New Poor Law of 1834. As medical training in Britain became increasingly reliant on the study of anatomy, the traditional source of corpses for dissection – the bodies of executed felons – fell woefully short of the demand generated by the nation's medical schools (Hurren, pp. 3–4). Doctors made up the difference by purchasing corpses from 'resurrectionists', who stole the bodies of the recently dead from graveyards: tempted by the high prices paid for fresh corpses, the Edinburgh body snatchers William Burke and William Hare soon began murdering the living, as well (Hurren, p. 5; Gasperini, pp. 10–11). The surgeon to whom they sold their victims, Robert Knox, claimed to be ignorant of their origins, but the public was sceptical: as the incident in Nottingham the following year suggests, many people were willing to believe that doctors might knowingly pay criminals to commit murders in order to supply bodies for dissection. Reports of attempted 'burkings' – murders, usually by suffocation, in order to procure corpses for anatomists – proliferated over the years that followed, especially after the exposure of a second resurrectionist murder-gang in London in 1831 (Durey, pp. 176–8; Gasperini, p. 11). By 1831, much of the British public clearly regarded doctors as being complicit in a system of murder, and associated them with what Tabitha Sparks describes as 'depraved, criminal, and godless practices'.[6] Nor was it lost upon the labouring classes that, in both London and Edinburgh, the resurrectionists preyed primarily upon the socially marginal, choosing their victims from among those least likely to be missed (Gasperini, pp. xii–xiii). The urban poor, who were least likely to be able to afford the fees of doctors in life, thus became the most likely to end up on their dissection tables after death.

It was in this tense atmosphere that Asiatic Cholera first reached Britain in 1831. The government responded by organising local Boards of Health throughout the country, tasked with tracking and monitoring cholera cases, constructing cholera hospitals, and burying deceased cholera victims in quicklime, whenever possible within twelve hours of their deaths (Durey, pp. 76–7, 89–92, 164–6; Morris, pp. 34–5).[7] This immense effort represented the first time that the British medical profession was deployed as an arm of the state, rather than being treated as a mere collection of private individuals: in all previous epidemics, the expectation had been that most doctors would simply save themselves by fleeing the affected areas (Brown, pp. 151–2). However, while the Boards of Health form a milestone in the history of British public health, the poor regarded them with intense suspicion. In their view, as Morris notes:

> What distinguished cholera from the other perils of life was not the danger of the disease itself, but the extraordinary and disturbing way in which the middle and ruling classes were behaving with their rules and regulations, Boards of Health, hospitals and subscriptions. (p. 101)

In 1831–2, cholera was overwhelmingly a disease of the poor, which flourished amidst the squalor of urban slums. Elite observers were swift to place the blame for this on the afflicted populations, arguing that the labouring classes laid themselves open to infection through their unhygienic habits and excessive drinking (Morris, pp. 85–6, 135–8; Durey, p. 195). Unsurprisingly, this analysis gained little traction with the poor themselves, who soon developed their own theories about what was really going on. Some argued that cholera did not really exist, and had been invented by a conspiracy of doctors as an excuse to extract additional public funds from an already overtaxed population (Morris, pp. 96–7). Others claimed that the government was using the cholera scare as a pretext for silencing radicals, or that it was deliberately inflating case numbers as part of a plot to terrify the people into submission, having been spooked by the Swing Riots of 1830 and the revolutionary Days of May in 1832 (Morris, pp. 98–100; Durey, pp. 190–1). Still, others concluded that the cholera hospitals had been built, not to cure people, but to kill them, in order to provide doctors with a supply of corpses for dissection (Morris, p. 99; Durey, p. 92).

Medical horror stories proliferated in the (literally) febrile atmosphere of 1831–2. Cholera burials were regarded with horror by the poor, as their rapidity left no time for customary mourning rituals, and many cholera victims were buried without shrouds or coffins in mass graves, in unconsecrated ground, a fate normally reserved for suicides (Morris, p. 105; Durey, pp. 164–7). The conviction thus took hold that these rapid burials were proof that the doctors had something to hide: the fact that they had poisoned their patients, perhaps, or that they had stolen their bodies for dissection. The heavy usage of opiates in cholera treatments aroused particular suspicion: doctors were said to be dosing patients with laudanum until they appeared dead, and then either vivisecting them or handing them over for live burial (Durey, pp. 126–7, 168–70). The darkest conspiracy theories linked the cholera outbreak to the recently completed 1831 census: cholera, they asserted, was nothing less than a state-sanctioned Malthusian murder plot, and the true purpose of the census had been to identify the most densely populated districts of the country, into which cholera was then deliberately introduced in order to bring the population down to more manageable levels (Morris, p. 99).[8] What united all these theories was their shared cynicism about the new alliance between the medical profession and the state represented by the formation of the Boards of Health, and their conviction that doctors and government alike were united in a malevolent conspiracy against the poor.

Relations between the medical profession and the people were strained even further by the passage of the Anatomy Act, which was first proposed in 1829 and ultimately passed in 1832. This act addressed the national shortage of corpses for anatomy training by decreeing that the unclaimed corpses of paupers should be given over to teaching hospitals for dissection (Hurren, pp. 4–6). Copies of the Act were pinned up inside workhouses, in the hope that the fear of having their bodies seized upon death would discourage the poor from seeking relief unless they were truly desperate (Hurren, p. 21). Coupled with the New Poor Law of 1834, which was founded on the Malthusian principle that relief had to be made as unappealing as possible in order to discourage the poor from irresponsibly increasing the pauper population, the Anatomy Act served to powerfully reinforce the popular perception of doctors as ghoulish henchmen of the state, ever willing to help lower the poor rates by culling the poor as long as they were paid a suitable bounty of human corpses. The fact that the New Poor Law also involved the creation of a network of state-appointed District Medical Officers points to the growing interdependence of the state and the medical profession during this period, which led to officials and doctors alike being regarded with such suspicion by the working classes (Brown, p. 173).

The distrust with which doctors were regarded by the populace was intensified even further by the widespread suspicion that they regarded the bodies of the poor, alive or dead, as opportunities for medical experimentation. Impoverished families who were unable to pay the medical bills of dead relatives sometimes handed over their corpses to clear their debts, while doctors who operated on the poor for free often did so because they were looking to practise new or unfamiliar surgical techniques, with results that sometimes proved fatal to their patients (Hurren, pp. 83, 223; Gasperini, pp. 55–6). Medical students, like Charles Dickens's Ben Allen and Bob Sawyer, were viewed as particularly dangerous in this respect, and the unpleasant practical jokes for which they were notorious did nothing to endear them to the general population (Hurren, pp. 77, 83–5; Durey; pp. 175–6). These attitudes are reflected in *The Pickwick Papers* (1836–7), in which Sam Weller – who frequently acts as the mouthpiece of the working classes – assumes that Allen and Sawyer have hired Mr Martin as a test subject, 'to take strong medicine, or to go into fits and be experimentalised upon, or to swallow poison now and then with the view of testing the efficacy of some new antidotes, or to do something or other to promote the great science of medicine'.[9] Sam's view of the medical profession in general is summarised by his bleak joke to Arabella: 'I only assisted natur, ma'am; as the doctor said to the boy's mother, after he'd bled him to death' (Dickens, p. 634).

The murder plot rumours of 1831–2 resurfaced during the politically volatile years of 1838–9, with the appearance of articles in the radical press claiming that a clergyman named 'Marcus' had developed a plan to prevent population growth by murdering the excess children of the poor using poison gas.[10] Marcus – whose name was surely intended to evoke that of Malthus – was the clearest embodiment to date of a conviction that had been taking root among the British poor since 1829: that their own government wanted them dead, and that the nation's doctors were willing to use the latest medical science to help bring this objective about. Under these circumstances, it is hardly surprising that many of the labouring classes avoided orthodox medicine as much as possible. Instead, they embraced homeopathy, herbalism, mesmerism and other forms of alternative medicine, and when all else failed they sought aid from traditional cunning men.[11] The fortunes of botanical medicine, in particular, were closely linked with those of the Chartist movement:

herbalism could easily function as a form of working-class self-help, whereas orthodox doctors, as the Chartists liked to point out, had every incentive to keep their patients sick in order to multiply their opportunities for collecting fees (Morris, p. 160; Brown, p. 222).[12] During the 1830s, when the reputation of orthodox medicine was at its nadir, these alternative traditions received so much support that their practitioners believed they would soon sweep away the existing medical establishment entirely.[13] It was in these years, during which many working-class people clearly viewed orthodox doctors as little more than state-sanctioned murderers, that the 'penny blood' Gothics first rose to popularity among the Victorian poor.

'Bad characters': Doctors and Villains in Early Victorian Popular Gothic

The association of nineteenth-century doctors with body-snatching, vivisection, and experimentation upon unwilling patients famously fed into the depiction of the various 'mad scientist' figures who populate the Gothic literature of the period, such as Frankenstein, Jekyll, and Moreau. In the popular Gothic fiction of the 1830s and 1840s, however, medical villainy had little to do with forbidden knowledge or attempts to 'play God': instead, it focused on the brutal reality that, to medical professionals, the poor were often worth more dead than alive. As Gasperini notes, dissection-obsessed grave-robbing doctors appear in both James Malcolm Rymer's *Manuscripts from the Diary of a Physician* (1844, 1847), and in Rymer and Thomas Peckett Prest's *Varney the Vampire* (1845–7) (pp. 35, 43, 82, 88–9). William Harrison Ainsworth's plague novel *Old St. Paul's* (1841) – which appeared in weekly instalments in *The Sunday Times,* a newspaper that had a large lower-class audience – has as its chief villain a cruel nurse, Mother Malmaynes, who murders plague victims under her care in order to rob them (James, pp. 90–2). Edward Bulwer-Lytton's *Lucretia, or the Poisoners* (1846), meanwhile, is preoccupied with the way in which medical knowledge may be turned to criminal ends, and includes among its villains both a murderous nurse *and* a brutal body-snatcher, an 'ogre' with eyes 'like that of the birds which feed on the dead', who threatens to turn those who cross him into 'meat for the surgeons'.[14]

The body-snatcher's description of his victims as 'meat' draws attention to the connections that can also be drawn between these concerns over body-snatching and the most famous penny blood villain of all, Sweeney Todd in *The String of Pearls* (1846–7). Todd is a barber rather than a doctor, but his trade was still adjacent to medicine – barbers were only definitively disaggregated from surgeons in 1842 – and while he and Mrs Lovett cook their victims rather than dissecting them, multiple contemporary sources compared anatomists to butchers.[15] Dissection rooms were called 'meat shops' by Victorian medical students, demonstrators in anatomy were known as 'Meaters', and anti-anatomy cartoons from the period made the connection explicit by depicting doctors buying dead bodies by the pound, hanging them on meathooks, and grinding them up into mincemeat (Gasperini, p. 143; Hurren, pp. 187, 183–5). The first reading of the Anatomy Act in 1829 sparked a panic in the Shadwell workhouse, whose inmates leapt to the conclusion that the authorities were literally butchering them in order to make soup from their bodies, and when the house of a Manchester woman was attacked in 1831 by a mob who accused her of kidnapping children to make into pies, the fact that a preparer of bodies for the local anatomy school lodged in her house was probably seen as proof of her guilt (Gasperini, p. 149; Durey, p. 182). It is also worth noting that one of the secondary antagonists in *The String of Pearls* is a private madhouse keeper, whose willingness to certify the sane as mad and to murder the patients under his care reflect yet another set of anxieties over the ways in which medical practices could be weaponised by the rich against the poor – a significant concern in an era when elite doctors were willing to diagnose Chartist activists as insane simply on the basis of their political beliefs.[16] Similar worries about the ease with which mercenary doctors could be persuaded to certify people as lunatics also appear in Rymer's *Diary of a Physician*, whose doctor-protagonist nobly refuses a bribe to do so, but soon discovers that not all physicians are as principled as he is.[17]

The longest and most influential of the penny bloods was Reynolds's sprawling serial *The Mysteries of London* (1844–8). The closest thing that it has to a primary antagonist is the Resurrection Man, who murders vulnerable Londoners and sells their bodies to surgeons. When it comes to medical villainy in *The Mysteries of London*, however, the Resurrection Man turns out to be only the tip of the iceberg. His murderous trade exists only because of the demand created by unscrupulous medical professionals, whom Reynolds portrays as almost vampiric in their desire for corpses:

> For some minutes before their arrival an individual, enveloped in a long cloak, was walking up and down beneath the shadow of the wall.
>
> This was the surgeon, whose thirst after science had called into action the energies of the body-snatchers that night.[18]

Driven by his uncontrollable 'thirst' to prowl around graveyards in a long cloak at midnight, this surgeon seems to be virtually undead already. Another is described as having devoted an outhouse to 'dissection and physiological experiment', because he is 'passionately attached to anatomical studies' – a description that carries a hint of necrophilia (p. 331). Of the various corpse-hungry doctors who appear in the *Mysteries*, the most thorough description is given to Dr Lascelles:

> He was devoted to the art which he practised, and was reputed the most scientific man of the whole faculty. His anatomical researches had been prosecuted with an energy and a perseverance which afforded occupation to half the resurrection-men in London, and more than once to the doctor's own personal danger in respect to the law. It was whispered in well-informed circles that he never hesitated to encounter any peril in order to possess himself of the corpse of a person who died of an unusual malady. His devotion to anatomy had materially blunted his feelings and deadened the kinder sympathies of his nature; but his immense talents, added to a reputation acquired by several wonderful cures, rendered him the most fashionable physician of the day. (p. 331)

The concern Reynolds articulates here – that the gruesomeness of 'anatomical researches' desensitised doctors to sympathy and morality, leading them to regard people as mere specimens for medical study – was one that was frequently expressed at the time (Gasperini, pp. 38–9). Lascelles himself is so 'deadened' that he keeps a row of severed human heads on a shelf, regarding any objection to this as mere 'prejudice' (Reynolds, p. 331). For Reynolds, the result was a blurring of the boundaries between respectable medicine and urban criminality, as doctors and criminals alike lived lives characterised by theft, secrecy and violence, as the references here to 'peril' and 'personal danger' attest.

In order to pursue his anatomical research undisturbed, Lascelles rents a house that is designed for, and inhabited by, criminals:

> 'I hired this room at an enormous rental. I did not, however, care about the high rate demanded of me for the use of the place, because it is not only in a most retired neighbourhood, but there is also a private and subterranean means of egress and ingress from another street, which is useful, you know, for one who has to deal with resurrectionists.'
>
> 'Then, for aught you know, doctor,' said the Earl, 'you may occupy an apartment in the house of bad characters?'
>
> 'What do I care?' exclaimed Lascelles. 'I could not well have such a laboratory as this at my own residence – my servants would talk about these human heads, and those plaster casts, and the galvanic experiments, and I should be looked upon as a sorcerer, or at all events with so much suspicion and aversion as to lose all my practice.' (Reynolds, pp. 169–70).

From Reynolds's pro-Chartist perspective, the irony here is that, for Lascelles and the earl, 'bad characters' refers, axiomatically, only to members of the criminal underclass. Just as William Burke went to the gallows (and to the dissecting room) while Robert Knox walked free, so Lascelles is shielded by his social class and professional status from facing any real consequences of his actions. Despite his hiring of body-snatchers, his underground tunnels, his midnight experiments and his secret rooms full of stolen human heads, it would clearly never occur to him to wonder whether he might conceivably be something of a 'bad character' himself.

Reynolds's fascination with the relationship between medicine and crime is ultimately embodied in the figure of Jack Rily, who is one of the main villains during the later stages of the *Mysteries*.

Rily is a medical student turned criminal, 'brought up to the medical profession', whose underworld nickname is 'the Doctor', and the narrative repeatedly draws attention to the ways in which his medical education has prepared him for his subsequent criminal activities (p. 259). His surgical skills assist him in acts of violence – most notably in his final knife-fight with his rival, Vitriol Bob – and his training in anatomy has left him desensitised to death and crime, as his speech to Mrs Mortimer makes clear:

> 'Ah! I understand you, my dear tiger-cat,' exclaimed Jack Rily: 'you don't admire the presence of the stiff 'un there. Lord bless you! if you'd only been my wife when I was a doctor, you would have become familiar enough with articles of that kind – aye, and have thought nothing of shaking hands with a resurrection man. But it's all habit; and so, since you would feel more comfortable if that bundle over there was moved, I'll just drag it into the back kitchen –and our friend here will doubtless amuse himself by burying it to-morrow night.' (p. 259)

Rily's remark that 'it's all habit' speaks to the widespread concern among the working classes who comprised Reynolds's audience that anatomical training inculcated the wrong habits in aspiring doctors: instead of teaching them to value life, it deadened their sympathies and taught them to associate with criminals. For Reynolds, the institutional embodiment of this system of medical inhumanity was the linkage between the Anatomy Act and the New Poor Law, as the Resurrection Man himself is all too aware:

> 'But do you think there's such people as resurrection men now-a-days?'
> 'Resurrection men!' ejaculated the reverend visitor, bursting out into a laugh; 'no, my dear madam – society has got rid of those abominations'.
> 'Then where do surgeons get corpses from, sir?'
> 'From the hulks, the prisons, and the workhouses,' was the answer.
> 'What! poor creatures which goes to the workus!' cried Mrs. Smith, revolting at the idea.
> 'Yes – ma'am; but the surgeons don't like them as subjects, because they're nothing but skin and bone.'

'Well, for my part,' exclaimed the widow, wiping away a tear, 'I think it's wery hard if, after paying rates and taxes for a many – many year, I should be obleeged to go to the workus, and then be cut up in a surgeon's slaughter-house at last.'

'Ah! my dear ma'am, these are sad times – very sad times,' said the sanctified gentleman. 'But a woman who does her duty to her fellow creatures as you do, need fear nothing; heaven will protect you!' (p. 319)

The 'sanctified gentleman' here is, in fact, the Resurrection Man in disguise, who knows full well that 'heaven' will do nothing to protect those sentenced to the 'surgeon's slaughter-house' by the laws of these 'very sad times'. Indeed, the fact that this apologist for the New Poor Law is actually a murderous resurrectionist in disguise can be interpreted as a symbolic reflection of the way that the Anatomy Act effectively transformed the state into an industrial-scale body-snatcher, pressing official ideology into the service of medical criminality.

To complete its gallery of medical criminality, *The Mysteries of London* also features multiple private madhouses, whose doctors are willing to certify inconvenient people as insane. Here, for example, is Dr Swinton:

> The Doctor himself was an elderly person, of highly respectable appearance, and of very pleasing manners *when* he chose to be agreeable: but no demon could exhibit greater ferocity than he, when compelled to exercise his authority in respect to those amongst his patients who had no friends to care about them. (p. 331)

Like Lascelles, Swinton maintains a double life, reflecting the different faces that the medical profession presented towards the rich and the poor. For Lascelles, this doubleness is embodied in the two homes that he maintains: the rich see him at his house in Grafton Street, where he performs his 'wonderful cures', whereas the poor encounter him at his secret laboratory, where he purchases their stolen corpses. In Swinton's case, however, the doubleness is hidden in plain sight. Just as the 'highly respectable' doctor actually behaves like a 'demon' towards his victims, so his 'cheerful' house is actually a prison:

It was by no means a gloomy-looking place, although the casements were protected by iron bars: for to mitigate that prison-like effect, the curtains were of a cheerful colour, and the window-sills were adorned with flowers and verdant evergreens in bright red pots. Moreover, the front of the house was stuccoed; and wherever paint was used, the colours were of the gayest kind.

The front door always stood open during the day-time, because there was an inner door of great strength which led into the hall; and a porter in handsome livery was constantly lounging about at the entrance. (p. 331)

It is only Swinton's friendless 'patients' who discover, to their cost, that the flowers conceal iron bars, that the porter is a guard and that behind the front door that is always open is an inner door that is always shut. His house thus acts as an emblem for contemporary working-class anxieties about the medical profession: that despite their show of superficial benevolence, behind closed doors doctors might behave cruelly, criminally and even murderously towards the impoverished patients who became subject to their 'authority'. Swinton is described as the kind of person who might, at any time, deliver a speech on the necessity of 'circulating a million of Bibles amongst the poor savages of the Cannibal Islands' (*Mysteries of London*, IV, p. 331). His smile, however, is described as 'showing his well-preserved teeth': a hint that this seemingly benevolent doctor, like so many of the other villainous medical professionals who haunt the popular Gothic literature of the period, has actually been the true cannibal all along (*Mysteries of London*, IV, p. 331).

'A hideous phantom stalking the streets': Tales of the Plague

Although the cholera epidemic of 1831–2 was undoubtedly socially traumatic, it left relatively little mark on British literary history. Admittedly, the fiction of the early 1830s was dominated by historical novels and 'silver fork' stories of high life, neither of which were well adapted to address such subject matter – but even with the rise of the 'penny bloods' and 'condition of England novels' in the 1840s, cholera found little place in their depictions of urban misery. Possibly the epidemic was too clearly attached to a specific historical moment to serve the purposes of writers who wished to write about injustice and poverty in general, rather than about the events of 1831–2 in particular. Or perhaps cholera – a disease whose causes were unknown, for which no effective treatment existed, and of which the only outcomes were recovery or rapid death – simply did not lend itself to narratively satisfying stories.

Epidemic disease does haunt the margins of the popular Gothic fiction of the period. *The Mysteries of London* includes a scene in which the Resurrection Man and his henchmen rob a plague ship anchored in the Thames, and while the infection in this case comes from Africa rather than Asia, the parallel with the Asiatic cholera of 1831–2 is made clear by the question that their employer, Mr Swot, asks them to test their willingness to undertake the mission: 'would you sleep in the same room with a man who had the cholera or the small-pox, for instance – supposing you got a thousand pounds each to do it?' (p. 83). The fact that the ship carries both gold and plague from Africa to London also makes clear the connection between Britain's imperial trade networks and its exposure to new forms of infectious disease – a connection frequently drawn at the time in relation to cholera, which originated in Britain's colonial territories in India.[19]

Varney the vampire can be read as a metaphor for contagion, insofar as his victims can become vampires in turn; and while it would be a stretch to read his vampirism as symbolic of cholera, the fact that he is created via medical experimentation and then goes on to inflict his unnatural condition on others is reminiscent of the rumours regarding the true origins of cholera which circulated in 1831–2 (Morris, p. 99). Furthermore, while Sweeney Todd's murder spree in *The String of Pearls* is hardly an infection in the conventional sense, the novel is clearly in dialogue with the public health measures introduced in the wake of the 1831–2 cholera epidemic. Todd's activities are revealed partly by the awful smell created by the remains of his victims packed under St Dunstan's Church – a detail that recalls the persistent worries in the period about the infectious miasmas arising from urban graveyards, which were thought to spread disease among the poor (Gasperini, pp. 152, 193).[20] As Rosalind Crone notes, the vaults of the real St Dunstan's were so packed with corpses that workers had to be bribed with brandy to remove them, and when one subsequently died his death was blamed on infectious 'effluvium' arising from the bodies – an event that may have inspired the corpse-discovery scenes in *The String of Pearls* a few years later.[21]

Elite perspectives on epidemic disease, meanwhile, are visible in Harriet Martineau's 1839 novel *Deerbrook*, whose hero is a physician in a country village struck by an epidemic of 'fever'. Whereas penny bloods focused on the ways in which the poor were victimised by doctors, in *Deerbrook* the situation is reversed, with the significantly named Mr Hope having to contend with the ignorance, prejudice and superstition of the rural poor. He is unjustly accused of body-snatching, poisoning children and carrying out unnecessary amputations 'for the sake of practice and amusement': at one point his surgery is even attacked by a mob, 'this being the place where the people expected to find the greatest number of dead bodies', an event which recalls the anti-medical riots of 1831–5.[22] Despite these provocations, however, Hope continues to patiently care for the people afflicted by the epidemic, as he maintains that 'their ignorance ... renders them unfit to take any rational care of themselves' (Martineau, p. 462). Throughout the novel, the enlightened selflessness of the doctor is juxtaposed with the superstitious behaviour of the poor, whose suspicion of the medical profession is depicted as merely yet another example of their self-destructive ignorance. Indeed, Martineau's obvious sympathy for doctors, coupled with her Malthusian defence of the New Poor Law, was probably one of the reasons why she was depicted in the radical press as being a supporter of the medical murder plot orchestrated by the fictitious poisoner 'Marcus' (Vargo, p. 57).

By far the most important disease novel of the period was William Ainsworth's *Old St. Paul's* (1841), whose subject was the plague of 1665. Drawing on Daniel Defoe's *Journal of the Plague Year* (1722), Ainsworth depicted the plague in apocalyptic terms as a 'hideous phantom stalking the streets', transforming London into a city of the dead.[23] His scenes of plague pits, sealed houses and sudden death must have resonated with audiences who still remembered the cholera quarantines and mass graves of 1832, and his depiction of the plague nurse Judith Malmaynes murdering and robbing her patients recalls popular anxieties over what might really have happened in Britain's cholera hospitals during the epidemic. At one point Ainsworth even explicitly connects the two epidemics, comparing a 'Dance of Death' held at St Paul's during the plague with the 'carnival pastime' made in Paris during the cholera epidemic 'in our own time' (p. 262).

Compared to penny bloods such as *The Mysteries of London*, however, *Old St. Paul's* offers a much more sympathetic depiction of the medical profession. Doctor Hodges, who acts as physician to the protagonists, is depicted as a good and dutiful man, while the crimes that were popularly attributed to doctors during the 1831–2 epidemic are displaced onto lower-class characters such as Judith Malmaynes and the coffin-maker Anselm Chowles. In 1832, Hood's satirical poem 'Ode to Malthus' had imagined misanthropic Malthusians actively hoping that cholera would spread in order to reduce the surplus population, and Cobbett had suspected doctors of exaggerating the disease in order to profit from it (Morris, pp. 96–9). In *Old St. Paul's*, however, it is not elite physicians but impoverished coffin-makers who are shown drinking toasts to the plague on the grounds that 'My coffins and coffers alike it fills' (p. 40). Anxieties about medical experimentation, so common among the working classes at the time, are voiced in the novel only by the comical servant Blaize, who worries that 'Doctor Hodges will kill me' because '[h]e is fond of trying experiments, and will make me his subject' – and whereas in *The Mysteries of London* such predictions would usually turn out to be accurate, in *Old St. Paul's* Blaize is mocked for his fear of doctors and his reliance upon alternative medicines (pp. 62–3). As well as trusting orthodox medicine, the protagonists survive the plague through strict self-isolation, cutting themselves off from the death-blighted city around them – the kind of policy that had been deeply unpopular with the poor during the 1831–2 epidemic, for whom quarantine measures were often incompatible with the economic activities they relied upon to survive. In *Old St. Paul's*, the Bloundel family weather the epidemic by locking themselves away with a year's supply of food and medicine – a measure that would have been an impossible fantasy for most labouring-class families in cholera-struck cities in 1831–2, many of whom lived hand to mouth, and would have struggled to lay in supplies for a week in advance, let alone a year.

These displacements and dismissals of contemporary anxieties suggest that Ainsworth's fundamental cultural loyalties lay with the middle classes, who formed the primary target market for his novels, rather than the poor. Despite its serial format and morbid subject matter, the attitudes towards medicine and disease expressed in *Old St. Paul's* are closer to those of Martineau's *Deerbrook* than to those of penny blood authors such as Reynolds and Prest. Consequently, it is instructive to examine the ways in which Ainsworth's novel was rewritten in the penny press. It was plagiarised by Prest as *A Legend of Old St. Paul's* in Lloyd's *Penny Sunday Times and People's Police Gazette*, but this rewrite de-emphasised the plague to focus on the repeated seduction plots of its aristocratic villain, Eustace St Clair. Compared to Ainsworth's original, Prest's plagiarism also shows more suspicion of the handling of the plague by the authorities, who are accused of manipulating the infection figures in St Giles by 'knavery and collusion'.[24] Doctor Hodges – who is renamed 'Doctor Stanley' – is still sympathetically depicted, but his role in the story is enormously reduced, and a heavy emphasis is placed instead upon the importance of popular medical self-help. As the plague rages the government appoints physicians and surgeons to tend to the poor, but the narrator is much more impressed by the fact that it also publishes directions for cheap remedies that the poor can make themselves, a measure which is described as 'one of the most charitable and judicious things that could have been done' (Lloyd, issue 49 p. 4). In this context it is worth noting that the first eighteen issues of the *Penny Sunday Times*, in which the story appeared, actually included a medical advice column, and offered a service whereby readers could write to the paper for assistance with medical problems on which they could not afford to consult a doctor: judging from the published replies, these included queries on cheap remedies, on navigating hospital bureaucracy, and even on finding affordable asylums for insane relatives (Lloyd, issue 4 p. 4, 12 p. 4). The paper also regularly carried advertisements for herbal pills and patent medicines: issue 104 alone carried advertisements for 'Parr's life pills', 'Nixon's Universal Herbal Ointment', 'Holloway's Ointment and Pills' and a hydropathy service (Lloyd, issue 104 p. 4).

Prest's fictional dethroning of the orthodox doctor in favour of cheap home-made remedies can thus be seen as an expression of the same culture of working-class medical self-help that was visible in the pages of the *Penny Sunday Times* itself. Epidemic disease, meanwhile, seems to have been viewed by the paper with a mixture of fatalism and grim humour. In issue 63, one issue after the end of Prest's plague tale, it carried a cartoon of a plague cart heaped with bodies, all with the characteristic blackened faces of cholera victims, with the caption: 'Going a black-bury-ing' (Lloyd, issue 63 p. 1).

A more aggressive rewriting of Ainsworth's novel can be found in the anonymous penny blood *Mysteries of Old St. Paul's* (1841), the publisher of which, George Vickers, would go on to publish Reynolds's *The Mysteries of London*. In this retelling, the benevolent Dr Hodges becomes an outright villain named Dr Calder, and whereas Ainsworth displaced contemporary anxieties about doctors onto the lower-class nurse and coffin-maker, here the nurse and coffin-maker alike are mere minions of the diabolic doctor, who conspires with them to rob and murder plague victims and betrays them to the authorities when they have outlived their usefulness. In Ainsworth's novel, Dr Hodges rebukes the coffin-makers for drinking to the plague's success, but in this rewrite the apothecaries *join in*, because they too stand to profit, while 'villainous surgeons' are actively colluding with the coffin-makers to steal valuable items buried with the dead (pp. 40–1).[25] Doctor Calder murders two people with his own hands over the course of the novel, and indirectly kills others by giving them sedatives to kill them in their sleep, an act which recalls popular anxieties about the misuse of opiates in cholera hospitals (*Mysteries of Old St. Paul's*, p. 117). His misdeeds go undetected because he has bribed the relevant officials, and when a crowd attacks his home yelling 'Bring forth the murderer! – the poisoner! – the hypocrite!', in scenes strongly reminiscent of the anti-medical riots of the 1830s, the narrator is clearly on the side of the mob (pp. 43, 136).

In a further sign of the author's scepticism regarding elite discourses over epidemic disease, this rewrite dispenses with the quarantine plotline. Ainsworth had held up the self-isolation of the Bloundel family as an ideal, but here the narrator mocks the 'weak-mindedness and foolish fears' of those who 'so far gave way as to resolve to close up their houses entirely' (p. 46). Like the cholera sceptics of 1831–2, this rewrite asserts that popular fear and medical corruption are worse problems than the disease itself, to which they actually contribute (Ainsworth, pp. 18, 118; Morris, p. 116). Ainsworth had depicted the comical servant Blaize as foolish because he distrusted doctors, but his equivalent here, Scrubb, is depicted as being foolish because he *does* trust them, and is consequently susceptible to medical scaremongering. The hero, Lawrence, tells Scrubb that 'your fears are worse than any contagion', and goes on to reject Calder's preventive medicines, declaring that he prefers to trust in God and that 'if it is to be my fate, I must submit' (pp. 18, 30). The herbal remedies of the housekeeper, Dame Trivet, are represented as being far superior to orthodox medicine, and their composition is described in sufficient detail to enable readers to make them themselves at home (pp. 10, 16–17). The novel's whole attitude towards epidemic disease is summarised in the dying speech of the plague nurse, Haggett: 'be just, be cleanly, be bold-hearted, but above all be a Christian, and you may defy the plague' (p. 136).

Mysteries of Old St. Paul's thus articulates in fictional form the popular attitudes expressed by the anti-medical riots of 1831–5: that the authorities were in league with corrupt medical professionals, that public health measures such as quarantines were more dangerous than the diseases they supposedly suppressed, and that orthodox doctors were grave-robbing murderers – another 1841 penny blood, *The Monument*, features a grave-robber who actually uses the alias 'Doctor Orthodox'.[26] In this view, good food and traditional herbal remedies afforded better protection against disease than any amount of 'doctor-drink', and epidemics were best encountered in a spirit of resignation and Christian courage (Ainsworth, p. 52). This rewrite clearly emerged from the same culture of medical self-help that made botanical medicine so popular among the working classes, and spoke to a population still traumatised by the 1831–2 cholera epidemic and the 1832 Anatomy Act. If Ainsworth's novel reflected the growing prestige that the medical profession was coming to enjoy in elite circles, then its penny blood adaptations expressed the fear and contempt with which doctors were still clearly regarded by many of the urban poor, especially in matters connected to epidemic disease.

Conclusion

In the overall history of British medicine, the anti-medical sentiment of the 1830s proved to be a temporary crisis. Contrary to the hopes of herbalists such as A. I. Coffin, the reputation of orthodox medicine improved rather than declined as the century progressed, and when cholera returned to Britain in 1848–9 it did not trigger anything like the level of civil disturbance that had attended the 1831–2 epidemic (Miley and Pickstone, pp. 141–52). The Boards of Health, which had seemed so sinister in 1832, no longer prompted the same anxieties when they were made permanent by the Public Health Act of 1848. The Victorian medical profession continued to consolidate its institutional authority, and while alternative practices such as homeopathy remained popular, their appeal gradually waned over the course of the second half of the nineteenth century (Gilbert, p. 3; Barrow, pp. 89, 102).

As the fortunes of the profession changed, so too did the depiction of doctors in British fiction. Sparks has pointed out that doctors in British novels tend to be portrayed much more positively after 1850, and even when they appeared as Gothic villains, it was in a new and grander style (p. 16). The Gothic doctors of the 1830s and 1840s are mere butchers, mutilating the poor in order to perfect the skills they need to profitably treat the rich, but by the 1880s medical villains like Dr Jekyll, Dr Raymond, and Dr Moreau had come to function more like dark magicians, capable of working miracles and creating monsters. The earlier texts express popular fears that doctors might know *too little*, their supposed 'cures' merely a mask for murderous greed and crude self-interest. By contrast, the later novels articulate elite fears that doctors might know *too much*, their medical science having advanced so far that it is able to reach into the darkest recesses of the brain and body to conjure up demons like Arthur Machen's Helen Vaughan or Robert Louis Stevenson's Mr Hyde.

However, while they lack the dark glamour of their *fin de siècle* equivalents, the Gothic doctors who appear in the penny bloods bear witness to the very real (and frequently justified) anxieties that their working-class readers felt regarding the medical profession. We know from writers such as Edwin Chadwick and Thomas

Southwood Smith how the great Victorian campaigns for public health appeared from above, and how they were understood by elite experts who viewed cholera and political radicalism as almost interchangeable symptoms of urban squalor (Poovey, p. 59; Sparks, p. 37). It is harder to know how these same measures were understood from below, among the impoverished populations whose tenements were scrutinised with such suspicion by Chadwick's new Boards of Health. Such people wrote little, or at any rate little that has survived: but they *did* read, and it is thus highly significant that the penny blood fiction that most appealed to them was littered with medical malefactors. Such works reflected popular attitudes towards a medical profession that must often have appeared to the poor as little more than an instrument of state terror, empowered to quarantine, confiscate, dissect and institutionalise at will: and in their distrust of official pronouncements and emphasis on homemade remedies, they provide a glimpse of those cultures of medical self-help and popular resistance through which the working classes endured the recurrent epidemics of the early nineteenth century, during which orthodox doctors often seem to have been regarded more as foes than friends.

Notes

1. Michael Durey, *The Return of the Plague: British Society and the Cholera 1831–2* (Dublin: Gill and Macmillan, 1979), p. 177.
2. Also see R. J. Morris, *Cholera 1832: The Social Response to an Epidemic* (London: Croom Helm, 1976), p. 101.
3. Also see Gavin Budge, *Romanticism, Medicine, and the Natural Supernatural: Transcendent Vision and Bodily Spectres, 1789–1852* (Basingstoke: Palgrave Macmillan, 2012), p. 123.
4. Also see Elizabeth Hurren, *Dying for Victorian Medicine: English Anatomy and its Trade in the Dead Poor, c. 1834–1929* (Basingstoke: Palgrave Macmillan, 2011), pp. 6, 97.
5. Louis James, *Fiction for the Working Man, 1830–1850* (London: Oxford University Press, 1963), pp. 165–7; Anna Gasperini, *Nineteenth Century Popular Fiction, Medicine, and Anatomy: The Victorian Penny Blood and the 1832 Anatomy Act* (Cham: Springer International, 2019), passim.

[6] Tabitha Sparks, *The Doctor in the Victorian Novel: Family Practices* (Farnham: Ashgate, 2009), p. 13.
[7] Also see Michael Brown, *Performing Medicine: Medical Culture and Identity in Provincial England, c. 1760–1850* (Manchester: Manchester University Press, 2014), pp. 163–4.
[8] Also see Dorothy Porter and Roy Porter, *In Sickness and in Health: The British Experience 1650–1850* (London: Fourth Estate, 1988), p. 148.
[9] Charles Dickens, *The Pickwick Papers* (London: Amalgamated Press, 1905), p. 643.
[10] Gregory Vargo, *An Underground History of Early Victorian Fiction: Chartism, Radical Print Culture, and the Social Problem Novel* (Cambridge: Cambridge University Press, 2018), pp. 11, 68.
[11] J. F. C. Harrison, 'Early Victorian Radicals and the Medical Fringe', in W. F. Bynum and Roy Porter (eds), *Medical Fringe and Medical Orthodoxy 1750–1850* (London: Croom Helm, 1987), pp. 198–9; P. S. Brown, 'Social Context and Medical Theory in the Demarcation of Nineteenth-Century Boundaries', in Bynum and Porter, *Medical Fringe*, pp. 217–21.
[12] Also see Harrison, 'Early Victorian Radicals', pp. 200–2; Ursula Miley and John Pickstone, 'Medical Botany around 1850: American Medicine in Industrial Britain', in Roger Cooter (ed.), *Studies in the History of Alternative Medicine* (Basingstoke: Macmillan, 1988), pp. 145–6.
[13] Logie Barrow, 'An Imponderable Liberator: J. J. Garth Wilkinson', in Roger Cooter (ed.), *Studies in the History of Alternative Medicine* (Basingstoke: Macmillan, 1988), p. 89.
[14] Edward Bulwer-Lytton, *Lucretia: or, the Children of the Night*, 2 vols (Leipzig: Bernhard Tauchnitz, 1846), II, pp. 13–14.
[15] Robert Mack, *The Wonderful and Surprising History of Sweeney Todd: The Life and Times of an Urban Legend* (London: Continuum, 2007), pp. 42, 87; Gasperini, *Nineteenth Century Popular Fiction*, pp. 51, 131.
[16] Eileen Yeo, 'Culture and Constraint in Working-Class Movements, 1830–55', in E. and S. Yeo (eds), *Popular Culture and Class Conflict 1590–1914* (Brighton: Harvester Press, 1981), pp. 154–86 (p. 160).
[17] James Malcolm Rymer, *Manuscripts from the Diary of a Physician*, 2 vols (London: E. Lloyd, 1844, 1847), I, pp. 32–8.
[18] G. W. M. Reynolds, *The Mysteries of London*, 4 vols (London: George Vickers, 1846–8), I p. 125.
[19] Pamela Gilbert, *Mapping the Victorian Social Body* (Albany: State University of New York Press, 2004), pp. xix, 142–6.

[20] Also see Margaret Pelling, *Cholera, Fever and English Medicine 1825–1865* (Oxford: Oxford University Press, 1978), pp. 58–9; Mary Poovey, *Making a Social Body: British Cultural Formation, 1830–1864* (Chicago: University of Chicago Press, 1995), p. 41.
[21] Rosalind Crone, *Violent Victorians: Popular Entertainment in Nineteenth-Century London* (Manchester: Manchester University Press, 2012), p. 190.
[22] Harriet Martineau, *Deerbrook* (London: Smith, Elder, and Co., 1817 [1839]), pp. 300, 307, 319.
[23] W. H. Ainsworth, *Old St. Paul's* (London: Collins Clear-Type Press, n. d.), p. 11.
[24] Edward Lloyd, *Penny Sunday Times and People's Police Gazette*, 49/4 (1841–3). It is probably not coincidental that St Giles was the London district hit hardest by the cholera epidemic of 1831–2.
[25] Anonymous, *Mysteries of Old St. Paul's: A Tale of the Plague* (London: George Vickers, 1841), pp. 32–3, 37–8.
[26] Rip Rap, *The Monument; or, the Great Fire of London* (London: Samuel Haddon, 1841), pp. 34–5.

7

'Mistress of the Broomstick': Biology, Ecosemiotics and Monstrous Women in Wizard's The Wild Witch of the Heath; or The Demon of the Glen

NICOLE C. DITTMER

'When a woman thinks alone, she is evil!'[1]

Upon the introduction to penny bloods, awfuls and dreadfuls, one could initially perceive them as 'pernicious' low forms of cheap, quasi-plagiarised stories amalgamative of canonical novels, periodicals and popular tales.[2] However, these neglected literary admixtures, while sometimes crude in form and language, intelligently navigate through, and expose deeper societal issues. They create intricate conversations between such discursive material as medical treatises and behavioural guides resulting in terrifying tales of the Gothic. Stemming from an early modern concern with corrupt female morals, as the above quote suggests, and their vulnerability to 'animal' influences and ungodliness, the Victorian penny, *The Wild Witch* utilises both literary and cultural attributes of sixteenth-century Scotland to illustrate the correlation of nature and women as 'wild and uncontrollable' in the ecosemiotic figuration of the Wild Witch.[3]

The Wild Witch of the Heath; or the Demon of the Glen: A Tale of the Most Powerful Interest (1841), a rather obscure penny blood published in 1841 under the pseudonym Wizard, is a residual vestige of the first wave of eighteenth-century Gothic literature. Demonstrating characteristics of foreboding environments, monstrous women and dark villains, integrated with constructed gender ideologies and folklore, this narrative explores early Victorian perspectives of dangerous femininity with depictions of witchcraft and the reactive environs. This chapter, then, will dissect the transgressive figuration of the witch through an ecoGothic and contemporaneous biological lens to demonstrate the concerns of gynophobia as they transition from the sixteenth to the nineteenth century. As an embodied representation of women's instinctual nature, the witch in Wizard's penny blood joins the conversation of female instability in the early Victorian period. Whereas Wizard presents the witch as a monstrous female figure, this penny is not a continuation of the Scottish sixteenth- and seventeenth-century witchcraft accusations, but a literary exhibition that juxtaposes anxieties of the woman–nature relationship and a forced female instalment into the role of nervous hysteric during the nineteenth century.[4]

Penny Bloods: Gothic Conversations of Monstrous Women

As Jarlath Killeen argues in 'Victorian Gothic Pulp Fiction' (2012), such serialisations as penny publications, or what he refers to as 'Victorian pulp', and their images of bodily violence are reflective of a shift of 'cultural hatred'.[5] In decades past, exhibitions of physical brutality were focused on the annihilation of political adversaries. However, it is during the nineteenth century that these violent images were diffused and unbiased towards inclusion (Killeen, pp. 43–4). No longer used as literary examples of punishment against enemies of the state, depictions of somatic violence and terror were reconfigured in the pages of penny serialisations to demonstrate that all individuals were capable of transgressions, or in the case of this chapter, women. This cultural shift of violence and hatred in Wizard's penny blood manifested from the intersection of scientific progression and the persistent suspicion of female biology. While the emerging nineteenth-century medical sciences deliberated over experimental theories of female neurology and reflex theory as the genesis for hysteria, authors and publishers of penny serialisations juxtaposed these discourses with the 'plunder[ed]' and 'plagiariz[ed] Gothic tales and popular novels' to fabricate an imaginative image of female monstrosity synonymous with the cultural shift.[6] Intertwining overt themes of violence, Gothic tropes, and relatively contemporaneous and lesser-known accusations of female instability, penny bloods and dreadfuls utilised this shift as a source of entertainment to 'attract and fulfil readers' and encourage sales, while functioning as harbingers for early Victorian society against women's supposed oppugnant 'nature'.[7]

Historically, nature and women were regarded as a monistic entity with a divergent double-sided ontology. Drawing a direct influential relationship from their reproductive systems, women were perceived by society as fragile beings, synonymous with nature and categorised as either saintly virgins or corruptive witches.[8] This timeless belief of conflicting 'womanhood' originated from the superstition that women were 'otherworldly' individuals who were able to produce living beings from their own bodies, a feat, Selma R. Williams asserts, that 'no man, not even a king, could do'.[9] It has been argued, most notably in the past several decades, that nature and women, due to this reproductivity, have been unequivocally intertwined.[10] Ecofeminist Carolyn Merchant, as an example, argues this is a negative affiliation that places women 'closer to nature', a persistent belief that encourages men to subjugate women in the 'social hierarchy' (p. 13). As nature itself is depicted in images suggestive of the fertile and nurturing earth mother, it is also imagined as chaotic and destructive. This identification of nature, most notably that of the earth, is traditionally imagined as the fertile mother responsible for the care and sustainability of 'her' inhabitants; a depiction that suggests order and stability for 'mankind'. However, nature is also imagined as a force of chaos, contradictions and instability that brings destruction, storms and violence against 'mankind'. This closeness to nature, as Merchant identifies, creates a belief that society should subdue women's assumed chaos and keep them 'in their place' (*Death*, p. 132). Therefore in the nineteenth century, gender ideologies and categorical roles 'according to the individual's reproductive organs' were constructed and regulated through popular rhetoric and literature.[11] Although this relationship that dichotomises women-nature and men-culture extends throughout the centuries, the Victorian period further emphasised the correlation of women-nature through progressive medical treatises, scientific research and penny serialisations.

Victorian Medical Sciences and Female Biology

Early Victorian medical sciences claimed progression in psycho-somatic studies of women. However, these discourses still tied reproductive biology to instincts and the unpredictability of nature. In this period, as Gail Turley Houston suggests, women were most impacted 'by the changing nature of medical practice', and therefore were subjected to the 'progressive' experiments that invaded the female mind-body.[12] Women were reductionistically figured, by the Victorian medical industry, according to their reproductive biology and environmental influences.[13] Categorically identified as sources of potential monstrosity, women in the early-Victorian medical literature were discursively anchored to their inherent nature as reflected in such texts as Thomas Laycock's *A Treatise on the Nervous Diseases of Women* (1840), inspired by Jean-Baptiste Lamarck's (1809) pre-Darwinian theories of evolution. Assumed figures of material instability, they were labelled as inferior and impaired by their fluctuating passions and metamorphic biology. Prior to Charles Darwin's tumultuous publication, *The Origin of Species* (1859), which argues for the emergence of the human from the animal, an early proponent of evolutionary progression, Lamarck correlates these biological transitions to environmental surroundings.[14] Whereas Darwin's theory became popular and prolific in the mid-period and well into the *fin de siècle*, Lamarck's preceding declaration encouraged and inspired early Victorian medical sciences to alter and enforce psycho-physiological approaches for the treatment of women. Namely, he offers a postulation which suggests that 'structures were adapted to their functions', therefore arguing that either the structure, with the involvement of special design, is responsible for creating function, *or* the function itself creates the structure.[15] The latter argument is the basis for the theory of 'inheritance of acquired characteristics', an epigenetic concept that aligns the function as the external influences and the structure as the living species (Lamarck, p. xlviii). When exposed to the instability of the environment, the body (and ultimately the mind) are modified by what Lamarck refers to as the 'nervous fluid' (p. lxix). Defined as a physiological impulse, this 'electric fluid' becomes metamorphosed, or what Lamarck calls 'animalised', when the nerves are affected in 'the bodies of the higher animals' (p. lxix). It is this particular fluid that is assumed to succumb to environmental affectation and inform biological modifications, which experts later attribute to psychological and behavioural transgressions.

It was believed that these 'physical and biological factors', informed by external sources, 'caused insanity' (Turley Houston, p. 271).[16] In the translation of *Philosophie zoologique, ou des considérations relatives à l'histoire naturelle des animaux* (1809), H. R. Elliott highlights Lamarck's proposal that if the 'environment remain[s] unaltered', the inhabitants residing therein have a high probability of remaining unaltered (p. xxx). These assumptions influenced the approaches by nineteenth-century medical experts, leading to the conclusion that the restriction of female activities would distance women from nature and align them with the expectations of culture and society.[17] The popular belief was that if women remained uncontrolled and exposed to their own nature, it would eventually lead to a degenerative state. Further creating a categorical chasm of antithetical ontologies for women, Victorian sciences encouraged the dichotomies of saint/angel/witch/whore by emphasising the vulnerabilities of women. For example, the prominent early medical expert Laycock reintroduced women's reproductivity as the impuissant source for behavioural instability and irrationality. The 'nervous fluid', previously introduced by Lamarck, was later incorporated into theories of reflex and hysteria by Laycock, who establishes that this excitability, or 'heat … peculiar to the females of the higher classes of animals', is drawn from their reproductive capabilities (pp. 71–2). Although the uterus was previously blamed for degenerative 'monomaniacal cunning', Laycock shifts the blame to the 'analogous structure', the ovaries, as the affective source connecting women's excitability to that of animals and nature (p. 72). His research, informed by Lamarck, incorporates studies of animal sexuality to determine the responsible factors for reflex theory and hysteria in human women. Formulating an argument that in both animals of the 'higher species' and women, Laycock asserts that 'there are certain physiological phenomena intimately connected with the reproduction of the species' (p. 71). The female reproductive system was then determined as the root cause for 'sexual desire, combativeness, and love of offspring', therefore giving rise to more severe behavioural reactions as 'cunning ferocity' and 'wakefulness' (p. 71). This 'generative nisus' of artful practices, Laycock contends, was inherently provided to women 'in place of those weapons of offence and defence' that 'men of the same species were typically granted' (p. 72). This belief of female deception and 'exalted perceptive faculties' determined by their ingrained nature, presented throughout history a gynophobic trepidation utilised to sanction female roles and behavioural regulation (p. 72).[18] Therefore early Victorian literature promoted reductive medical sciences that centred on the biologically informed behaviours of women and their relationship with non-human nature.[19]

An Early Modern Tale of Gynophobia and Ecosemiotics

Although the hysterical woman and the assumed connection to her biological nature became part of the popular rhetoric in the Victorian medical industry, Wizard exhibits the inherent connection between the hysteric and the supernatural monster in his ecosemiotic figuration of the witch. Eco-semiotics, then, is defined by Winifred Nöth as 'the study of sign processes which relate organisms to their natural environment'.[20] Therefore, by examining the anachronistic placement of the witch in Victorian popular penny fiction, it allows for an interpretation of the meaning of the female figuration in conjunction with the ecoGothic environment. As literature reflective of social and cultural anxieties, this ephemeral penny blood draws on these pervasive concerns to construct semiotic figurations of monstrously transgressive women in the ecoGothic mode. In their introduction of *EcoGothic* (2013), Andrew Smith and William Hughes assert that this approach examines how the Gothic form as a symbol of fear, 'sexual, injured, dismembered and celebrated', can be exhibited and 'positively remembered in a literary landscape'.[21] Likewise, David Del Principe asserts that the ecoGothic 'examines the construction of the Gothic body' from an inclusive perspective that asks how the figure can provide deeper understanding 'as a site of articulation for environmental and species identity'.[22] As a figuration of 'fearful' female nature exhibited as a traditional she-monster, Wizard's witch is that point of 'articulation' where dangerous women's assumed identity is founded within this dystopian, or volatile, 'literary landscape'. Interactive with an environment of desolation and volatility, the Wild Witch responds to, what Del Principe refers to as humans' refusal to face their 'nonhuman' origins and biological ancestry (p. 2). She functions, then, as a Gothic figuration composed of contemporaneous social anxieties and desires, and embodies what Allan Lloyd Smith argues is a return of the 'repressed and denied', a reminder of the past with the potential to corrupt the present social structure.[23] This 'return' of communal phobias is prevalent in Wizard's witch as the once 'buried secret', who re-emerges again in the Victorian period to act as a harbinger of female monstrosity (Smith, p. 1). Examining these two perspectives utilising this ecoGothic approach, this chapter juxtaposes the early Victorian fears of women's nature and the environment within the penny blood's figuration of the witch.

Witches, as archetypal symbolic figures of non-human nature and female corruption, were utilised as literary figurations in penny bloods to demonstrate the 'unholy merging of woman, flora, and fauna'.[24] Fred Botting, in his elucidation of the Gothic genre and mode, contends that transgressions, both of the 'social and aesthetic limits', highlight their significance and necessity, and work to redefine their boundaries.[25] According to Botting, Gothic literature, and for the sake of this chapter, penny publications, assume these attributes to emphasise the threat of 'social and moral transgression' (p. 4). These transgressions are utilised to exhibit the effect of neglected social rules and behavioural regulations. As an embodiment of transgressions, such as the rejection of boundaries, societal expectations and historical perceptions, the figuration of the witch, then, is evaluated in this chapter under the stipulation of nineteenth-century sciences, hysteria and the fear of female instability.

Concerns of female witchcraft seemed to have waned during the Age of Enlightenment; however, these fears were transformed from a supernatural element to a medically informed affliction.

Prior to the nineteenth century, women's so-called fragile nature and spirituality were determined as vulnerable to external sources, such as the devil (Parker, p. 184).[26] However, with the medical movements of the Victorian period, women, in light of such influential discourses of Darwin, Lamarck and Laycock, were connected with their biology and animal instincts. This 'new ideology', as Marianne Hester suggests, changed the perception of women from the 'powerful and threatening witch' to that of the controllable 'hysterical woman', thereby realigning female gender restrictions from a spiritual-religious designation to that of a scientific subordination.[27] As embodiments of excess and transgression, the witch and hysterical woman were conflated as a monistic figuration to function as a nineteenth-century cautionary tale.

Following the transition of societal values and Victorian perspectives about dangerous women, penny bloods, most notably Wizard's *The Wild Witch*, adopted this transitory trend into its pages of Gothic.[28] Indeed, as Kristine Moruzi and Michelle J. Smith point out in the Introduction to *Young Adult Gothic Fiction* (2021), '[t]he Gothic is constantly being reinvented in ways that address the current historical moments.'[29] As proponents of Gothic literature, some penny tales, as Anna Gasperini identifies in *Nineteenth Century Popular Fiction, Medicine, and Anatomy: The Victorian Penny Blood and the 1832 Anatomy Act* (2019), incorporated the contemporaneous politics of the body and the medically informed sentiments of the period, to illustrate the 'violation' of the individual – in this case the Victorian woman – and create terrifying tales founded on social discourses.[30] The exhibition of witches used in *The Wild Witch* function with the traditional expectations of being 'synonymous' with their settings and, as Elizabeth Parker points out in *EcoGothic and the Forest* (2021), act as 'conduits' for the expression and exploration of society's gynophobia and 'environmental anxieties' (p. 184). Utilising the façade of the witch as the figure of anti-hierarchy, chaos and destruction, Wizard juxtaposes this archetype with the early Victorian theories of hysterical women. While the terminology of the presumed she-monster has changed to reflect contemporaneous scientific rhetoric, the foundation of the woman–nature connection has not. This is owing to the emergence of the mind–body–nature connection prolific in the growing medical industry infusing Victorian discourses with a bio-semiotic influence of female degeneration and corruption. As Royce Mahawatte suggests, '[i]f medical epistemologies revived horror in the nineteenth century', it is clearly the penny bloods, or what he calls 'the cheap literature of the 1840s', that made this mind–body politic horror 'virulent' (p. 94). This specific penny publication, then, brings attention to the key conflicts of the early Victorian period and acts as an intersection of progressive medical sciences, gynophobia and ecophobia through bio- and ecosemiotic figurations of a literary female monstrosity.

Setting up a narrative that echoes supernatural depictions of early modern witchcraft, while writing during a time of the scientific 'progress' for female psychosomatic practices, Wizard takes an ominous approach to the woman–nature connection. In the fifteenth-century text, the *Malleus Maleficarum* (1486), also known as the 'Hammer of Witches', Heinrich Kramer and James Sprenger assert that 'all witchcraft comes from carnal lust, which is in woman insatiable', thereby linking female sexuality (natural instincts) and destructive monstrosity (p. 47). Several hundreds of years later, while the Victorians no longer participated in the traditional witch-hunts, they maintained this link between female sexuality, social corruption and inherent dangers. Although the meanings of witchcraft, or witch trope, change, as Elizabeth Reis argues, so does the interpretation of women's roles in society (p. xiii). Similar to the nineteenth-century categorisation of the female hysteric, labels of 'witch' and 'witchcraft' helped to strategically force women into constructed roles that allowed the policing of 'female normativity and acceptability' (p. xii). Seemingly, the definition of witch changed from the early modern period to the Victorian era, as Reis asserts; however, 'the fear of women's power has not' (p. xii). For example, when the reader is introduced to the eponymous witch figure in *The Wild Witch*, Wizard expertly invokes the Scottish sentiment and cultural beliefs of the sixteenth century while hinting at the implications of women during the Victorian period:

> At the time of our narrative, when the people of Scotland yielded to the belief of every idle and superstitious tale of the times, the mountains were inhabited by a wild and mysterious being, whose

supernatural power (real or imaginary) was universally believed and feared by all.[31]

Referred to as a 'being' or later on, as an 'it', the witch is regarded as an evil spirit, or 'prognosticator' of 'severe calamity' (p. 17). Attributing events such as hysteria, combativeness, indulgence and sexual aggression to the antiquated beliefs derivative of historical gendered perspectives, new medical studies focused on these physiological-psychological consequences drawn from an inherent biological source, connecting women to non-human nature. Women, as reduced to their reproductive functionalities and biological metamorphoses were characterised as unstable, volatile and vulnerable to external and internal influences.[32] Labelled as 'wild and uncontrollable', women and nature were regarded as inferior, and thereby much nineteenth-century literature tended to utilise this conflictual ontological rhetoric to both perpetuate the dangers of female instability and create terrifying stories for entertainment (Merchant, p. 11).[33]

As traditional with penny literature, *The Wild Witch of the Heath* is an amalgamation of different textual forms. Wizard combines sixteenth-century plays, Gothic tropes and progressive medical and scientific discourses of the Victorian period to create a tale of horror that echoes the centuries-old perpetuation of the woman-nature-monster stereotype. While not directly borrowing from these sources, Wizard intertwines such sentiments of Lamarck and Laycock in his figuration of the witch. For example, Laycock ascertains that the 'vernal and autumnal' or 'equinoctial' shifts illustrate the 'natural history' of the hysteric, and the 'state of the atmosphere in which thunder-storms prevail' has a significant impact on the nervous woman (pp. 149, 199). Taking this nature-influencing-hysteric into consideration, the witch in *The Wild Witch* can be read as an inversion of this relationship in which the female figure informs the environment. Witches, then, were employed in this particular penny as a Gothic-semiotic response to the 'progressive' medical interment of women as uncontrollable hysterics. Drawing on former fears of the spiritual susceptibility and the danger of female 'nature', this blood utilises the fiendish character to illustrate the transgressive behaviours of supposedly monstrous women. A text that prompts instant recollection to those familiar with William Shakespeare's plays, *The Tempest* (1623) and *Macbeth* (1606), this penny blood draws together elements of the chaos of non-human nature and monstrous women with supernatural characteristics of the Gothic novel.

Wizard begins the tale, and unveils the overall plot, with Viscount Dunbardon's overwhelming desire to impart revenge on his nemesis while plotting to kidnap and marry the angelic Isabella. To achieve this task, Dunbardon, both protagonist and villain, travels through the Scottish wilderness to visit a 'wild' group of 'uncouth female figures' and 'withered hell-cats', a collection of prophetic 'hags' who gesticulate and dance 'around a huge blazing fire' upon the heath (p. 5). While not speaking in rhyming couplets, these Macbethian witches instruct Dunbardon on his fate while simultaneously summoning a demon, a wild witch, and manifesting environmental responses of 'loud and terrible peals of thunder [that] shook the earth from its foundation'; an atmospheric response so terrifying that 'the forked and vivid lightning angrily darted in long and repeated flashes from the blackened clouds' (p. 5). Although Wizard begins this story with the introduction of this supernatural collective, not one of these three sisters is the eponymous 'Wild Witch of the Heath' but the sources responsible for calling her into existence. Drawn directly from the earth, ensconced within a 'bright blue, sulphurous flame', the 'strange being' known as the Wild Witch appeared as if ceremoniously birthed from nature (p. 18). This added exhibition of feral and chaotic women producing a monstrously wild and powerful witch alludes to the Victorian concern about corruptive heredity and destruction of lineage. Therefore, in this opening sequence, Wizard draws attention to the purpose of this novel: that women, once out of societal confines, are seamlessly intertwined with 'nature' and responsible for destruction and harm against civilisation. In doing so, this scene purposefully creates a relationship between the environment and the women involved, thereby constructing an ecosemiotic figuration in the Wild Witch that functions as a point of rhetoric about the ongoing discussion of female instability.

These interactions between species and nature become what Timo Maran refers to as 'a matrix of qualitative meaning connections' that are informed by the biological needs of its inhabitants.[34] 'In an external view', as established by Maran, the environment is a 'composition' of resources that benefit and 'interface' with its inhabitants (p. 8). The environment, then, metamorphoses based on the necessities of the relative species. Nature, then, according to ecosemiotics, mirrors the impingement of influences on the species's 'early individual development' (Maran, p. 9). In short, as the 'biological structures' of the figure changes, the surrounding environment, 'interpretations' of, and 'active behaviors' towards it also shift to accommodate the individual (Maran, p. 9). Thereby, Wizard's witch is a representation of the contemporaneous social concerns of the assumed unstable female biology who informs the surrounding environs, causing an ecoGothic exhibition.

The Witch and the Wildness of Nature

The shared dynamic of the ecosemiotic environment-inhabitant and the ecoGothic are juxtaposed in the cyclically informed relationship of the witch and the evocation of the wildness of her environs. In a prior publication about the relationship between gynophobia and monstrous women, I argue that 'the natural environment is not considered a neutral sphere but a mirrored representation of the wild, unpredictable behavior of women' (Dittmer, p. 197). Aligning with the ecosemiotic loop of affectation informed by female biology, nature, as the 'feminine domain of power', is perceived as 'wild and bestial without definitive borders or ideologies' (Dittmer, p. 197). With the 'sudden appearance' of the 'WILD WITCH OF THE HEATH', Wizard presents this 'wild and terrific' animalistic image that would 'strike terror into the boldest heart'; a sensation also suggested by the capitalisation of her name when addressed (p. 26). In the many interactions with the witch, the environment intervenes to provide the reader with an explicit interrelation between monstrous women and nature. For example, in this introduction, the protagonist confronts the witch while she stands 'on the brow of the mountain', instantly exhibiting a sense of power and superiority (p. 26). Wizard, then proceeds to emphasise her wildness by claiming:

> In her right hand she clutched a huge black snake, which emitted volumes of fire from its mouth: and in her left ... she held a long, black wand of ebony, around which was coiled another snake of much smaller dimensions than that which she grasped in her other hand. (p. 26)

Drawing attention to the fire-breathing serpents in the witch's grasp, Wizard is quick to invoke images of Eve and her corruption of 'mankind' in Christian theology. However, unlike the patriarchal environment from which Eve is forcibly removed, the witch's surroundings suggest a female-dominated habitat:

> huge toads, with bloated bodies, and eyes like two blazing coals protruding from their heads ... strange and uncouth shape[s], with forms of unnatural dimensions, now sat gibing and gibbering ... from every dark recess. Large black cats, of a size equal to a mastiff, purred ... with their bristled backs, causing the same acute pain as if each hair had been a packing-needle. Faces detached from bodies, and headless forms ... phantoms, each more hideous than the other, appeared. (p. 147)

This depiction of the witch's environs is not only a perversion of the Christian garden of life, but a distinct Victorian admonition of the capability of female corruption. Inhabiting an antithetical setting to the fertile Garden of Eden, the Witch, also referred to as 'Spirit of the Mountains', utilises her surroundings as a source of power and influence (p. 26). Indeed, when addressed by the bandito, Pietro D'Arste, using society's presumptive, and derogatory, moniker, the Witch exhibits her ecosemiotic connection with her domain:

> Scarcely had he given utterance to the latter sentence, when the moon, the moon which was before bright in the heavens, suddenly changed to a blood-like hue, and all was buried in impenetrable darkness, save when the lightning momentarily illuminated the scene. (p. 26)[35]

The 'bright in the heavens' to the bloody moon transformation, the instant darkness, and the elemental atmospheric disruption reflect the popular belief that the witch is a sympathetic figure to her natural surroundings.[36] Wizard's reference to the transgressive moon, while executed to create a Gothic impression, once again draws from Laycock's treatise about the afflicted female and the environment. The moon, as Laycock argues, is an influential source on the 'vital organisms' (p. 148). Likening his theory to the 'findings' of Pythagoras, Laycock perpetuates the belief that the lunar cycle informs the menstrual, or biological, cycle, and therefore is a direct source of affectation for potential female instability (p. 146). At each new moon cycle, Laycock asserts, there are points of lunar influence that inspire the strength of the hysteric's reaction. He claims that the 'equinoxes' and 'solstices' of the 'solar influence' are also considered as influences on the hebdomadal period (p. 146).[37] This reactive affectation of the witch-nature scenario demonstrates how the 'landscape', as Parker asserts, is 'commonly read as a binary space' (p. 1). Similar to the female dichotomies of Victorian 'angel' and 'whore', nature is also categorised under the good/bad parallel of 'wonder and enchantment' or 'dangerous and terrifying' (Parker, p. 1). The witch–environment reaction to the informal acknowledgement brings attention to the assumed instability of women's behaviour while also drawing attention to the woman–nature relationship.

Throughout history, the witch, in particular, has a known relationship to non-human nature. As Merchant clarifies, the witch is the embodiment and a 'classical symbol of the wilderness and violence of nature' (p. 127). A figure bound to nature's environs and simultaneously controlled by the biologics of feminine 'nature', the witch, then, maintains the ability to manipulate the environment while succumbing to her own instincts. Parker notes that 'women and nature are portrayed as in dark sympathy with one another', a relationship that is clearly exhibited in this text (p. 114). This sympathetic relationship is demonstrated in the witch's actions and the resounding reaction of the environment. Vociferating a cry of 'Behold!', the witch waves her 'wand' and her 'command was seconded by a loud and long peal of thunder' (p. 27). With this simple directive, Wizard clearly exhibits the long-assumed cause-and-effect interrelationship of women–nature. However, the continued response of a 'tremendous crash' and 'loud deafening sounds' emitting 'from a whole forest of wild animals', reveals the anxiety about this particular partnership (p. 27). The witch, with her ability to invoke violent and 'wild' environmental responses, functions as a semiotic figuration that speaks to the Victorian concerns about hysterical women's biological instability and behaviours. As a historic figure of terror, violence, and corruption of values, the witch and her embodiment of biological degeneration and animism is used to demonstrate society's need for women–nature domination.

Expanding upon what Louis James refers to as one significant 'element of the Gothic story', the *Wild Witch* adopts the use of 'supernatural powers' to provide a 'heightened significance to the conflict between the evil villains and immaculately pure heroine' and environmental depictions of 'good' and 'evil'.[38] This dichotomy is clearly illustrated in the landscape of Wizard's penny dreadful through the gazes of the male characters Dunbardon and D'Arste, and the virginal love interest, Isabella:

> The evening was calm and serene. The beauty of the prospect, and the silence that required around, inspired their minds with rapture and devotion to that supreme Power, who formed the glorious scene. A few streaks of purple appeared to glow in the west; and at length the sunburst from behind a dark azure cloud in all his retiring splendour – his bright golden beams slanting in a glorious majesty upon the mountain tops. (p. 20)

When isolated from society and distanced from uncontrolled women, D'Arste, Dunbardon and the angelic Isabella pause to appreciate the sublimity of nature. Without the influence of the corruptive she-monster, the environment radiates with the 'splendour' of the 'supreme' God's blessings (p. 20). In contradistinction to these images of serenity in the absence of female instability, the male invasion of the witch's 'abode' recalls the potential ferocity of the woman–nature relationship:

> Dark and gloomy mountains everywhere met the eye, retiring in long perspective until their summits were obscured in the clouds ... Dark glens, deep and frightful chasms on every side met their view ... The howling blast descended on the valleys its mournful sighings [sic] along the rocks; the distant roar of torrents concealed

from the eye, and the humming of bees, threw a strain of melancholy over the spirits. (p. 122)

While the natural environment is on its 'best behaviour' and providing bliss to 'deserving' humanity, it is praised as a creation of the male Christian God; however, when 'unruly' or destructive, it is segregated from creationism and solely aligned with the chaos of women. These different perspectives of the sublime versus the desolate depictions of nature not only allude to the antiquated beliefs that men are orientated as cultivated and structured, while women, as beings from nature, are chaotic (Parker, p. 114). Clearly echoing the argument that '[w]omen, like the natural elements, are considered dangerous and lack reason', Wizard highlights the dichotomous roles of both the socially controlled woman and the female who rejects these restrictions (Dittmer, p. 198). As a source of instability and irrationality, the unrestricted female, according to Victorian constructs, was monstrous and corruptive. It also highlights how witches 'with demonic aid', as Stuart Clark postulates, were believed to 'interfere with elements and climate'.[39] The traditional distinction of the witch as 'the symbol of the violence of nature' who 'raise[s] storms, cause[s] illness, destroy[s] crops, obstruct[s] generation, and kill[s] infants', is clearly demonstrated in Wizard's figuration as a perpetual warning to Victorian society to remind readers that, while the label of dangerous women has changed, the underlying concerns have not (Merchant, p. 132).

Gothic Harbingers of Social Concerns

In conclusion, the early Victorian period, while bidding a temporary farewell to the first wave of Gothic literature and entertaining the progressive medical hypotheses of transgressive female behaviours, gave birth to publications that exacerbated real-life issues into dreadful tales of terror. Just as Sally Powell posits in 'Black markets and cadaverous pies' (2004), and Rosalind Crone reiterates in *Violent Victorians* (2012) that James Malcolm Rymer's *The String of Pearls* (1846–7) is responsible for drawing attention to the social concerns about increased commercialism and industrialism through its cannibalistic atrocities and consumption of meat pies, Wizard's *The Wild Witch of the Heath* is profound in correlating the image of the hysterical woman with that of the ephemeral witch.[40] Drawing from the biological concerns that conjoin the 'reproductive functions' of women, modifications of behaviour due to environmental affectations and folkloric superstitions of witchcraft, the penny bloods, dreadfuls and awfuls, were not only sources of horrific entertainment, but harbingers of catastrophe. As Elaine Showalter once stated, the psychology of the nineteenth century was informed by Gothic literature, while Gothic literature was informed by medical discourses of the period, thus creating a perpetual feedback loop.[41] Preceding the later *fin de siècle* rhetoric and literature that circulates these notions of degeneration, penny publications entered during the newly formed progressive medical cycle of the 1840s. Popular sources of information and entertainment for the working class, pennys joined, and further informed, the conversation of the woman–nature connection.

As one of the earliest penny bloods to enter the popular rhetoric of the early Victorian period, Wizard's *The Wild Witch*, clearly juxtaposes concerns of female reproductivity, instability and corruption exhibited in the figuration of the Wild Witch and her surroundings. In the final chapter of his novel, Wizard resolves the conflict with the destruction of the protagonist/villain Dunbardon by the hand of the Wild Witch. He leaves the reader with the powerful image: '[o]n the shafts of lightning, on the wings of the wind, on the forked glare of the thunderbolt, may still be seen, as the harbinger and pilot of the storm, THE WILD WITCH OF THE HEATH' (p. 158). Once again, attention is drawn to the relationship of woman––nature. However, while concluding the novel with these final words, Wizard creates a sensation of terror and pending doom. Although readdressing the witch in all capitals to accentuate her power, he also provides an image of female interminability. Similar to the 'witches' of the sixteenth and seventeenth centuries, the concept, or representation, of the Wild Witch lives on. Formulating a bridge between the witches of centuries past and the female hysterics of the nineteenth century, *The Wild Witch of the Heath* is truly a harbinger of Victorian rhetoric.

Notes

1. Heinrich Kramer and James Sprenger, *The Malleus Maleficarum* (New York: Dover Publications, 1971), p. 43.
2. Patrick Dunae, 'New Grub Street for Boys', in Jeffrey Richards (ed.), *Imperialism and Juvenile Literature* (Manchester, 1989), pp. 12–33 (p. 16); B. G. Johns, 'The Literature of the Streets', *Edinburgh Review*, 164 (1887), 40–65 (43).
3. Carolyn Merchant, *The Death of Nature: Women, Ecology, and the Scientific Revolution* (New York: HarperCollins Publisher, 1980), p. 117.
4. J. Goodare, 'The Scottish Witchcraft Act', *Church History*, 74/1 (2005), 39–67. The time period and setting of Wizard's penny title is contingent with the Scottish Witchcraft Act of 1563. One of many Acts set forth to retaliate against the movement of witches in Europe, the Scottish Act, similar to those enacted by England, Wales and Ireland, set in motion that the practice of witchcraft, or the affiliation with individuals who practised, were listed as capital offences.
5. Jarlath Killeen, 'Victorian Gothic Pulp Fiction', in Andrew Smith and William Hughes (eds), *Victorian Gothic: An Edinburgh Companion* (Edinburgh: Edinburgh University Press, 2012), pp. 43–65; quoted in 'Introduction' by Smith and Hughes, p. 8.
6. Michael Anglo, *Penny Dreadfuls and Other Victorian Horrors* (London: Jupiter Books, 1977), p. 11.
7. Rosalind Crone, *Violent Victorians: Popular Entertainment in Nineteenth-century London* (New York and Manchester: Manchester University Press, 2012), p. 163.
8. Refer to medical treatises: Thomas Laycock, *A Treatise on the Nervous Diseases of Women: Comprising an Inquiry into the Nature, Causes, and Treatment of Spinal and Hysterical Disorders* (London: Longman, Orme, Brown, Green and Longmans, 1840); Robert Brudenell Carter, *On the Pathology and Treatment of Hysteria* (London: John Churchill, 1853); Forbes Winslow, 'Woman in Her Psychological Relations', *Journal of Psychological Medicine and Mental Pathology*, 4/13 (January 1851); conduct books: Sarah Stickney Ellis, *The Women of England, Their Social Duties, and Domestic Habits* (New York: D. Appleton and Company, 1839), *The Daughters of England: Their Position in Society, Character, and Responsibilities* (New York: D. Appleton and Company, 1842), and *The Wives of England: Their Relative Duties, Domestic Influence, and Social Obligations* (New York: D. Appleton & Company, 1843), John Ruskin, 'Lecture II, Lilies: Of Queens' Gardens', in *Sesame and Lilies*, Harvard

Classics, 28 (London and New York, 1865); and poem: Coventry Patmore, *The Angel in the House* (London: John W. Parker and Son, 1858).

9. Selma R. Williams, *Riding the Nightmare: Women and Witchcraft from the Old World to Colonial Salem* (Ne w York: Perennial, 1992), p. 11.

10. Refer to Sherry B. Ortner, 'Is Female to Male as Nature is to Culture?', in M. Z. Rosaldo and L. Lamphere (eds), *Women, Culture, and Society* (Stanford: Stanford University Press, 1974), pp. 68–87; Anja Höing, 'A retreat on the "river bank": perpetuating patriarchal myths in animal stories', in Douglas A. Vakoch and Sam Mickey (eds), *Women and Nature? Beyond Dualism in Gender, Body, and Environment* (Abingdon and New York: Routledge, 2018), pp. 27–42; Stacy Alaimo, *Bodily Natures: Science, Environment, and the Material Self* (Bloomington: Indiana University Press, 2010). Ortner and Höing both discuss the woman–nature relationship as a negative stipulation that hinders female progression; Alaimo, on the other hand, argues that this embeddedness is not only a positive juxtaposition, but a source for potential power and success.

11. Nicole Dittmer, 'Malignancy of Goneril: Nature's Powerful Warrior', in Krishanu Maiti and Soumyadeep Chakraborty (eds), *Global Perspectives on Eco-Aesthetics and Eco-Ethics: A Green Critique* (New York and London: Lexington Books, 2020), pp. 195–202 (p. 196).

12. Gail Turley Houston, 'Insanity', in James Eli Adams, Tom Pendergast and Sara Pendergast (eds), *The Victorian Encyclopedia, vol. 2* (Danbury, CT: Grolier Academic, 2004), pp. 270–3 (p. 271).

13. See Laycock, *Nervous Disorders*, Winslow, 'Psychological Reactions', Carter, *On the Pathology and Treatment of Hysteria* and Isaac Baker Brown, *On the Curability of Certain Forms of Insanity, Epilepsy, Catalepsy, and Hysteria in Females* (London: Robert Hardwicke, 1866).

14. Charles Darwin's three-volume approach, *The Origin of Species* (1859), *The Descent of Man* (1871), and *The Expression of Emotions in Man and Animals* (1872), inspired the degeneration theory which later became a point of distress and a reason for medical and social control as well as contributing to the re-emergence of the Gothic and transgressive monstrosities during the *fin de siècle*.

15. Jean Baptiste Pierre Antoine de Monet de Lamarck, *Zoological Philosophy: An Exposition with Regard to the Natural History of Animals*, ed. H. R. Elliott (London: Macmillan and Co., 1809/1914/2012), p. xlviii.

16. This belief was prolific in Victorian society, and such scholars, as Vieda Skultans in *Madness and Morals: Ideas on Insanity in the Nineteenth Century* (1975) determines that factors such as excessive behaviours, sexual

17 repression, reproductivity and living in an industrial civilisation were viewed as causes for nervousness and hysteria.

17 In Winslow's 1853 dissertation about hysteria, behaviour and female fragility, he explores the concept of human generativity from non-human nature. Echoing the concerns of Lamarck and Laycock, Winslow stipulates that humans possess an internal 'microcosm' compiled of 'all the power, properties, and faculties of the lower animals'; therefore they have the potential, not only to progress, but also to 'retrograde' (p. 21).

18 For example, Winslow perpetuates Laycock's claims and gynophobia by later stating that women suffer 'from irregular action of the ovaria' and thereby their system 'degenerates' into an eventual 'artful' and 'monomaniacal cunning'. Winslow, 'Woman in Her Psychological Relations', p. 32.

19 In 1848, surgeon John Millingen furthers the claim that women are 'more under the control of matter' and that 'she is less under the influence of the brain than the uterine system', thereby vulnerable to a hysterical predisposition 'predominating from the dawn of puberty' (p. 160); see John Millingen, *The Passions; or Mind and Matter* (London: John and Daniel A. Darling, 1848). Similarly, the British psychologist Winslow correlated this hysterical disposition to personal desires (of spouse or offspring) that are 'common in every female animal', thereby continuing the discourse that hysteria emerges during the stages of reproductivity when 'love of one kind or the other is the ruling passion' which results in 'her whole nature' being 'imbued' with passionate 'love'. Winslow, 'Psychological Relations', p. 32.

20 Winifred Nöth, 'Ecosemiotics and the Semiotics of Nature', *Sign Systems Studies*, 29/1 (2001), 71–81 (71).

21 Andrew Smith and William Hughes, 'Introduction', in Andrew Smith and William Hughes (eds), *Ecogothic* (Manchester: Manchester University Press, 2013), p. 3.

22 David Del Principe, 'Introduction: The EcoGothic in the Long Nineteenth Century', *Gothic Studies*, 16/1 (May 2014), 1–8 (1).

23 Allan Lloyd Smith, *American Gothic Fiction: An Introduction* (New York and London: Continuum, 2004), p. 1.

24 Elizabeth Parker, *The Forest and the EcoGothic: The Deep Dark Woods in the Popular Imagination* (London: Palgrave Macmillan, 2020), p. 184.

25 Fred Botting, *Gothic* (New York and London: Routledge, 2012), p. 4.

26 See also Elizabeth Reis (ed.), 'Introduction', *Spellbound: Women and Witchcraft in America* (Lanham and Oxford: SR Books, 1998), p. xiii.

Both Parker and Reis discuss the relationship of the witch with the devil. It was believed that the witch made a pact with a demon or the devil itself in which her soul was renounced for power and an infusion of animism that rejected hierarchical confines of society.

27 Marianne Hester, *Lewd Women and Wicked Witches: A Study of the Dynamics of Male Domination* (Routledge, 2003), p. 145.

28 This common thread of dangerous women can be found in such pennys as James Malcolm Rymer's *The String of Pearls* (1846–7) with Mrs Lovett, the baker of humans; George W. M. Reynolds's *Wagner, the Wehr-Wolf* (1846–7) and its maliciously deceptive Nisida of Riverola; Malcolm J. Errym's (an anagram of James Malcom Rymer) *The Dark Woman, or Days of the Prince Regent* (1861) with the criminal figuration of the metamorphic Dark Woman; and Septimus R. Urban's (also a pseudonym for James Malcolm Rymer) *The Vendetta; or a Lesson in Life* (1863), later known as *The Wronged Wife, or the Heart of Hate* (1870), through the destructive Bertha Mason-esque figuration of Agatha Jefferies.

29 Kristine Moruzi and Michelle J. Smith, 'Introduction', in Kristine Moruzi and Michelle J. Smith (eds), *Young Adult Gothic Fiction: Monstrous Selves/Monstrous Others* (Cardiff: University of Wales Press, 2021), pp. 1–14 (p. 1).

30 Royce Mahawatte, 'Horror in the Nineteenth Century: Dreadful Sensations, 1820–80', in Xavier Aldana Reyes (ed.), *Horror: A Literary History* (London: The British Library, 2020), pp. 77–101 (p. 98). In Mahawatte's investigation of penny horrors he, similarly to Anna Gasperini's *Nineteenth Century Popular Fiction* and Joseph Crawford's chapter in this collection, 'A Tale of the Plague', explores how literal and figurative 'burking' and cannibalism were key sources for the creation of these sources of literary horror.

31 Wizard, *The Wild Witch of the Heath; or. The Demon of the Glen, A Tale of the most Powerful Interest* (London: T. White, 1841), p. 16.

32 This belief seemingly originated in the Aristotelian sexual theory that promoted the concept that women's mental, spiritual and physical frailty were vulnerable, thereby easily deceived, causing 'melancholic humors' that burdened their overall being. See Merchant, *Death of Nature* and Edward Clayton, 'Aristotle: *Politics*', *The Internet Encyclopedia of Philosophy*, ISSN 1260-a11. https://iep.utm.edu/aris-pol/ 27 July 2005.

33 For additional information on female 'monstrosity' and the rhetoric of female instability in popular novels, refer to Nicole C. Dittmer's

forthcoming monograph *Monstrous Women and the Victorian EcoGothic* (Lanham: Lexington, 2022).

34 Timo Maran, *Ecosemiotics: The Study of Signs in Changing Ecologies* (Cambridge and New York: Cambridge University Press, 2020), p. 8.

35 I use the term 'derogatory' when referring to the name 'Spirit of the Mountain' because in the serialisation, it is a nickname that encapsulates the social terrors of the witch. However, it also strips the female antagonist of her material being, thereby assisting in the degeneration of her agency.

36 Refer to Lisa Kröger and Melanie R. Anderson, *Monster She Wrote: The Women Who Pioneered Horror & Speculative Fiction* (Philadelphia: Quirk Books, 2019).

37 This he determines in studies of sexual cycles of birds and their 'moult' during the summer solstice. Working with the French physician Philippe Pinel, Laycock also hypothesises that 'paroxysms of insanity' frequently result from the stimulation of sexual instincts.

38 Louis James, *Fiction for the Working Man 1830–1850* (London: Oxford University Press, 1963), p. 77.

39 Stuart Clark, 'Inversion, Misrule and the Meaning of Witchcraft', *Past & Present*, 87 (1980), 98–127 (120).

40 Sally Powell, 'Black markets and cadaverous pies: the corpse, urban trader and industrial consumption in the penny blood', in A. Maunder and G. Moore (eds), *Victorian Crime, Madness and Sensation* (Aldershot: Ashgate, 2004), pp. 45–58 (p. 46); Crone, *Violent Victorians*.

41 Elaine Showalter, 'On Hysterical Narrative', *Narrative*, 1/1 (Winter 1993), 24–35 (31).

Section III
Mode, Genre, and Style; or, Gothic Storytelling and Ideologies

8

A Highwayman and a Ventriloquist Walk into an Inn ... Early Penny Romances and the Politics of Humour in Jack Rann *and* Valentine Vaux

CELINE FROHN

> It was frightful, but by the crushing blow of the cleaver, one of Gray's eyes had been forced from its socket – it hung by a bleeding filament – round – glassy and fixed.[1]

With a subject matter conventionally labelled as penny dreadfuls, or penny bloods, is it a surprise that many studies focus on the blood and violence that Victorian penny serials contain?[2] The quotation above demonstrates one of the instances of gore and terror to be found in penny fiction from the 1840s. While penny dreadfuls have increasingly become the subject of academic study, including in the present volume, many studies focus on violent content.[3] Occasionally this tendency leads to a disregard of non-violent content in penny fiction. Jarlath Killeen, for example, writes that penny dreadfuls are sensationalist fiction with plots that 'were merely vehicles to get the reader from one scene of gore, violence and torture to the next'.[4] I argue for a more holistic approach: to study the *humorous* content alongside the horrifying. Violence in penny fiction is often couched in humour – a mode which can negate or undermine the Gothic potential present in the texts. Additionally, the episodic nature of penny fiction, where the main character moves through seemingly unrelated and repetitive adventures, is better understood when integrating humour within its analysis. This chapter focuses on two early penny romances from 1839–40, allowing us to trace some of the generic origins of the penny dreadful: *Jack Rann, Alias Sixteen-string Jack* by James Lindridge (1840) and *Valentine Vaux* by Thomas Peckett Prest (1839–40), a plagiarism of Henry Cockton's serial *The Life and Adventures of Valentine Vox, the Ventriloquist*.[5] Both of these texts feature tropes that evoke Gothic resonances: in *Jack Rann*, the horrifying spectacle of public execution of the eponymous Jack; in *Valentine Vaux*, the reality-distorting ventriloquial capabilities of Valentine. Yet the way these tropes have been embedded in the wider narrative precludes feelings of terror, fear or disgust, or other emotional states ascribed to the Gothic.[6] This negation through humour points us towards what I argue characterises early penny dreadfuls: a playful attitude towards violence, where harm or discomfort is nullified by humour. *Jack Rann* and *Valentine Vaux* make for a useful comparison, as they are published around the same time period at the start of the penny publishing boom of the 1840s, and they share similarities in their construction as they both draw from the picaresque tradition of the eighteenth century, like Henry Fielding's *Jonathan Wild* (1743). The picaresque episodic format underpins the sequences of events in both *Jack Rann* and *Valentine Vaux*, where the reader follows the main characters in a string of largely causally unrelated adventures. According to Ulrich Wicks, 'the picaresque mode satisfies our impulse for a vicarious journey through chaos and depravity.'[7] Both texts engage with the mode in their own way: while *Jack Rann* follows the adventures of a highwayman as he robs many unsuspecting victims and typically escapes capture, Valentine Vaux seeks victims to prank through ventriloquism for his own amusement. While the traditional picaresque hero – the *picaro* – is defined by his position as outsider, both Jack and Valentine are part of a constant negotiation between belonging and exceptionalism. The episodic plot, and the humour that is reiterated repeatedly during it, provide a necessary touchstone to understanding the narrative form and the appeal of the penny dreadful, existing in conjunction with, and often undermining, the Gothic potential of the tropes present in the text.

Jack Rann is a reimagination of the life story of John Rann, an English highwayman active in the 1770s. He gained the nickname of 'Sixteen-String Jack' because of the number of colourful ribbons attached to his breeches.[8] On 19 October 1774, Rann was sentenced to death, and he was executed on 7 December in the same year. Like other highwaymen such as Dick Turpin and Jack Sheppard, Rann's short albeit eventful criminal career became the subject of much speculation and fabrication. After his death, two pamphlets were published containing different accounts of his life, and he became the subject of a play by William Leman Rede in 1823.[9] Lindridge's *Jack Rann* starts with the eponymous Jack as a peasant boy of sixteen years, selling food at the Bath market. After a conflict with a local poacher and reputed thief, Jack flees to London, where he eventually is taken in by a gang of thieves, who introduce him into a life of crime. Jack participates in a string of humorous robberies and spends his time drinking and exchanging farcical stories with his fellow gang members. The causal relationships between the series of robberies are tenuous at best, and events often repeat themselves. Jack is captured and stands trial three times, being released twice, while the third time leads to his execution. He is finally captured by soldiers led by Sir John Fielding. Jack is convicted of theft and spends his last days in Newgate as 'guest', rather than a prisoner, and entertains several of his friends until his solemn execution concludes the narrative. Before focusing on the public execution which terminates the text, it is important to contextualise it within the politics of the text – more specifically, the politics of humour.

Throughout Jack's picaresque adventures, farce plays an essential role. While Jack commits crimes, the text takes a playful attitude that interprets property crime as a joke. Jack's robberies are cast in a comic light through the usage of farcical tropes that minimise the perceived suffering of the victims of his robberies and threats. Jack's first robbery takes place at an inn, one of the many drinking spaces that populate the text. The transient and socially equalising nature of the inn, where travellers from different classes mingle and move on, lends social ambiguity to Jack.[10] As Jack and Clayton, a fellow robber, enter the inn, the landlord is introduced as a comic stereotype of a drunk: 'his round rubicund face ornamented with such a brilliant specimen of a "jolly nose," as would leave not a shadow of doubt in the beholders [*sic*] mind, that the tapster had a strong partiality for the liquors he dispensed' (p. 46). The landlord's propensity to drink his own wares make him a suitable victim for the ensuing prank. In the context of the farce, the 'victim "asks for" punishment by this stupidity', and as a result, is 'tortured shamelessly'.[11] Clayton and Jack terrify the landlord, accusing him of providing them with sub-par drinks. While the landlord is described as 'panic-stricken' and 'horror-struck', this emotional state is limited to the landlord, and the reader is not expected to mirror his horror. In fact, the scene exhibits a sense of playfulness. Clayton and Jack are merely acting; there was nothing wrong with their drinks, and the reader is in on the 'joke' that the landlord is in no real danger despite his fear. The scene escalates when Clayton demands to 'forbear corporeal punishment only upon one condition' (p. 48):

> Pouring half of the brandy and water from out of each vessel, [Clayton] deliberately filled them up with an equal admixture of Hollands and rum; then beckoning the landlord, he bade him, on the pain of instant flagellation, to drain them instantly to the dregs. (p. 48)

The landlord complies after Clayton gives him a 'smart lash with the whip', and falls down 'dead drunk', passing out because of the excess of alcohol (p. 48). The landlord's self-indulgence is what instigates his downfall, a humorous reversal that creates laughter. That this sequence is meant to be comic is explicit in the text: when the landlord collapses, 'a burst of laughter greeted the fall' (p. 49). For good measure, the joke is repeated several times over, including his wife calling him a 'drunken beast' and 'pummelled [him] soundly', and the ostler, in an idiosyncratic accent, exclaiming 'Hollo! What drunk agin!' (p. 49).

Although Jack's actions generally might not be considered as quite heroic, he is nevertheless a sympathetic and attractive character. He is neither a true chivalrous hero nor a fool or buffoon. I argue that this ambivalent heroism is typical of the hero in the penny blood: part of the perceived realism of the penny blood is how its heroes and their acts are more mundane than the epic feats of the classic hero.[12] Jack is no Robin Hood – he robs only for his personal gain rather than for some higher cause – yet his robberies do not make him a repulsive character. This is illustrated in the continuation of the scene: after the fainting of the landlord, Jack and Clayton rob the other gentlemen present in the inn, who laugh at the landlord's humiliation described above:

> On [Clayton's] return to the parlour, he was greeted with a peal of laughter, the squire declaring it was 'the richest joke he had ever seen'.
> 'And the beauty of it is, gentlemen, it is not the only spree I intend to have to-night; Jack, guard the door, and the first man that disobeys my orders, shoot him through the head.' (p. 50)

While the squire and the gentlemen were the audience before, they now become the subject of the second joke. The incongruity between the previous joviality and the intense physical threat uttered in immediate succession creates a comic effect. At the same time, it implicates the threat of violence and robbery into the comic vocabulary of the narrative by their concurrence. Robbery, in *Jack Rann*, is humorous business. While two of their victims struggle, the third admonishes his companions to simply hand over their valuables. He is cooperative:

> 'Don't let me detain you, gentlemen – I perceive it is useless to deceive you,' and saying these words, he placed his watch and purse upon the table; 'they are the only valuables I have about me – if you doubt my word, search me.'
> 'I'll be d——d if I do!' said Clayton, 'I should hope I know an honest man when I see him; thank you sir – your'e [sic] a gentleman;' and he bowed politely, 'much obliged to you'.
> The other returned the salutation good-humouredly, and by way of a joke, observed that he 'hoped soon to have the pleasure of meeting him again,' a wish in which both Rann and Clayton joyously concurred. (p. 52)

Being a well-behaved participant in the robbery earns the man respect from Jack and Clayton, and as a result, better treatment; he is not searched, unlike his companions. This character 'plays along' with the joke, and therefore does not invite ridicule and violence in the way the innkeeper does. Not only does cooperation lead to less violence; in the comic reversal of the text, playing along is seen as honourable, deserving of the classification of a gentleman. It points towards the class politics that are present in the text: a true gentleman does not mind being stolen from. Jack overwhelmingly steals from rich middle-class and small country gentry. When he does take money from working-class individuals, it is often freely given. On the surface, this is related to the 'suffering' that robbery causes – it is assumed, by the text, that the middle class and gentry can stand having some money taken off them without any particular hardship. It is easier to laugh at victims that are not significantly harmed. The lack of harm is an important limit on the use of physical violence as well; while the terror Jack inflicts on the innkeeper is a form of emotional violence, he constantly admonishes his fellow highwaymen not to use physical violence. When planning the robbery of a house, they plan 'to decamp without doing any violence, disturbing any of the house, or committing any further depredations' (p. 91). Jack's repeated insistence of 'no violence' defines the limit of play – 'no violence' means no *lethal* violence, which would ruin the joke. This mechanism complicates the reading of penny bloods as merely promoting violence and gore. While violence is certainly present in *Jack Rann*, it is couched in playful language, and has to abide by certain moral limits. The potential horror of the (especially emotional) violence which might arise in a close identification with the victim (a mechanism that the female Gothic exploits) is precluded through its farcical framing.[13] As we will see, the violence in *Valentine Vaux* functions in a similar fashion.

The consequences of Jack's robbery of the middle class and gentry go beyond the humorous: by constantly blurring the boundaries of property and possessions, by intruding into private spaces and taking objects that are owned by others, Jack symbolically claims their social status for himself. The doubleness that this creates, of both belonging and not belonging, constitutes the humorous uncertainty that the text exploits over and over. The joy that characters express after being robbed by Jack is not merely one of perverse pleasure – it is an expression of admiration and recognition of an equal. After having already been robbed by Jack and Clayton once, the squire claims that 'nothing would give me greater pleasure than to see [Sixteen-String Jack] and Clayton seated at my table' (p. 163). Jack's uncertain social status is part of the constant renegotiation and anxiety that surrounds him as a picaresque hero. As Wicks writes of the picaresque hero, his 'essential characteristic is his inconstancy – of life roles, of self-identity – his own personality flux in the face of an inconstant world' (p. 242). Part of this flux is enacted through disguise, as Jack assumes several false identities throughout the story. The disguise in *Jack Rann* takes the shape of comic disguise, leading to farcical situations of misrecognition, displaying an anxiety surrounding class and class perception. Jack utilises his 'favourite disguise of a country gentleman' to gain admission to various spaces, like middle-class households or Newgate Prison without suspicion (p. 155). As a highwayman, he enjoys a certain rank, being called 'Captain' by his gang members, and even being recognised as a fellow military man by Captain Manby (p. 152). Yet, the categories of highwayman and gentleman are opposites, comically brought together:

> 'You are a gentleman, sir,' said the Beau, with a bow of exquisite grace.
> 'I am, sir,' answered our hero, with equal politeness, 'OF THE ROAD, and therefore as a preliminary measure, am under the necessity of demanding your money or your life.' (p. 135)

The Beau later calls him 'the most gentlemanly vagabond I ever met in my life!' (p. 135). The text suggests that neither highwayman nor gentleman are Jack's 'true' identity; Jack says that 'for the spree of the thing [I must] shake off the Count and appear in propria personæ as the play writers say – as Sixteen-stringed Jack the dashing knight of the road', speaking about both his presentation as Count and as highwayman in the same terms (p. 147). In *Jack Rann*, disguise is a visual deception – it depends on the other party seeing and recognising certain markers of class. Although disguise can also involve the assuming of a different voice (so important to the humour in *Valentine Vaux*), the disguise in *Jack Rann* relies solely on surface presentation. Laughter is created by the various incongruities created by the gang members pretending to be members

of the upper class. Like the eighteenth-century masquerade and its
'identity play', disguise has the potential to spill across the carefully
drawn 'boundaries of ludic make-believe'.[14] The text questions:
what makes a man a gentleman? Is it birth, values, conduct, or the
perceptions of others? Can Jack Rann be a gentleman despite his
low birth? The importance of the issue is underlined by the fact
that, despite the general comic tone of the text, Jack's relationship to
gentility is never ridiculed. The issue of class is never fully resolved,
revealing class to be an unstable category. Towards the end of the
narrative, Jack is caught by Sir John Fielding, and convicted to be
executed:

> Jack saw at once the odds were against him. 'Sir John,' he said, frankly
> extending his hand, which the worthy magistrate took and shook
> heartily, 'I am your prisoner, and it gives me some pleasure in this
> dark hour to confess so, for you are the only man in England worthy
> of taking me'.
> 'My duty is a painful one, Mr. Rann,' said the good man, a tear
> of commiseration appearing in each eye, 'but it must, nevertheless,
> be fulfilled.' (pp. 400–1)

The relationship between Jack and authority, as embodied by
Fielding, is therefore complex: although the narrative ends with
his capture, Jack retains his paradoxical status as gentleman highwayman even while incarcerated in Newgate, a position legitimised by
the fictional Fielding.[15] The resistance to casting Jack as penitent
and regretful criminal underpins the narrative's interpretation of
state power. At the same time, it undermines the Gothic potential of the threat of impending death. The decision for Jack to be
executed at the end of the narrative seems to have been deliberate
rather than a genre convention – the 1823 play by Rede, which
Lindridge borrows from liberally, does reprieve its hero at the end
of the narrative; as does the seminal work of highwayman fiction,
The Beggar's Opera (1728).

Despite the death sentence, Jack's last few days act as a capstone
to a life well lived, spent in quiet contemplation with loved ones.
Unlike the horror that accompanies being faced with (unnatural)
death in Gothic literature, Jack spends his time receiving visitors in

'a private apartment allotted to him by the governor' and cautions his friend that 'what can't be cured must be endured' and he might 'as well laugh as pine [his] time away' in Newgate (Botting, p. 48; *Jack Rann*, p. 403). Comparing Jack's incarceration with a popular contemporary novel illustrates how *Jack Rann* avoids any fear or terror in its final chapters. In Charles Dickens's *Oliver Twist* (1837–9), published a year prior to *Jack Rann*, the gang leader and 'receiver of stolen goods' Fagin 'raved and blasphemed' and 'howled and tore his hair' while he awaits his execution in a cell in Newgate.[16] In his fear of death, Fagin himself has become a source of horror to his guards: as he walks around his cell 'with gasping mouth and burning skin […] in such a paroxysm of fear and wrath', even his guards 'recoiled from him' (p. 446). Fagin figures in a Gothic space, where faced with the sublime obliteration of the self, rationality no longer signifies. Lindridge's descriptions of Jack's response to the same premise – the death penalty after a life of crime – is diametrically opposed. While his friends mourn his impending death, Jack remains heroic and attractive, calm, and collected. Jack argues his conscience is clear because he has not committed murder, merely property-related crimes: '[were] my hand stained in blood to the wrist, He might have terror for me […] but, thank heaven, it is for no murder that I am about to suffer […] and for the rest, why should I care?' (p. 408). This quotation indicates how firmly the text functions in the farcical mode – it is by following the rules of the farce (no lethal violence) that Jack's execution signals a natural end to the time of play and a return to conventional morality, rather than a true punishment of a criminal.

Despite the public appetite for hangings in the 1840s, which led contemporary commentators like Dickens and Thackeray to express their horror at the perverse enjoyment of the public when faced with a spectacle of death, the reader of *Jack Rann* is not invited to partake in this pleasure rooted in a spectacle of human suffering.[17] After a parting monologue where he admonishes others not to follow in his footsteps, Jack merely 'ceased to exist' (p. 412). The elision of the hanging itself shows a refusal to engage with the material realities of death and the emotional states connected to it. The scene gives the impression of Jack merely stepping off stage rather than going through the act of dying, and his disappearance signals the end of the farce. The text avoids the uncomfortable ethical and emotional dynamics of real-life executions, where criminals admired by the public would be executed in front of large celebratory crowds. On the surface the order is restored by the end of the text by way of Jack's execution, yet the text manages to unsettle conceptions of authority by casting Jack's life in an alternative light. Although the death penalty is enacted, it does not provide the narrative closure that signals a return to the normal social order. The subversive potential of a text like *Jack Rann* partially lies in its part of a cycle of telling and retelling of criminal tales, implying that even after the fictional death of Lindridge's version of Jack Rann, the text is always open to further retelling in a different moment of time.[18]

Where *Jack Rann* undermines authority and unsettles class distinctions, *Valentine Vaux* shows how a similar plot structure is used to present an essentially politically conservative text. The predominant theme of both Cockton's *Valentine Vox* and Thomas Peckett Prest's plagiarism *Valentine Vaux* is that of ventriloquism: a skill of projecting one's voice across space and emulating it to make it sound like other people or animals. In both stories the main character, Valentine, is highly proficient at ventriloquism, and plays tricks on those around him which lead to farcical situations and laughter. Contrasting *Jack Rann* and *Valentine Vaux* not only helps in tracing the range of politics available to working-class readers in penny fiction, but also shows a broader pattern emerging in which humour takes precedence over gore or horror, and how the farcical framing precludes the ambiguity and liminality the Gothic mode thrives on. On the surface Jack's adventures are similar to Valentine's – both often rely on misdirection of the senses. Valentine uses auditory misdirection, while Jack uses visual misdirection through his various disguises. Both texts engage with farce as a mode, yet the meanings created in their contexts are vastly different. On a basic level, both *Valentine Vox* and *Valentine Vaux* are the story of a young ventriloquist, Valentine, who travels to London to live with a friend of a relative, called Septimus Bramstone in *Valentine Vaux*. Bramstone is a rich bachelor, whose brother, and his son (Harry and Arnold) have prematurely claimed his inheritance for themselves. They perceive Valentine as a threat and decide to secure their inheritance by committing Bramstone to an asylum. In *Vox*, the bachelor (named

Goodman in this version) is initially released because of the guilt-stricken conscience of his brother; in *Vaux*, Bramstone is liberated by Valentine, aided by several policemen. The plot points are strung together in a similar way: chapters that further the plot are alternated with Valentine seeking entertainment, usually in the form of a ventriloquial prank. The structure of the humorous ventriloquial scenes in *Valentine Vaux* is fairly constant throughout the text. This, in itself, is part of the 'joke': as was recognised by Henri Bergson, the French philosopher who wrote an essay on humour in 1900, repetition is one of the key characteristics of comedy.[19] Following roughly the same script, the reader already knows what to expect by the precedent that has been set, only increasing the comic value. The scenes are instigated either by Valentine consciously seeking entertainment, or by him simply coming across an opportunity as he wanders through London. Very few of his pranks occur within the domestic space, which is connected to the sense of staging in *Vaux*: the idea that Valentine induces others to amuse him as if it were a performance, while he directs the action from a safe distance. Valentine uses ventriloquism to 'throw' his voice to make it sound as if someone else made an inappropriate comment. An early example of this is when he heckles a chimneysweep, yelling 'sweep!', followed by derisive laughter, making it seem like a baker ridiculing him:

> 'What do you mean by running against me, you ugly man's child?' demanded the indignant baker.
> 'Vy I means to hinsult yer, as yer hinsulted me jist now,' replied chummy, poking his nose so near to the baker's mouth that it was in evident danger of being snapped off.
> 'Who insulted you?'
> 'You!'
> 'When?'
> 'Vy jist now! Didn't yer call across the road arter me, and didn't yer set up a grin that would have frightened even a Cheshire cat?'
> 'It's a lie!' (p. 8)

This kind of exchange, appearing in the first issue of the story, is typical for the comic script the other ventriloquial scenes follow. A heckle receives an instant response; the accused denies having had anything to do with it; the parties argue until they start a physical fight ('[the chimneysweep] lent the baker two or three such smart taps upon the face, that he was obliged to throw down his basket and act upon the defensive') (p. 9). As mentioned above, a requirement of farcical violence is that it figures within certain limits. Jessica Milner Davis writes, 'The aggression is both sufficiently precise to be psychologically valid and yet sufficiently delimited to qualify as play' (p. 85). The discussion on the humour of violence by William Hazlitt, a nineteenth-century literary critic, resonates with Davis's remark:

> In what relates to the laughable, as it arises from unforeseen accidents or self-willed scrapes, the pain, the shame, the mortification, and utter helplessness of situation, add to the joke, provided that they are momentary, or overwhelming only to the imagination of the sufferer.[20]

In *Vaux*, the fleetingness of pain is induced by the momentum of the narrative: within a sentence or two, the story moves on to another topic. Spending time on the suffering of the characters would deflate the joke, and therefore it is paramount that the subjects of Valentine's pranks are removed from the narrative stage the moment they have served their purpose. Importantly, Valentine is in control of when the time for play ends, for example deciding 'the matter should not end here' when he continues his ventriloquial deceptions (p. 86). This example illustrates the distribution of power between the characters; Valentine determines the duration of the prank, who deserves to be pranked and when the joke is 'done'. It is an extension of the power fantasy that Steven Connor ascribes to Cockton's Valentine: 'a fantasy of exercising absolute control over people and events, while remaining himself absolutely invulnerable to detection and retribution'.[21] This assessment holds for Prest's Valentine as well.

Although ventriloquism had become a common act in popular entertainment in the first half of the nineteenth century, it also has the potential to unsettle.[22] Ventriloquial anxieties are exploited in the Gothic novel *Wieland: or, The Transformation* (1798) by the American author Charles Brockden Brown, in which the titular character Wieland and his family are terrorised by the ventriloquial effusions of Carwin. At the climax of the novel, it is revealed to the narrator,

Wieland's sister Clara, that Theodore Wieland has murdered his wife and children because a voice (which he interprets as God's command) told him to do so. Clara hears voices coming from near her bed at night, threatening to shoot her, though there is no one to be seen. Her reaction is one of terror: 'My heart began to palpitate with dread of some unknown danger [...] My terrors urged me forward with almost a mechanical impulse.'[23] The ventriloquism in *Wieland* is 'ghostly', disembodied speech from impossible origins.[24] Van Elferen has theorised that in Gothic literature, sound or its absence creates uncanny effects, as 'sound suggests presence even when this presence is invisible or intangible, and is thus closely related to the ghostly'.[25] This effect of ghostly presence which ventriloquism can create is utilised in *Wieland*; in *Valentine Vaux*, however, sound is no longer uncanny. If a person is terrified at the voices or sounds Valentine creates, this fear is always mediated through Valentine's laughter. Despite *Valentine Vaux* embracing Gothic tropes such as asylum incarceration, disembodied voices and repetition in its plot, it creates a laughter that is an expression of joy rather than fear. In the categorisations by Peter Bailey, *Valentine Vaux*'s laughter is a 'noise of merriment', rather than a 'noise of terror'.[26] While the Gothic thrives on ambiguity and liminality, *Vaux*'s characters are quick to ascribe a source to any voice or sound they come across. In a particularly silly passage set in the Tower of London, Valentine throws his voice in a statue of Henry the Eighth to frighten a family with a shockingly bad knowledge of history, calling them fools:

> 'Is that figure alive?' at length asked Mr. Jonas Jenkins, in a tone of mingled terror and amazement.
> 'Alive, lor' bless you, not as I knows on,' answered the horror-struck warder. 'It's only an effigy, sir, and though I've been here for the last ten years I never heard him speak a word before, as I'm an honest man'.
> 'He called me a fool, at any rate,' exclaimed Bob, indignantly, 'and king or no king, I'm blest, if I'm going to stand that sort of caper.' (p. 101)

Even when faced with a terrifying voice coming from a statue, the characters in *Vaux* take these situations in their stride, and deal with the seemingly impossible at face value. Fear soon morphs into anger, a particularly ineffective anger as Bob is arguing with a statue. Prest's characters solve the aural mystery (a voice coming from an impossible place) by accepting that it is indeed coming from this place, however improbably. It is this willingness by the subjects of Valentine's pranks to 'play along' with these situations, as it were, that constitutes the humour in *Valentine Vaux*. As any ambiguity is immediately resolved in the text, however, even a voice coming from a place it should not, fails to become uncanny.

The power differential between Valentine and his victims is tied in directly with the politics of the text. His victims are either defined by their occupation (a baker, a blacksmith, a costermonger); persons who overstep their class boundaries and are therefore already ridiculous, which Prest describes as 'exquisites'; and persons who engage in politics, which again makes them a target by virtue of the ridiculousness of politics. One such justification can for example be found when Valentine causes a dandy to be soaked in water; in this instance it is not just for Valentine's benefit that the person receives a punishment, as 'The punishment to which this puppy had been subjected was highly approved of by the generality of the company on board' (p. 79). This illustrates both how Valentine's victims are 'deserving', while at the same time giving more insight on who decides this. Valentine's actions are justified by the authorial voice, as well as supported by a majority of bystanders. Although there is a small minority who think he has 'gone too far', overstepping the limit of play, the assessment made by Valentine (and the authorial commentary which underwrites his decisions) carries more weight. Valentine intervenes in overtly political spaces several times; politics makes fools out of us, even if one is part of the upper layers of society, as in the House of Lords, where the politicians are described as 'rabid gentlemen', one of whom 'abus[es] his foe after the elegant style of a Billingsgate fishwoman' (pp. 50–1). Yet this does not mean that difference in status becomes obsolete within the farcical framing – Prest is much harsher on radical politics and socialism.

When Valentine comes across a meeting of 'that truly vicious society the "Socialists"', the tone of the narrative shifts from ironic to scathing. Rather than seeking amusement, Valentine, 'though detesting the tenets of this class of men, resolved to enter the place, if it were only for the purpose of convincing himself whether men and women could be so utterly depraved in principle as report had stated' – a stark contrast to his usual motivations (p. 186). The scene is mainly concerned with 'socialist' views on marriage, which are a distorted interpretation of Robert Owen's stance on marriage and divorce. Owen gave lectures on the topic in the 1830s, arguing that marriages without affection should be allowed to be disbanded, to protect vulnerable women from abusive marriages as well as preventing people becoming unhappy for life in unsuitable matches.[27] In Prest's reading, the socialists aim to 'prove that marriage is opposed to the happiness of mankind, and, consequently, that the sexes ought to live together in a state of nature' (a stance not supported by Owen's lectures) (p. 186). More specifically, the lecturer claims that 'We are for a community of goods – every thing is to belong in common to one another, and why, therefore, I ask you, should not our women be common also?' (p. 188). To Valentine, this stance goes against 'common decency', and he is discouraged by the amount of women in the crowd, but he 'consoled himself with the certainty that there were always enough of good people in the world to prevent any very wide-spreading evil resulting from such a filthy sink of corruption' (p. 186). When Valentine ventriloquially interferes, it is not with the intention to amuse; it is to vent his disapproval. The socialists are insidious exactly because they succeed in overstepping the boundaries of convention, especially sexual convention. The speaker, for example, is looking for a fourth partner, and to Valentine's disgust, the women in the audience show an interest in filling this position. While the structure of the scene at the socialist meeting is similar to the comic script the reader has become very familiar with at this point in the text, its tone is diametrically opposed to the usual farcical humour Valentine's ventriloquial exploits express. The crimes of the socialists are so extreme, the text reasons, that even the trickster Valentine cannot abide their ideology. When the lecturer argues for the rights of women to separate from a husband who has for example become imprisoned, Valentine becomes the mouthpiece of conservative familial values:

> 'Curses light upon the woman who would forsake the husband who has fallen into trouble!' cried Valentine [...] 'In difficulties a

man should be strengthened and supported by the tender care of his wife, and yet there are hollow miscreants who would deprive him of this; – perhaps his sole remaining consolation upon earth!' (p. 189)

This speech might seem surprising coming from a character who has little compassion for anyone except perhaps his rich benefactor, and actively goes out of his way to annoy others. What Valentine is expressing in this speech is therefore not a call for wives to have pity on their husbands who might fall on hard times, but a defence of the status of monogamous heteronormative marriage as a moral obligation and a pillar of civilisation. The section continues with Valentine exclaiming, 'I am, indeed, bigoted, as you call it, to the cause of virtue', calling the lecturer's words 'language that would be a disgrace even to a barbarian' (p. 189). Under the pressure of Valentine's disruption, the socialist meeting erupts in violence, only to be disbanded by the police.

The police play an important role throughout the text, restoring order after Valentine's ventroquilism-induced chaos. Part of the dynamic between Valentine and the police can be explained through the sense of play that the text espouses – for the text to present itself as play, it is necessary that there is no real lasting consequence to Valentine's antics. The reader is periodically assured that his victims went home safe and sound, though perhaps slightly worse the wear as a result of their fighting, dunking or mudding. When Valentine requests help from the magistrate to save his benefactor from being wrongfully held captive, it becomes clear that Valentine is not antithetical to authority. In fact, the police's support is easily secured, and in the following scene, he retains power and agency, while the policemen follow his directions. While Valentine and the police, at a glance, might seem to have oppositional interests (Valentine causing disorder, while the police return crowds back to order), when placed together in the pattern of the narrative, they underpin conventional authority and the inevitable triumph of order. While allowing for the fact that Valentine himself is not completely beyond the control of these forces (as he too is aware of the possibility of arrest), he affirms their validity by drawing on their authority. Valentine's destabilising potential as a trickster – or as a picaresque hero – is therefore limited.[28] His speech at the socialist meeting reveals Valentine's true relationship to power: he is opposed to any shift in the structures of power present in early Victorian society. His pranks only highlight how he stands apart from those he tricks – including his often working-class victims. Valentine respects and supports the power invested in the police and magistrate, indicating that his temporary rebellions are not meant to go beyond any boundaries of permitted behaviour, but instead reveal where those boundaries lay and reinforce them through laughter, or lack thereof, such as at the meeting of the socialists.

Contrasting *Jack Rann* and *Valentine Vaux* shows how laughter is always political – it matters who laughs, and at what. While Jack undermines middle-class domesticity and safety by not only stealing members' possessions, but by his own uncertain class identity, the middle-class Valentine ridicules working-class people or others whom he deems to be overstepping their class boundaries. Valentine's tricks hold no threat to existing hierarchies. Both texts sideline the Gothic mode despite the Gothic tropes they include (sensory misdirection, Gothic spaces like asylums and prisons, execution) in favour of farcical humour. Despite the violence that is part of the narratives, like Jack's threats and Valentine's brawling crowds, the harm is minimised through narrative strategies aimed to reduce the reader's sympathy with the victims. As such, it complicates the reading of penny bloods only relying on gore and blood to engage its readership – it is not suffering that texts like *Jack Rann* and *Valentine Vaux* foreground, but the joys of chaos within delineated rules of play, both inside and outside corrective state power.

Notes

[1] James Malcolm Rymer, *Ada the Betrayed; or, The Murder at the Old Smithy. A Romance of Passion* (Fairford: Echo Library, 2015), p. 515.

[2] This chapter is based on research conducted as part of a PhD degree at the University of Sheffield, funding for which was generously provided by the Elisabeth Brandenburg Foundation, the Dutch Culture Fund, Hendrik Mullerfonds, Stichting Niemijerfonds and Fundatie van Renswoude.

3   Some recent excellent studies include Anna Gasperini, *Nineteenth Century Popular Fiction, Medicine and Anatomy: The Victorian Penny Blood and the 1832 Anatomy Act* (Cham: Palgrave Macmillan, 2019) and Ted Geier, *Meat Markets: The Cultural History of Bloody London* (Edinburgh: Edinburgh University Press, 2017).
4   Jarlath Killeen, 'Victorian Gothic pulp fiction', in A. Smith and W. Hughes (eds), *The Victorian Gothic:. An Edinburgh Companion* (Edinburgh: Edinburgh University Press, 2012), pp. 43–56 (p. 50).
5   James Lindridge, *Jack Rann, Alias Sixteen-string Jack* (London: G. Purkess, 1840) and Timothy Portwine, *The Adventure of Valentine Vaux; or, The Tricks of a Ventriloquist* (London: E. Lloyd, 1840). Timothy Portwine is a pseudonym of Prest. The name 'Vaux' might have been inspired by Vauxhall, the pleasure gardens in London which the character Valentine Vox attends in the course of the story. Another interpretation is that Vaux is a tongue-in-cheek echo of the French word faux, or false – as Valentine Vaux is a 'false' version of Cockton's story.
6   Fred Botting, *Gothic* (London: Routledge, 2014), pp. 2–3.
7   Ulrich Wicks, 'The Nature of Picaresque Narrative: A Modal Approach', *PMLA*, 89/2 (1974), 240–9 (242).
8   There seems to be some confusion about the actual number of strings. It is unclear whether there were sixteen strings in total, or sixteen on each knee.
9   Leman Rede, *Sixteen-string Jack* (London: G. H. Davidson, 1823).
10 Susanne Schmid, 'Eighteenth-Century Travellers and the Country Inn', in S. Schmid and B. Schmidt-Haberkamp (eds), *Drink in the Eighteenth and Nineteenth Centuries* (London: Pickering & Chatto, 2014), pp. 59–70 (p. 62).
11 Jessica Milner Davis, *Farce* (London: Methuen & Co Ltd, 1978), p. 26.
12 For a discussion of the characteristics of the classic hero, see Dean A. Miller, *The Epic Hero* (Baltimore: Johns Hopkins University Press, 2000).
13 For an extensive analysis of the 'female Gothic' plot, see Robert Miles, *Ann Radcliffe: The Great Enchantress* (Manchester: Manchester University Press, 1995).
14 Dror Wahrman, *The Making of the Modern Self: Identity and Culture in Eighteenth-Century England* (New Haven: Yale University Press, 2006), p. 159.
15 For the gentleman highwayman, see Robert B. Shoemaker, 'The Street Robber and the Gentleman Highwayman: Changing Representations

and Perceptions of Robbery in London, 1690–1800', *Cultural and Social History*, 3 (2006), 381–405.

[16] Charles Dickens, *Oliver Twist, or, The Parish Boy's Progress* (London: Penguin Books, 2003), p. 445.

[17] V. A. C. Gatrell, *The Hanging Tree: Execution and the English People 1770–1868* (Oxford: Oxford University Press, 1994), pp. 59–60; Andrew Smith, *Gothic Death 1740–1914: A Literary History* (Manchester: Manchester University Press, 2016), p. 108.

[18] See Lincoln B. Faller, *Turned to Account. The Forms and Functions of Criminal Biography in Late Seventeenth- and Early Eighteenth-Century England* (Cambridge: Cambridge University Press, 1987), p. xi.

[19] Henri Bergson, *Laughter: An Essay on the Meaning of the Comic*, trans. Cloudesley Brereton and Fred Rothwell (London: Macmillan and Co., 1911).

[20] William Hazlitt, *Lectures on the English Comic Writers* (London: John Templeman, 1841), p. 16.

[21] Steven Connor, *Dumbstruck: A Cultural History of Ventriloquism* (Oxford: Oxford University Press, 2004), p. 320.

[22] John A. Hodgson, 'An Other Voice: Ventriloquism in the Romantic Period', *Romanticism on the Net*, 16 (1999).

[23] Charles Brockden Brown, *Wieland; or The Transformation, and Memoirs of Carwin, the Biloquist* (Oxford: Oxford University Press, 2009), p. 54.

[24] Stefan Schöberlein, 'Speaking in Tongues, Speaking without Tongues: Transplanted Voices in Charles Brockden Brown's *Wieland*', *Journal of American Studies*, 51/2 (2017), 535–52 (538).

[25] Isabella van Elferen, *Gothic Music: The Sounds of the Uncanny* (Cardiff: University of Wales Press, 2012), p. 3.

[26] Terminology paraphrased from Peter Bailey, 'Breaking the Sound Barrier: A Historian Listens to Noise', *Body and Society*, 2/2 (1996), 49–66 (51–2).

[27] Robert Owen, *Lectures on the Marriages of the Priesthood of the Old Immoral World, Delivered in the Year 1835, Before the Passing of the New Marriage Act* (Leeds: J. Hobson, 1840), pp. 86–90.

[28] Barbara Babcock-Abrahams '"A Tolerated Margin of Mess": The Trickster and His Tales Reconsidered', *Journal of the Folklore Institute*, 11/3 (1975), 147–86 (159).

9

Gothic Ideology and Religious Politics in James Malcolm Rymer's Penny Fiction

REBECCA NESVET

Gothic writing originated as anti-Catholic propaganda. The Gothic, Robert Mighall explains, tends to contrast a supposedly 'enlightened now' with a 'repressive or misguided then': usually, a Protestant 'now' and Catholic 'then'.[1] A work that presents 'particularly strong argumentation supporting the idea that the Gothic tradition actually grew out of anti-Catholic polemic' and that this tradition encompasses penny dreadfuls, is the late Diane Long Hoeveler's *The Gothic Ideology: Religious Hysteria and Anti-Catholicism in British Popular Fiction, 1780–1880* (2014).[2] Hoeveler shows that anti-Catholicism is the reigning ideology not only of Gothic classics but of mass-market chapbooks.[3] As Franz Potter explains, the chapbook was a 'legitimate downmarket manifestation' of the Gothic novel that targeted the same audience as the penny dreadful a generation earlier, although, as Andrew King has pointed out, actual readership of popular print was far more socio-economically diverse.[4] Hoeveler's discovery of the essentially anti-Catholic 'Gothic ideology' of the chapbooks and mainstream Gothic writing raises an important question: how did penny bloods and dreadfuls, the Victorian descendants of the Romantic-era 'lower-class Gothic imaginary', represent Catholicism and, more generally, sectarian politics? Hoeveler acknowledges this question in her coda, leaving it largely for other scholars to answer.

In response to her invitation, I consider the representation of Catholicism in the work of one of the most prominent, influential and prosperous authors of penny bloods and dreadfuls, Sweeney Todd's creator James Malcolm Rymer (1814–84). Over time, Rymer's usage of the Gothic ideology evolves dramatically. In his early penny dreadfuls, Rymer demonises Catholicism. In later works, Rymer dispenses with overt anti-Catholic political rhetoric but repurposes the anti-Catholic tropes that had become firmly established as the paraphernalia of British Gothic storytelling. The new ideological purposes to which he applies these tropes include promotion of a limited toleration of the Catholic population that had been legally emancipated in 1829, and of other minority monotheistic faiths. In these ways, the anti-Catholic Gothic ideology identified by Hoeveler haunts Rymer's widely read Victorian penny oeuvre even as his views about Catholicism and religious diversity evolved.

An Inherited Ideology

Rymer's inheritance of the Gothic ideology originated close to home, as his father, the Edinburgh-born, London-based engraver and author Malcolm Rymer (1775–1835) wrote a Gothic novel that incorporates that ideology absolutely. Malcolm Rymer's novel, *The Spaniard, or, The Pride of Birth* (1806) is plagiarised from a Gothic chapbook that Hoeveler highlights as a prime example of the Gothic ideology, Richard Cumberland's *The History of Nicolas Pedrosa* (1799). This chapbook deploys nearly every anti-Catholic cliché of the early Gothic tale, including an early modern continental setting (Madrid), a lecherous Catholic clergyman, superstition, the Inquisition, torture and a proto-Protestant hero who ultimately seeks freedom in England. In plagiarising it as *The Spaniard*, Malcolm Rymer recycles these clichés to critique aristocracy but also lauds the Reformation. This aspect of *The Spaniard* is bolstered later in the same writer's verse 'Address' to a Regency-era mutual improvement society. The 'Address' celebrates printing in London as a vehicle of political liberty, commemorating by name the late medieval printer and publisher William Caxton.[5] In the words of

Caxton's modern biographer N. F. Blake, Caxton is 'generally honoured as the man who introduced printing into England' and had this reputation in the nineteenth century.[6] As England's Gutenberg, Caxton may therefore be read as a medieval proto-Protestant just as Nicolas Pedrosa clearly is.

Like Malcolm Rymer, his son Gaven Rymer, an artist and engraver (d. 1842), insisted that London folk culture was fundamentally Protestant and explicitly anti-Catholic. In 1834, Gaven Rymer published six street scenes depicting London folk creativity, including a depiction of Guy Fawkes Day. In Gaven Rymer's composition, a group of working-class men and boys boisterously transport an effigy of Fawkes through the London streets. The effigy is disturbingly dressed as a modern Londoner, not a denizen of the seventeenth century, while a staid middle-class couple look on (Figure 2).[7] There is an undercurrent of danger, as the Guy, slumped in a makeshift sedan chair, looks more human than scarecrow, and wears the same types of clothing as his bearers. That this London

Figure 2 G. Rymer. 'Guy Fawkes, or, the Fifth of November'. From Rymer's *London Scenes*. 1834. Image: London Picture Archive.

crowd might be participating in the persecution of a human being, someone not unlike themselves, and a fellow Londoner undermines the picture's jollity. Perhaps it is why the couple in the background, staring past the crowd and effigy at the picture's spectator, look somewhat concerned. In this picture of Gaven Rymer's, to be a Londoner is to be insistently Protestant and vigilant against English Catholicism's most notorious spectre.

A Gothic Miscellany

Gaven's brother James Malcolm Rymer achieved success in the 1840s as an author of penny bloods published by Edward Lloyd. In Lloyd's pages, Rymer firmly branded himself a Gothic novelist. His first two bestsellers, *Ada, the Betrayed, or, The Murder in the Old Smithy* (1842–3) and *Jane Brightwell* (1842–3), first appeared as serials in Lloyd's *Penny Weekly Miscellany*. Slightly misquoting Scott's *Rokeby* (1813), the verse epigraph of the 1843 omnibus edition of volume 1 of *Lloyd's Penny Weekly Miscellany* promises 'tale[s] of war for knight', 'beauty' and 'goblins grim'.[8] This epigraph promises that the omnibus will contain many of the key ingredients of early Gothic fiction, including a medieval setting, a chivalric romance, and a heroine ('beauty') in distress. Rymer might have seen the Gothic formula as an easy, guaranteed money-maker. As Michael Gamer observes, as early as the 1790s, the Gothic seemed 'an attractive and potentially lucrative aesthetic, particularly for writers ambitious for popular success'.[9] However, like the 1790s Gothic novelists, Lloyd assumes a Protestant reading nation. The 1843 *Lloyd's Weekly Miscellany* editorial 'Why Should We Despair?' claims that three million Irish people have given up alcohol, with a 'very, very rare' relapse, and adds that 'as Protestants, we smile at the old legends of the Catholic church' but consider the progress of temperance in Ireland a genuine miracle'.[10] *Lloyd's Penny Weekly Miscellany* imagines its readers as English Protestants whose relationship to colonised Catholics is paternalistic.

The first volume of *Lloyd's Penny Weekly Miscellany* also explicitly condemns the Catholic clergy. The non-fiction article 'Story of the Crusades', whose anonymous author I cannot determine, claims that 'the ruling passion of those times' is 'religious enthusiasm', and adds that the Muslims whom the Crusaders encountered ('the polite natives of the east') are described accurately as 'barbarous, illiterate, firm, and savage' men 'in terms not unlike those which preceding historians had deployed in describing the incursions of the Goths and Vandals, as they overturned the Roman empire' (p. 89). The Crusaders are prototypical Grand Inquisitors: 'in the ardour of rage and victory, they put thousands of Turks and Jews to the sword' and 'assembling all the Jews, burned them in the temple' (p. 89). *Lloyd's Penny Weekly Miscellany* blames this violence on the Church: 'the pope and clergy continued to recommend this sacred war with increasing ardour' (p. 90). Economically, 'the court of Rome profited by' the Second Crusade while even a traditional English hero of the Crusades appears a mindless maniac: 'Richard Coeur de Lion' beheads three thousand Turks to demonstrate 'the rage of the conquerors' (p. 90). This characterisation is indicative more of the Church community than it is anti-monarchic, as the historian praises a king, Saladin. The monarch whose people the Crusaders attacked is 'exemplary for his piety and his temperance' (p. 90). A modest antithesis of Percy Bysshe Shelley's 'Ozymandias', 'during his last illness he ordered his shroud to be carried throughout the city, while a crier went before the procession and proclaimed with a loud voice: 'This is all that remains of the mighty Saladin' (p. 90). In this conception of history is an implicit critique of Catholic theological and temporal leadership.

The Black Monk and *The Ordeal by Touch*

As Rymer continued writing for Lloyd, he exploited Gothic ideology. *The Black Monk, or, The Secret of the Grey Turret* (1844–5) is a pastiche of Matthew Lewis's *The Monk* and a sizeable fraction of Ann Radcliffe's oeuvre. Published in March 1844, within two years of Rymer's hiring by Lloyd as a major contributor to his *Miscellany*, it succeeded his popular success *Ada, the Betrayed*. Taking no aesthetic or philosophical risks, *The Black Monk* is a paint-by-numbers Gothic romance. Set during the reign of Richard I, it inhabits the world of the Crusades article from the previous year's

Miscellany. The eponymous monk Morgatani is scheming, licentious, transnationally politically involved, covetous, vengeful and homicidal. He is also a Jesuit – four centuries before St Ignatius Loyola founded the Society of Jesus. Editor Curt Herr finds this anachronism a minor 'historical miscalculation' amidst 'an engrossingly enjoyable read' and an 'example of the penny dreadful at its peak form', but to thus minimise it is really to miss *why* this work seems a 'prime example' of the Gothic genre of the penny blood.[11] By displacing the Jesuits to the twelfth century, Rymer makes the Counter-Reformation much older than the Reformation, and the supposed tactics of its Jesuit proponents a fundamental aspect of the Church that Henry VIII opposed. In other words, the error removes the Counter-Reformation's context as a reaction to Protestantism, making its supposed abuses seem to have belonged to the medieval era and therefore not in reaction to suppression of Catholicism in Protestant England.

One of Rymer's immediately subsequent productions for Lloyd's fiction factory, *The Ordeal by Touch, a Romance* (1846) more audaciously deploys Gothic ideology to represent the Reformation as an essential way-station on the English nation's journey towards class equality and democratic government, and implies that this narrative is widely known. To see how this agenda functions in *The Ordeal by Touch*, it is necessary to understand this title's publication context. Lloyd advertised a competition for amateur authors of serial fiction, with the prize being extremely well-paid publication of the winning entry in his periodical *Lloyd's Entertaining Journal*. *The Ordeal by Touch* was publicised as the 'prize romance for which one hundred guineas were paid'.[12] In reality, it was written by Lloyd's long-time house author Rymer.[13] In *The Ordeal by Touch*, Rymer represents Reformation anti-Catholicism as an origin of Victorian working-class English political self-determination. Specifically, *The Ordeal by Touch* deploys the Gothic ideology to show the Reformation as a populist movement that aims, anachronistically, towards the sort of political liberty envisioned, for instance, by Milton.

In the one-volume edition of *The Ordeal by Touch*, this agenda first appears in the Preface. The supposed amateur author declares that he has set his romance early in the reign of Henry VIII because the Reformation is a key event in English history. 'At no time in the

Figure 3 *The Ordeal by Touch*, p. 1.

history of this country', this Preface explains, 'were there so many strange and romantic adventures as when that great change was taking place in the habits, feelings, and manners of society', i.e., the Reformation (p. i). The Preface further defines the Reformation as 'the abandonment of the superstition and the priestcraft of papal rule' in favour of the 'much more tolerable and milder dominion of a Reformed Church' (p. i). In response to the Reformation, the Preface adds, the 'Church of Rome' resorted to 'every description of crime, including murder ... to crush [its] opponents' (p. i). In this Whig narrative of English history, the Reformation is inherently progressive and Catholicism inherently evil. By rejecting Catholicism, England starts on a long but certain path to the abolition of tyranny.

The romance's opening gambit reinforces this narrative of history. Rymer begins *An Ordeal by Touch* with a description of a Tudor-era painting of the protagonists supposedly exhibited at present – that is, in 1847 – at the Royal Academy. A woodcut of the alleged painting forms the instalment's illustration (Figure 3). At the centre is an apparently martyred early Tudor gentleman, laid out on a table like an anatomy lesson or a medieval effigy, bleeding from an evidently recent and mortal wound. The deceased is foregrounded by his grieving widow and many small children. In the upper background, two Catholic clerics loom, superstitiously overseeing the titular ritual, the 'ordeal by touch', in which the dead man's wound erupts with blood at the touch of his suspected murderer. The two clerics' shepherds' crooks simultaneously announce their vocation and suggest that in having failed to protect the dead man from murder and his family from want, they have failed at their pastoral responsibilities.

Rymer's ekphrasis of this imaginary painting frames the Reformation as the cataclysm from which a better present is in the process of emergence. In the opening dialogue, a Tudor courtier discusses with one of the pictured priests whether England has ever had popular government. The priest asks whether 'the people have governed' in England; the courtier concludes that they have not yet, 'but like an infant Hercules, a people is beginning to feel that it has strength and power' (p. 4). As *The Ordeal by Touch* continues, we learn that the clerical establishment as represented by the iconic corrupt, licentious *incognito* Jesuit (again, anachronistic) Father Georges publicly known as Sir Rupert Brent – the figure who in the illustration is being forced to touch the wound. The bleeding victim, Ranulph Hensman, is the heroic secretary to the proto-Protestant Lord Warden, who has collaborated with his employer to save the life of Henry VII; Georges/Brent is indeed his attempted murderer; Hensman's body bleeds when Georges/Brent touches it because Hensman has survived the murder attempt. If Hensman is the text's embodiment of the Anglican Church, that ecclesiastical body leads a charmed life, resurrecting itself despite Catholic attempts to kill it, and thereby surviving into the Victorian present to be celebrated at the Royal Academy.[14]

Further entrenching the anti-Catholic ideology of *The Ordeal by Touch*, when Brent/Georges demands a trial by combat, the latter's faction is represented in that combat by a historical hero of the Reformation-era Protestant literary establishment, the Tudor poet Henry, Earl of Surrey, who thereby saves the heroine, Mrs Alice Hensman: poetry will defend Protestantism, English womanhood and the English nation from the Catholic menace. Notably, Mrs Hensman, a virtuous married mother of several children and a good Protestant, enjoys a popular romance. Though written in manuscript, this work is proto-Gothic and obviously presented as a direct ancestor of penny dreadfuls like Lloyd's. Rymer claims that Alice 'dipped into a short anecdotal sketch, called the "Haunted Horn"' (p. 77). Rymer states that this kind of reading material is imbued with Protestant rhetoric and popular with the nascent Protestant reading audience. He calls *The Haunted Horn* an exposé of medieval Catholic tyranny: it 'was strikingly illustrative of feelings and habits even then beginning to be on the wane among the better informed [*sic*] classes, and those who were making war upon the Romish supremacy' (p. 77). Sixteenth-century reading habits, this passage suggests, indicate that the Gothic literary tradition has always been both anti-Catholic and politically progressive.

While *The Ordeal by Touch* makes Protestantism the ideology of English pursuit of democratic rule, it refuses to make a hero of Henry VIII. In the guise of the prize-winning amateur author, Rymer is remarkably conspicuous in his anti-monarchic conviction. He approves of Henry VIII's 'war ... against monasticism' but 'give[s] no credit whatsoever' to that 'bluff Majesty' the King, because he pursued Reformation out of self-interest ('motives ... of a private and personal nature') and because 'he was as incapable as a broomstick of any nobler elevating principle' (p. 33). Henry VIII was not a particularly bad king; rather, Rymer condemns all kings. 'Like most of our monarchs', Henry was 'something of the brute, and something of the fool ... gross sensuality being the load-star [*sic*] of all his actions, as has likewise been the case with most of our monarchs' (p. 33). In another distinctly anti-monarchic passage from *The Ordeal by Touch*, a Protestant crowd tries to protect a Jesuit messenger from execution, to which Henry VIII has personally condemned him. 'Who shall say nay to the king's commission?', one demonstrator asks. 'Why, we, to be sure', is the response, 'We, the citizens of London!' (p. 81). They even insist that despite his Catholicism, he is their equal and a part of the citizenry: 'What citizen would betray another? ... None who are citizens!' (p. 81). These Londoners protect the condemned man not because they appreciate or pity him, but, nearly anticipating the parliamentarians of the era of the Civil War, to show their opposition to personal monarchic rule. In case the reader does not yet recognise this crowd as an ancestor of the Chartists of the 1840s or the Peterloo martyrs, Rymer spells that out too. While 'the people in the time of Henry VIII had scarcely begun to consider themselves a distinct and important portion of the body politic whose interests required to be seen to' in Rymer's own time, 'a great amount of intelligent people have found out that they are the real source of all power, and the real strength of a state, and will no longer be cajoled out of those liberties, which they have a right to demand' (p. 81). Rymer clinches the argument with a return to Gothic anti-Catholicism: in the Tudor era, the English people apathetically believed they could not 'possibly exist without the licentious, debauched, and scheming priesthood' (p. 82). Rymer renders political awakening and rejection of Catholicism synonymous.

Rymer's final statement on the matter ties Protestantism to Chartism by envisioning a straight line of societal evolution from the Reformation to a classless, equitable society. He prophesies that 'it must and will come to pass in this country, that 'the doctrine of every man being his own parson' will dominate, and the Church of England clerisy will fail just as had the pre-Reformation Catholic priesthood (p. 82). The 'trade of religion' will be transformed so that 'younger sons of noble families' and 'insipid sons of the middle classes' will no longer monopolise clerical appointments, and the clergy will no longer be a refuge for men unable or unwilling 'to be ... useful member[s] of society' (p. 82). Moreover, from the Reformation, 'a popular movement' will 'shake the power of the Jesuits to its foundation and free England from it for ever [*sic*]' (p. 86). This is the English Jerusalem imagined not by the Reformation, but by the Chartists – and, due to the hoax of the amateur prize-winner, this vision appears to emanate from the people and thereby fulfil that utopian vision.

Towards Toleration?

At about the same time in Rymer's career, his views on religious politics began to evolve. With them changed his use of the Gothic ideology in his penny fiction. As I have argued in two earlier publications, Rymer's *The Lady in Black, or, The Widow and the Wife* (Lloyd, 1847) adopts an urban mythological villainess, 'Miss Whitehead, the Bank Nun', a vengeful laywoman who dresses like a nun and exemplifies the Gothic stereotype of the hypocritical nun. In *The Lady in Black*, Rymer humanises and rehabilitates the 'Bank Nun', claiming that she and her family were genuinely harmed by the London financial industry, and in particular by one member of it, the Gothically rapacious villain Simon Godfrey, financier.[15] In *The Lady in Black*, the nun-like Lady is no longer evil, but she is dispossessed, made homeless and persecuted just as were the actual nuns of the Reformation era.[16] In her image, the Gothic guilty fascination with the dissolution of the monasteries haunts central London, very literally – though without providing a Whiggish justification of the dissolution.

Rymer ecumenically repurposes the Gothic ideology in his most enduring work, the Lloyd penny blood *The String of Pearls, a Romance* (1846–7). Later updated as *The String of Pearls, or, the Sailor's Gift* (Lloyd, c. 1850) and then *The String of Pearls, or, the Barber of Fleet-Street, a Domestic Romance* (Lloyd, 1850), this penny blood is the earliest tale of the pseudo-historical murderous Fleet Street barber Sweeney Todd. In the original 1846–7 penny blood, published serially in *Lloyd's People's Periodical and Family Library*, the human remains that Todd conceals in the crypts of St Dunstan's Church produce a stench that is noticed with alarm first by the church's congregation and minister, and then by the churchwardens and, finally, the visiting bishop. Explaining how this 'stinkification' came to be so long ignored by the church authorities, Rymer opines that 'in the great city of London, a nuisance of any sort ... requires to become venerable by age before any one thinks of removing it'.[17] Like other noxious metropolitan institutions, the corruption of the Church – perhaps figurative as well as biochemical corruption – is held sacred.

The bishop and ecclesiastical bureaucracy's response to the problem reflects poorly on them, allowing Rymer to demonise the Anglican clergy as horrifically out of touch with the people and tolerant of corruption and murder; that is, to transfer the anticlerical critique, directed by earlier Gothic novelists against the Catholic Church, against the Anglican establishment instead. However, the vestigial anti-Catholicism of the Gothic ideology leaks through this updated Gothic narrative. The source of the stench is a kind of mockery of the Eucharist, as Todd has been converting human remains to food for congregations of people. Todd is even somewhat monkish: unmarried, no family, itinerant, playing up his supposed asceticism, yet a closet drunk, doing scurrilous things in the crypts. And yet, in the three Lloyd editions of *The String of Pearls*, Rymer explicitly attacks the Anglican and Protestant Churches only. His jibes at Nonconformism include Todd's handing out of evangelical pamphlets to a murder victim's widow and children in lieu of more transferable alms, and the subplot involving a priest who sexually harasses and maritally pursues heroine Johanna Oakley and turns out to have murdered a string of wives, desecrated the corpse of at least one of them, and escaped from prison in Australia. While this character is as rapacious and deceptive as the Gothic monk, he is a self-declared Dissenting minister. Any organised religion, Rymer suggests, can be susceptible to the corruption that Gothic literature imputes to the Roman Catholic Church – which is a kind of argument for equal toleration of all denominations. Like *The Lady in Black*, *The String of Pearls* recycles the Gothic conventions of *The Monk* and its ilk, but with new and less explicitly anti-Catholic meaning.

Reynolds's Miscellany

After *The String of Pearls* (1850), Rymer continued to repurpose Gothic anti-Catholic imagery, but his substituted meanings became more radical, perhaps on account of a change in his employment. In the early 1850s, Lloyd's fiction business fell apart. He abandoned it to focus on news journalism. In 1854, Rymer found new regular literary employment with George W. M. Reynolds, specifically writing fiction for *Reynolds's Miscellany*, one of Britain's most popular periodicals and the most prominent penny paper of its day. Reynolds was a far more committed Chartist than Lloyd, especially in the immediate aftermath of the 1848 failure of the Third Chartist Petition. Rohan McWilliam articulates the prime difference between Lloyd's politics and Reynolds's. Lloyd's publications advanced liberalism, a form of progressive thought that advocated cooperation between classes, class equality and free trade, and eschewed imagining the abolition of the class hierarchy itself. Reynolds dreamed of such abolition, and, to achieve it, wrote fiction in what McWilliams calls the 'Chartist Gothic' mode.[18] 'Derived from the horrors and dark shadows of Gothic fiction', the Chartist Gothic proposes that 'power and wealth, rather than having been modernised by the liberalisation of the economy, remain with the aristocracy'; the middle class plays only a negligible role in this struggle, and 'Britain remains divided between riches and poverty' (McWilliam, p. 200). Reynolds was openly distrustful of nearly all organised religion. His earliest publication, *The Errors of the Christian Religion Exposed: By a Comparison of the Gospels of Matthew and Luke* (1832), vehemently argues that the Gospels should not be read literally as history and that their ahistoricity undermines Christian theology.[19] Later, however, Reynolds opposed representation of the Catholic Church as a uniquely corrupt or evil institution, and was interested in building ecumenical bridges, perhaps on account of his youthful sojourn in France, a country for which he developed a lifelong love. As the Reynolds scholar Michael Diamond explains, Reynolds 'wanted to correct the pro-Protestant bias of previous historians', arguing during the controversy over Cardinal Wiseman's appointment as the first modern Catholic bishop of London that the popes are generally no more venal than Britain's late Stuart and Hanoverian kings, the heads of the Church of England.[20] Hardly a defence of Catholicism, this rhetoric uses anti-Catholic ideology as a stick with which to beat the Anglican Church, its adherents and the Hanoverian contingent of the British monarchy – perhaps as indicative of ecclesiastical institutions. Reynolds's views on religion might best be summed up in a caricature from a *Comic History of England* published by the printer of *Reynolds's Miscellany* and many of his novels, John Dicks: Gilbert Abbott A'Beckett's 'The Clerical Weathercock'. Drawn by the renowned John Leech sometime before A'Beckett's death in 1856, the Clerical Weathercock (Figure 4) cheerily points his flock in any direction the political winds blow him.[21]

Employed by Reynolds from 1858 to 1862 to write fiction exclusively for *Reynolds's Miscellany*, Rymer seems to have adjusted his reinvention of the Gothic ideology to advance views on religion compatible with Reynolds's. An interesting example is Rymer's 1858 *Reynolds's Miscellany* serial *The Sepoys, or, Highland Jessie: A Tale of the Present Indian Revolt*. Composed while the Indian Revolt was in progress, inspired by the apocryphal and profoundly imperialist myth of the clairvoyant 'Highland Jessie' Brown, *The Sepoys* peddles

Figure 4 'A Clerical Weathercock'. Author's Collection.

a Chartist message with international scope to Reynolds's readers, who were located not only across Britain but beyond, including in British-colonised India. *The Sepoys* makes an impassioned plea for transcultural, interreligious solidarity against the East India Company's colonial kleptocracy, explicitly endorses intermarriage as a way of achieving just rule of India without full independence, and depicts the Revolt as an international offshoot of Britain's more or less failed Chartist movement, which had petered out after three failed major petitions (1839, 1842 and 1848) and the 1855 death of its controversial national leader, Feargus O'Connor. In the first instalment of *The Sepoys*, Rymer introduces *The Sepoys* as a tale so authentic it is almost describable as news journalism, billing it as 'a faithful account of the Perils and Adventures of Two Families in India ... and the numerous romantic Episodes of the Rebellion ... from authentic and exclusive sources'.[22] The cast is headed up by Jeffur Ahib, a Muslim prince from a region in northern India. Young, handsome, martial and just, Jeffur is respected by India's Hindus and Muslims. (The novel recognises no other Indian religious constituencies.) Except for his hereditary political status, Jeffur is the kind of ideal political leader of which the Chartists dreamed. His foil is the Hawkins family, a nasty assortment of nabobs clearly unfit to rule and functioning in India as the aristocracy does in the Home Counties. The Hawkins patriarch is Mr Vernon Hawkins of Delhi, an 'old civil servant of the East India Company', which company pillages India not only in reality but in the backstories of several earlier Rymer penny serials, including *The Dark Lady* and *The String of Pearls* (p. 130). Vernon's sons have names that recall *translatio imperii*: Captain Hannibal Hawkins and his younger brother Mr Caesar Hawkins, suggesting that the British Empire in India, like the empires of Carthage and Rome, might be destined to pass away should it become too tyrannical.

On the day the Revolt reaches Delhi, Jeffur visits the Hawkins house to petition Mr Hawkins. Like the Chartists, he begs the propertied on behalf of their victims:

> I come from a poor ryot, near the villages named Choree. The young Sahibs, in their eagerness for the chase, trampled his little patch of vegetation; and a lighted cigar, flung on the thatch of his hut, burnt

the thatch and soon reduced it to flames. Compensate the poor man, Sahibs, for he and his have had to take refuge among the tombs, for a fever is vexing the blood of his youngest child. (p. 130)

Like the Parliaments of 1839, 1842 and 1848, the Hawkins men dismiss this petition. Caesar Hawkins insists that as a 'gentleman', he has a right to 'a little amusement' (the destruction of Choree's livelihood) (p. 130). 'What's to compensate me, I wonder, for knocking up my best horse and losing a dog?', he asks (p. 130). Vernon insists that he will not discuss grievances with any indigenous people, including Jeffur. Vernon claims to 'never argue with a native'; he communicates with 'natives' only by instructing them 'to call at the proper office, and see the proper authority, who, after proper consideration in the proper official way, will do the proper thing when and how he thinks proper' (p. 130). In other words, he invokes a monstrous colonial bureaucracy to dismiss indigenous petitioning categorically. Jeffur, flummoxed by this response to his own petition, goes away – leaving the Hawkinses susceptible to the violence of popular revolution, which erupts almost immediately upon Jeffur's departure.

Cleaving to Reynolds's views, *The Sepoys* recycles Gothic imagery to deliver a Chartist Gothic message, and also advance toleration of all monotheistic religions within an inherently anticlerical ideological framework. Jeffur rescues his English beloved Bessie Hope from the colonial residence in Cawnpore by the aristocratic Nana Sahib, a historical local leader of the revolt. Notorious in Britain for having murdered the English women and children that he actually imprisoned at Cawnpore, and committing their bodies to the Residency's well, Nana Sahib functions in *The Sepoys* as a Gothic villain typical of early Orientalist Gothic texts such as William Beckford's *Vathek* or Southey's *Thalaba the Destroyer*. Rymer's Nana has 'bloodstained eyes implacable as a tiger in their rage', a harem and a drinking problem (p. 84). At the same time, his followers are characterised as religious fanatics, not unlike early Gothic monks: 'Blood shall flow till the sacred Ganges is tinted with the lifestream' of English ('Feringhee') victims; and he calls 'revenge ... the Hindoo watchword [password]' (p. 84).

As the serial progresses, however, Rymer makes a plea for religious toleration and even intermarriage. While consistently demonising the supposedly polytheistic Hindus, Rymer lionises Jeffur and depicts his and Bessie's romance in positive, even heroic terms: 'I do love him – I *will* love him! He is not of my creed or my people, but God will let me love him!' (p. 100). For 1866, this is a bold endorsement of anti-racist, interfaith love. That endorsement is considerably undermined by the details of their marriage. It takes place at 'St. John's Cathedral, in Calcutta' (p. 126). This location detail implies that Jeffur has accepted his wife's faith and abandoned his own. Religions other than Anglicanism are tolerable in *The Sepoys* only if, in political alliance and intermarriage, they are ultimately diluted or erased. The Gothic ideology's insistence upon the unique virtue of English Protestantism defines the very final paragraphs of the Chartist Gothic fable *The Sepoys*.

'The church of another clime'

Rymer makes a similar move *vis-à-vis* intermarriage specifically between an English Protestant and an English Catholic in *A Mystery in Scarlet* (1866), a leading serial of the likely final penny periodical he edited, *The London Miscellany*. By 1866, Catholicism's fortunes had changed considerably. In the wake of the Great Famine, England's Catholic population increased with emigration from Ireland.[23] Many Tractarians converted to Catholicism, including, most prominently, John Henry Newman. In 1850, Bishop Wiseman was installed. Four years later appeared the first modern edition of the sixteenth-century Catholic martyr-poet St (Fr) Robert Southwell, SJ. The Gothic Revival in architecture physically resurrected the aesthetic ghosts of medieval Catholicism; it tried to reconstitute the very objects and spaces that the iconoclasts of the Reformation had demolished, such as Charing Cross's replica monument. Amidst this resurgence, *A Mystery in Scarlet*'s George II plots against his secret legitimate elder brother, the legitimate king, driving him from Britain along with his daughter and heiress Bertha and her fiancé, the heroic Captain Weed Markham. Bertha was raised in 'the church of another clime', Rymer states: the location seems to be either France or Italy.[24] While this love plot promises toleration of British Catholics as part of *A Mystery in Scarlet*'s political messaging, it still identifies Catholicism as decisively foreign ('another clime') and so not British. Furthermore, Bertha's marriage to the Protestant Markham and her resignation to anonymity and to never becoming Queen invalidates the situation's potential to change Britain's ecclesiastical establishment. Like Jeffur's faith, Bertha's is approved because destined for erasure – hardly an improvement upon the open, obvious anti-Catholic rhetoric of *The Ordeal by Touch*.

Tracing the Gothic ideology of anti-Catholicism through the penny dreadful as represented by Rymer's copious, influential oeuvre both reinforces and challenges current critical assumptions about the relationships between the penny dreadful, the Gothic and the sectarian politics of religion in Britain. This longitudinal reading of Rymer confirms Hoeveler's theory that the penny dreadful grows out of the Gothic chapbook, taking the chapbook's virulent anti-Catholicism with it as a matter of generic identity, but it also shows that not all penny fiction subscribes to that ideology, nor is penny fiction homogeneous or monolithic in its treatment of religion. I have shown that Rymer appropriated the Gothic ideology from chapbooks and Romantic-era Gothic literature, including his father's *The Spaniard*. At the time of the *Queen's Magazine*, Rymer cynically believed that recycling Gothic tropes would enable him to achieve literary popularity, so for some years, he produced Gothic pastiche. Later, established as an anonymous but successful top writer at Lloyd's publishing house, Rymer experimented more liberally with his use of Gothic conventions and his treatment of religion. Some of his penny dreadfuls articulated relatively liberal ideas about toleration for Catholics and religious pluralism within an imperial context, particularly after his parting from Lloyd and employment by the progressive Francophile Reynolds. Even as Reynolds's exclusive hired writer, Rymer did not fully let go of the Gothic ideology – or, perhaps, like a Gothic ghost, it would not let go of him. Embedded in the recognisable conventions of Gothic literature, this ideology proved impossible for Rymer to fully abandon. Instead, he repurposed its tropes to promote social and political causes other than the suppression of Catholicism. Consequently, those tropes persist in his fiction, and through it, function as important generic identifiers of the penny dreadful.

Notes

1. Robert Mighall, *A Geography of Victorian Gothic Fiction: Mapping History's Nightmares* (Oxford: Oxford University Press, 1999), p. xiv.
2. Monika Mazurek, *The Unknown Relatives: The Catholic as Other in the Victorian Novel* (London: Routledge, 2019), pp. 147–50.
3. Diane Long Hoeveler, *The Gothic Ideology: Religious Hysteria and Anti-Catholicism in British Popular Fiction, 1780–1880* (Cardiff: University of Wales Press, 2014), p. 4.
4. Franz J. Potter, *Gothic Chapbooks, Bluebooks, and Shilling Shocks, 1797–1830* (Cardiff: University of Wales Press, 2021), pp. 2–4; Andrew King, *The London Journal, 1845–83: Periodicals, Production, and Gender* (Aldershot: Ashgate, 2004), pp. 5–6.
5. Rebecca Nesvet, '*The Spaniard* and Sweeney Todd', *Notes and Queries*, 64/1 (2017), 112–16 (115–16).
6. N. F. Blake, *William Caxton and English Literary Culture* (London: Hambledon, 1991), p. 5.
7. G. Rymer, 'Guy Fawkes, or the Fifth of November: Plate No. 6 from 'London Scenes', 1834, Lithograph (London Metropolitan Archives, no. 1–239–846). That this 'G. Rymer' is Malcolm's son Gaven, the engraver, is indicated by the absence of any other contemporaneous G. Rymer, engraver, combined with 'G. Rymer's' publication of another engraving in his brother James Malcolm Rymer's short-lived periodical *The Queen's Magazine* in 1842. The brothers' publishing collaboration ended with Gaven's death in July or August 1842.
8. *Lloyd's Penny Weekly Miscellany*, 1 (1843), unpaginated title page.
9. Michael Gamer, 'Gothic Fictions and Romantic Writing in Britain', in Jerrold P. Hogle (ed.), *The Cambridge Companion to the Gothic* (Cambridge: Cambridge University Press, 2002), pp. 85–104 (p. 89).
10. *Lloyd's Penny Weekly Miscellany* (London: Edward Lloyd, 1843), 244. Hereafter *LPWM*.
11. Curt Herr, 'Introduction', in James Malcolm Rymer, *The Black Monk, or, the Secret of the Grey Turret*, ed. Curt Herr (London: Valancourt Books, 2014), pp. vii–xix (p. xv).
12. James Malcolm Rymer, *The Ordeal by Touch, a Romance* (London: Lloyd, 1847), p. 1.
13. Helen R. Smith, *New Light on Sweeney Todd, Thomas Peckett Prest, James Malcolm Rymer, and Elizabeth Caroline Grey* (London: Jarndyce, 2002), p. 20.

[14] If Ranulph Hensman's unusual name is intended to recall Ranulph Higden, the medieval historian most famous for writing the *Polychronicon*, the association further entrenches Hensman in a medieval proto-Protestant pantheon. Translated into English by John of Trevisa, the *Polychronicon* was published by Caxton, linking Higden posthumously with proto-Protestant publishing.

[15] Rebecca Nesvet, 'The Bank Nun's Tale: Financial Forgery, Gothic Imagery, and Economic Power', *Victorian Network*, 8 (2018), 83–7.

[16] Rebecca Nesvet, '1837: "Miss Whitehead, The Bank Nun"', *BRANCH*, ed. Dino Franco Felluga (2020), https://www.branchcollective.org/?ps_articles=rebecca-nesvet-miss-whitehead-the-bank-nun.

[17] James Malcolm Rymer, *Sweeney Todd, the Demon Barber of Fleet Street (Sweeney Todd)*, ed. Robert L. Mack (Oxford: Oxford University Press, 2007), p. 150.

[18] Rohan McWilliam, 'Sweeney Todd and the Chartist Gothic: Politics and Print Culture in Early Victorian Britain', in Sarah Louis Lill and Rohan McWilliam (eds), *Edward Lloyd and his World: Popular Fiction, Politics, and the Press in Victorian Britain* (London: Routledge, 2019), pp. 198–215 (p. 199).

[19] Stephen Basdeo, 'Errors of the Christian Religion Exposed', *Reynolds's Miscellany*, 26 July 2021.

[20] Michael Diamond, 'From Journalism and Fiction into Politics', in Anne Humpherys and Louis James (eds), *G. W. M. Reynolds: Nineteenth-Century Fiction, Politics, and the Press* (London and New York: Routledge, 2008), pp. 91–8 (p. 95).

[21] Gilbert A'Beckett, *A Comic History of England* (London: John Dicks, c. 1880), p. 53.

[22] James Malcolm Rymer, *The Sepoys, or, Highland Jessie: A Tale of the Present Indian Revolt*, Reynolds's Miscellany, 20–1/504–41 (1858), 81.

[23] Carol Engelhardt Herringer, 'Roman Catholicism in Britain and Ireland: On the Margins and in the Majority", *Victorian Review*, 46/2 (2020), 156–8 (157).

[24] James Malcolm Rymer. *A Mystery in Scarlet*, The London Miscellany, 1 (1866), nos. 1–18, p. 18.

10

'Muddling about among the dead': Found Manuscripts and Metafictional Storytelling in James Malcolm Rymer's Newgate: A Romance

SOPHIE RAINE

The Newgate Tradition

Newgate Prison with its underground passageways, confined cells, and criminal associations, was a locale that writers of penny dreadfuls could hardly resist featuring in their Gothic narratives. Indeed Newgate Prison is featured in a host of penny titles including Edward Ellis's *Ruth the Betrayer* (1863), George W. M. Reynolds's *The Mysteries of London* (1844–6), and the anonymously authored *The Wild Boys of London; or, the Children of Night* (1864–6). The impression of Newgate in the Victorian imagination had been established by the *Newgate Calendar* in the eighteenth century with *The Newgate Calendar or the Malefactors Bloody Register* (1773) and *The New and Complete Newgate Calendar* (1795). The criminals of Newgate retained readers' interest as evidenced through various reincarnations of the calendar in the nineteenth century such as *The Chronicles of Crime or, The Newgate Calendar* (1841), various iterations of the Calendar by Andrew Knapp and William Baldwin in 1824 and 1826, and a penny dreadful version of the calendar, *The New Newgate Calendar* (1863). While the late eighteenth-century calendars focused on seventeenth-century criminals such as notorious highwaymen, the 1841 calendar would include a combination of historic and contemporary cases dating from 1700 to the early Victorian period. Newgate's presence in contemporary Victorian fiction and its associations to a historic past render it as a Gothic vestige, a term used by Robert Mighall to describe an anachronistic site incongruously present in a modern setting.[1]

As Stephen Knight has identified, however, the 'community and rural security blanket of *The Newgate Calendar* was ... inappropriate to the cities'.[2] Knight analyses George W. M. Reynolds's *The Mysteries of London* (1844–8) to reveal how this work of crime fiction updated the traditional Newgate style to focus on a 'lost community' model (p. 9). By the 1830s, according to Knight, crime fiction needed a main character to act as an 'expert guide' who was adept at navigating the 'contradictory evidence, multiple identities, baffling possibilities, all in the anonymous enigmatic, threatening modern city' (p. 29). This chapter argues that James Malcolm Rymer builds upon and contributes to the rejuvenation of the Newgate form through his work *Newgate, a Romance* (1846–7). What is particularly striking about Rymer's text in comparison to *Mysteries* is that the contradictory evidence present in Newgate is the text itself, as its frame narrative contributes to a distorted and fragmented narrative. Rymer's work is engaging in a more conscious, or at least more self-reflective way with the Newgate tradition than texts such as *Mysteries* as it features the discovery of a manuscript similar in style to *The Newgate Calendar*. Rob Breton has recognised *Newgate* as 'the only self-consciously deliberate Newgate novel'. However Breton further suggests that the text's use of 'sensational features' of the Newgate form and 'mixing in a wide assemblage of gothic tropes' reduced the Newgate novel to 'a set of quick and easy conventions'.[3] While the text does make use of the conventions of the *Newgate Calendar* (the anonymous author, the composite nature of the documents, historical accounts told through a frame narrative), the text's homage to the Newgate form, and its defence of the hybrid nature characteristic of the penny dreadful makes it a serial worth further consideration.

While for many penny titles, Newgate's role in the narrative was often peripheral or placed as an obstacle to overcome in a subplot, Rymer's *Newgate* reincarnates the encyclopaedic, miscellaneous form of the *Newgate Calendar* to provide a sensational tour of this Gothic vestige for the interloping reader. Utilising the composite nature of the Newgate tradition, Rymer reflects upon the process of producing, writing and preserving penny dreadfuls. The text, therefore, does not only return to the past, but uses an exploration of the past as a lens through which to analyse the present condition and future of working-class fiction. In *Newgate*, the reader and narrator move through the Newgate investigation concurrently uncovering the secrets of Newgate through archival research and physical exploration of its subterranean vaults. Through its frame narrative, polyphonic mode of storytelling and temporal ruptures, Newgate Prison is presented as a space where the past and the present collide, thus allowing Rymer to comment upon the ways in which historical records can be distorted, reimagined and misrepresented. In particular, Rymer expresses concern as to the preservation of less officious or more plebeian narrative forms with characters in *Newgate* resorting to oral storytelling as a way of preserving their stories. There is a clear affinity between the works that comprise the 'Newgate school' and the penny dreadful, with both forms continuously adapting and restyling themselves; as Gary Kelly states, 'each kind of Newgate narrative informed the others on the ever-changing field of struggle that was Newgate discourse.'[4] The contribution to existing bodies of knowledge is something that numerous penny titles strove to do by incorporating journalistic pieces, medical reports, statistical information, all within a framing fictional narrative; while the extent of this differs for each penny title, the synthesising of extra-textual materials and sensational fiction is something which numerous scholars have noted.[5]

Evoking the format of the *Newgate Calendar* was consistent with the stylistic conventions of the penny writers. This approach is also characteristic of the *Newgate Calendar* which 'satisfied the popular fascination with crime and criminals by gathering together accounts of the lives, trials, confessions, punishments and/or escapes from, or evasions of the law of celebrated criminals'.[6]

Unearthing Gothic Manuscripts

The found manuscript as a trope has been present within the Gothic tradition since its inception, most notably made famous by Horace

Walpole's *The Castle of Otranto* (1764), where the author claimed the text had been found in a lost archive. The overuse of this trope has been acknowledged by numerous scholars including Diane Long Hoeveler, who states that 'the unearthed manuscript was such a tired convention that it was both ridiculed and valorized in several later gothic (or antigothic) novels'.[7] When deployed in the context of penny publications, however, the trope takes on a renewed significance and, as well as being a homage to early Gothic, reveals similarities with this method of storytelling and the characteristic narrative form of the penny dreadful. The penny dreadful tended to veer towards a composite narrative framing using snippets of journalism, plagiarised newspaper articles, medical reports, and a whole array of extra-textual material embedded within its narratives. Similarly to the recovered manuscript, the penny dreadful was constructed through a diverse range of extra-textual sources, including newspaper reports, legislation and numerous other forms of non-fictional sources. As Anna Gasperini writes of the form, it comprises 'a gargantuan combination of scattered pieces'.[8]

The manuscript referred to in this chapter will be the manuscript 'found' by the narrator, rather than the penny serial itself, which is also purported to be an amalgamation of a number of reputable sources and posits itself as investigative journalism and historical research. Despite the text's preface emphasising the factual nature of the narrative and the manuscript contained within, as well as numerous narrators professing to uncover the truth, the unreliable narrator, falsified accounts of criminals and the emphasis on 'romance' indicate to the reader the complex challenge of preserving the past, recording the present and the responsibilities of writers conducting these to be conscious of this when producing art. As Timothy C. Baker argues, '[m]etafictional elements, including found manuscripts and clear forgeries, arguably highlight the extent to which any text, or work of language, fails to represent the past objectively or completely.'[9] Rymer's text not only draws the reader's attention to the questionable authority of 'found manuscripts' or other historical sources, but actively engages in this discussion by consistently, intentionally undermining the authority that was established in the preface of the text. Rymer demonstrates how both official documentation and works of literature are limited in representing both the present and the past due to their narrow range of sources and negation of marginalised voices, specifically those of the working classes. Moreover, Rymer contests the idea that fiction has a duty to be accurate and suggests that the nineteenth-century obsession with investigative journalism, statistics and the verifiability of archives has diluted the romance of the Gothic genre and sensational literature more broadly. The found manuscript allows the narrator and therefore the reader to vicariously experience the romance of a historical past and the lives of criminals. The information given to the narrator, however, is incomplete and fragmented. Thus the narrator begins a journey of discovery by seeking to uncover what has been lost in this amateurish archive. The research undertaken to either continue or complete parts of the manuscript has the narrator simulating the experience of the penny fiction writer who, with an assemblage of materials, weaves together a narrative. This is particularly relevant to Rymer's own authorial style, as Helen R. Smith has noted how he had previously deployed the trope of the 'found manuscript' in *Manuscripts from the Diary of a Physician* (1842, 1847) and *Leaves from the Note-books of a Queen's Messenger* (1848).[10] Rymer therefore allows the reader to vicariously experience his authorial processes.

The blurred line between fiction and fact in the text is communicated through the series of characters who encounter the manuscript and become corrupted by it, engaging with these 'historical' stories to the point of obsession. The narrator of Newgate comes into possession of the manuscript when he meets an unnamed old man, sometimes referred to as 'the stranger', who offers to tell him all the secrets of Newgate. After accompanying the old man to his home in an offal cellar connected to the underground vaults of Newgate, the narrator witnesses the true extent of the stranger's obsession when, during an incomprehensible raving monologue, he states that Newgate is his 'destiny' and reveals how he has devoted his life to uncovering the secrets of the prison. Following this, the old man accidentally falls down a well in the offal cellar and dies, leaving the manuscript to the narrator. Before his death, the old man laments that 'the romance of the old prison has departed' and thus establishes the quest at the heart of the narrative, both Rymer and the narrator's mission: to revive the romance of Newgate.[11]

This obsession is passed on to the current narrator who becomes entirely absorbed in the narratives, seeking out the final resting places of the characters detailed in the documents, researching their executions, and, eventually, becoming involved in the criminal underground of Newgate himself, such is the pernicious and corrupting influence of the document. Rymer is, perhaps, making a satirical remark regarding the supposedly corruptive nature of the penny dreadful in that those who cannot separate fact from fiction, reality from fantasy, are their own undoing. Dani Cavallaro writes that the quintessential Gothic text is a 'composite entity wherein disparate narrative strands parallel the split subjectivities of both characters and readers', which 'in being fashioned by their writers and readers, simultaneously construct the readers' identities by incarnating their most inveterate desires and fears'.[12] The narrator becomes captivated by Newgate to such an extent that his companion remarks that he is so preoccupied with 'muddling about among the dead' that he has lost interest in the above-ground world (p. 415). The manuscript is instrumental in removing the identity of the narrator so that he can pursue a variety of other identities, recreating the movements of the criminals of Newgate and separating himself from his reality. The fragmented nature of the manuscript enables this as the missing portions urge him to investigate; on the other hand, the minute details present in some documents in the manuscript, such as the blueprint of the vaults underneath Newgate, allow him the tools to conduct his discovery. The present, the modern, becomes abandoned in pursuit of the past; the narrator becomes estranged from his own world and an outcast in searching for the artefacts of the past and the remnants of the dead.

The fragmented manuscript demonstrates that texts that profess to be based on true events will only ever have access to part of the story and be limited in perspective. As the narrator explains to his companion following the dissatisfying conclusion of one of the stories, 'you must recollect that it is impossible every episode of human nature contained in these pages should have so very special a reference as to invest Newgate with any new interest' (p. 403). The manuscript is likened to the penny dreadful form itself with its ever-adapting nature. Rymer raises critiques of the form itself – incomplete narratives, derivative from other texts and itself – and answers them. The narrator acts as a mediator between Rymer and the reader, and explains the shortcomings of the form and the limitations of the author. Rymer's critiques of the form woven into the narrative constitute Newgate as metafiction. Though usually a term ascribed to postmodernist texts, this is clearly present in the work of Rymer. Patricia Waugh remarks that metafiction is 'writing which consistently displays its conventionality, which explicitly and overtly lays bare its condition of artifice, and which thereby explores the problematic relationship between life and fiction'.[13] Though Rymer continually asserts the authenticity of the document, the consistent commentary on the difficulty of retelling events accurately for potential future generations undermines this significantly and therefore intentionally exposes its artifice.

Another issue raised with the preservation of historic fact and its insertion into fiction is the inaccuracy of official sources. The narrator states that 'we must recollect that these are the chronicles of the building, gathered probably from a number of previously undiscovered sources, and that they carefully, in all likelihood, exclude anything that is not strictly authentic' (p. 404). This assertion is contradicted in the text, however. When the narrator explores the documents surrounding the case of Captain Hawk in a story entitled 'The Shadow of Death; or, the Coffin Cell', he finds that the official documentation and the manuscript are conflicting. While the manuscript indicated to the narrator that Hawk died in his cell before his execution, he finds a newspaper article in the collection of papers detailing Hawk's public execution. Following up on this, he discovers that this had been written beforehand, and that this was common practice according to one of his acquaintances who is said to know the 'secrets of newspapers' (p. 128). He is informed that

> Books are criticised which the critic never saw. Plays are praised or condemned which, in one or two cases, have not been acted, so you must not be surprised at a last dying speech and confession being printed before a man is hanged, and probably the printer would, if he were alive, excuse himself by saying that Captain Hawk ought to have been hanged, and that his not being so was no fault of his. (p. 128)

Rymer here further draws attention to the inaccuracy of newspaper reporting, thus reasserting the argument that history or research in general must cover a broad range of sources rather than accepting the printing press as infallible and without further scrutiny. In doing so, Rymer portrays an inverted world where the press creates stories that are fantastical, based on assumptions, and penny serials are asserted to have foundations in fact and corroborated by numerous sources. This role reversal furthers the distrust of the narrative, and in fact, of all works which profess to accurately document current or historical events. This had been alluded to previously within the Captain Hawk narrative where the narrator of that tale writes:

> The public press – which must write to live, as well as live to write – then, as now, found it necessary, in some measure, to pander to popular taste, and something daily about the popular highwayman was generally to be found as palatable food for gossip. (p. 74)

This was applied not only to the public press but is a sentiment that had been frequently used to describe the pandering nature of cheap popular fiction, particularly penny dreadfuls. As an article in the *Globe* (1839) wrote on the subject of literary piracy, '[l]iterature will, in fact, cease to control and regulate popular tastes. The most vulgar tastes will, on the contrary, control and regulate popular tastes.'[14] In *Newgate*, it becomes difficult to disentangle press reportage from fictional works, as both are accused of pandering to public tastes, engaging in sensationalising stories for profit, and prone to distorting or misrepresenting the truth. Though it is difficult for the reader to differentiate truth from fiction in this narrative, it becomes clear that the secrets being exposed are not only those of Newgate, but those of the printing press. In doing so, Rymer explores 'the possible fictionality of the world outside the literary fictional text' (Waugh, p. 2). Rymer cautions readers to be critical of all things they read by demonstrating through his fictitious 'found manuscript' the ease with which a writer can construct a fictional narrative and present it as fact.

Sophie Raine

Temporal Ruptures and Newgate's Spectres

The role of the manuscript in *Newgate*'s narrative illustrates the pitfalls of attempting to accurately record history, while simultaneously revealing the importance of imaginative literature. The dichotomising of fact and fiction is disrupted not only through the fragmented form of the manuscript, but also through the use of temporal shifts which occur in the narrative. As the narrator attempts to recreate or recall the past, he ends up reimagining it and altering it. *Newgate*, however, celebrates the literary potential that can result from the recycling and repurposing of legendary characters from the past whilst simultaneously warning the reader against uncritically accepting these stories as fact.

The intrusion of the past into the present occurs at the beginning of the narrative when the narrator enters the home of the stranger. Before the stranger falls to his death, he has the following conversation with the narrator:

> 'Newgate is my destiny. I never set foot within what may becalled its public walls. That low arched doorway conducts to all its subterraneous cells and gloomiest passages. Hush – hush! who speaks? Where are we now, Charles? Be careful, oh! be careful.'
>
> A feeling at the moment came over me that he was dying. His strange and abrupt transition from the present to some picture of the past which was traced upon his imagination, convinced me that delirium had seized upon him. …
>
> 'Hush – hush!' he cried. 'Stir not, move not; like bloodhounds they are upon your path – they will drag you to a scaffold, but I must first be killed. You see the door that leads to the vaults of Newgate. A strange hiding-place for a convicted felon.' (p. 10)

The old man's obsession with Newgate has led to his internment in a purgatorial space whereby he is not part of the past, nor is he engaged with the present. The two, for him, become interchangeable, shown in this episode of delirium. His authority as a historian or chronicler of the past is marred by this incomprehensible outburst.

The manuscript's new owner, the main narrator, wilfully invokes the ghosts of the past in order to fuel his imagination. One of the first instances of this is where Rymer's narrator ruminates on the chilling story of Captain Hawk and May Boyes. As he sits alone in his home, he begins, in a trance-like state, to imagine he is among them in the present day:

> I see Sir John, the great Sir John, who came in with the conqueror, and lost him in the crowd ... Yes, there he sits, conversing with ancient authors. Poor ancient authors, we pity you! The conversation of Sir John must be a treat indeed ... Euripedes [sic], Sallust, Pliny, sit you down, and converse with the great Sir John Boyes, who came in with the Conqueror. (p. 126)

The focus on narrators moves to include ancient authors of classics in this unusual and particularly reflective scene. Even when removed from the Gothic vestige of Newgate, the spectres of past prisoners intrude upon the contemporary Victorian home and pursue the reader through imaginative means. Moreover, the choice of guests the narrator imagines is particularly significant. By placing his own character (Sir John) among great classic writers and philosophers such as Euripides, Sallust and Pliny, Rymer suggests that his own creation, Sir John, possesses similar attributes. Rymer's text not only utilises the style of the penny dreadful in its tendency to look back at historic figures and reimagine their stories, but is active in creating a legacy for its own characters. The adaptation of the Captain Hawk story into its own serial, which was reprinted by Lloyd as *Captain Hawke; or, May Boyes; and the Shadow of Death* in 1851, attests to Rymer's desire to secure a literary legacy. As indicated through the continuation of the May Boyes tale through his own serial as previously mentioned, Rymer prophesies the long-lasting impact of his characters and boldly situates them in an established literary canon preserving them for posterity.

Conversely, the narrator's multiple journeys under Newgate transport him and the reader back in time to experience the tales in the same environment that they were conceived. The next section of the narrative moves away from archival research into a more practical exploration of underground Newgate. The narrator uses the blueprint contained within the document wallet to navigate his way to the coffin cells described in the narrative:

> A holy sort of awe crept over me. The delusion was perfect, and, as I sat down again without attempting, or even wishing now to light a candle, I could believe myself carried back a hundred years, and so should scarcely have been surprised to see the highwayman standing in his fetters before me. (p. 136)

Though the narrator claims his purpose in exploring Newgate is to uncover the truth, his motivations are grounded in a type of Gothic tourism. His desire not to disturb the past by altering the space even with a candle shows his fallacious belief in the past being alterable. The ghosts that linger under Newgate are conjured through the romantic imagination of the narrator rather than an actual spectral presence, highlighting that the haunting space of Newgate itself remained in the public imagination due to various texts surrounding its mystery. This experience is similar to what Emma McEvoy describes in *Gothic Tourism* in her analysis of Dennis Severs's house in Spitalfields:

> Severs' House blurs the boundaries between art and life and between temporalities. Things from both the past and present are placed side by side. The smell of rot that pervades the larger attic room, is not just pretend rot, a prop, a narrative device, a literary description. It exists here and now, as supposedly it did in the 1830s at the time of Victoria's coronation.[15]

The space under Newgate likewise exists in a paradoxical state: it is both a static symbol of a certain historical epoch, and part of modernity through the immersion of its visitors in the present day. As McEvoy goes on to state, Severs's house is 'a locale where the spaces of imagination are commandeered; where the material is spiritualized and the spiritual is materialized' (p. 90). The vaults under Newgate are a material reality, but from engagement with the manuscript, this space, to the narrator, becomes more than its physical reality and takes on a spiritual presence through the effect of literature. This period of criminal history becomes tangible as the space under Newgate, and can be referred to as what Mikhail Bakhtin finds as a chronotopic site, in that '[t]ime, as it were, thickens, takes on flesh, becomes artistically visible; likewise space becomes charged and responsive to movements of time, plot, and history.'[16] In the narrator's perception of history as fluid and adaptable, the very ability for it to be reimagined is what leads it to be both intriguing and misleading. In the underground space, the movement to present tense indicates a further time shift, and places the ghosts of the past firmly in the present as the narrator states:

> A sudden chill comes over me. My blood runs cold. What is it? Moving— yes, moving! Great God! it is the shadow upon the wall! The shadow of death which the excited imagination of Captain Hawk had made out to be the spirit of his father come to warn him of death, and to lead him to perdition. (p. 136)

The ghost of the past, the ghost which appeared to Hawk, becomes a present-day haunting and can move, like the narrator, through shifts in time.

Rymer's caution over statisticians and historians removing the romance of both history and literature is revealed further when the narrator expresses caution over a second visit to underground Newgate, stating that 'a second approach to anything which is strange and wonderful, and which has taken a strong hold of the imagination either in the way of the beautiful or the terrific has a strong tendency to expel the charm' (p. 187), as with Severs's house, which demands an 'ideal spectatorship' where 'visitors are expected to exert their imagination, but within certain limits: to have neither too little nor too much imagination' (McEvoy, p. 89). The narrator further asserts that curiosity is not enough to convince him to visit Newgate, and that it is not sufficient to simply want to 'wander about the gloomy passages and dream of the past', just as with the Gothic tourist McEvoy describes, attempting to place restrictions on his own imagination (*Newgate*, p. 319). Despite this assertion, however, the narrator makes repeated trips to Newgate and his exploits in the 'above ground' world are consumed by his Newgate investigation. Though he purports that his investigation is in aid of factual research, it is clearly driven, as indicated by the haunting presence of the manuscript's characters, by his romantic fascination with the space and its spiritual and literary significance.

Sophie Raine

Oral Storytelling, Polyphonic Voices, and the Penny's Literary Legacy

By utilising the manuscript trope, Rymer incorporates a range of narrators throughout the text who all compete for authority and narrative space. The polyphonic nature of Rymer's text provides a commentary on the way that non-fictional sources such as political and social histories and fictional works are recorded and preserved. In addition to the direct criticism of the way that officials or journalists document significant cultural or political events such as executions of high-profile criminals, Rymer further shows the inherited biases created through inaccurately transcribed oral histories. Moreover, the various narrators add further information to the documents held by the main narrator, supplementing crucial information; this suggests that a complete and accurate history is made impossible through the negation of less credible voices or less authoritative forms such as anecdotes.

The first keeper of Newgate's history, the unnamed old man who provides the manuscript to the narrator, describes himself as a 'living chronicle of those things which have been' (p. 9). The old man, however, as previously mentioned, dies shortly after, thereby exposing the limitations of record keeping and preservation. As with the decaying manuscript which is showing signs of wear, the reader is reminded of the perishable nature of working-class narratives. In a way, Rymer has a prescience about the knowledge that these texts will need to be preserved. Indeed, Rymer compiled various cuttings from his periodicals into sketchbooks and distributed them among his acquaintances; Rymer's desire to safeguard his precious yet perishable work has materialised, as these sketchbooks have since been donated to the British Library.[17] As numerous serials were not being collected into volumes, it was clear their longevity was severely limited in comparison to other forms of literature. These living chronicles are essential as a way of keeping working-class literature alive, and the difficulties of preserving the histories of marginalised groups such as the working classes; literature, for Rymer, was at risk of being diluted through the conservation of more authoritative, usually wealthy, sources. It can further be interpreted that Rymer was attempting to maintain and promote the tradition of oral storytelling; reading serial publications aloud would have been practised by many of Rymer's readers.

In *Voice and the Victorian Storyteller* (2005), Ivan Kreilkamp provides a thorough account of the decline of oral storytelling and how this was revived through the Victorian novel, which 'subsumes, transcends and reproduces speech'.[18] The penny dreadful is perhaps one of the most adept forms of Victorian fiction to do this by reproducing a multitude of voices, particularly evident in the work of George W. M. Reynolds, who often incorporated his own Chartist speeches in his prose – and vice versa, as thoughtfully examined by Mary L. Shannon in *Dickens, Reynolds, and Mayhew on Wellington Street: The Print Culture of a Victorian Street* (2016). Kreilkamp further argues that '[i]t becomes the novel's task to present the death of the speaker as a resurrection in print. By reincarnating the charismatic speaker as the author, the novel promises to reconstitute a society of dispersed and isolated readers as a community' (p. 23). Though in the case of *Newgate*, the charismatic storyteller is the narrator himself (and subsequently a variety of other characters who temporarily assume the role of the narrator), the relationship between the reader and the storyteller is explored throughout the text. Rymer represents the reader in the text – the narrator as reader of the manuscript, and his friend who listens as he narrates the stories contained within. As such, the characters in the text constitute this community of readers as they interject, scrutinise, and ask the questions that the reader may want to ask. The narrator presenting the story as it is unveiled to him aligns him to Rymer's readership and gives an interactive element to the text, a method of oral storytelling in the age of the printing press. The narrator indeed tries to create a sense of dialogue by positioning himself too as a reader. This is particularly made evident with the completion of the May Boyes story in which the narrator comments. While it would have been 'intrusive' to make 'any personal remark' during the narrative, once the story ends, the narrator confides the profound effect the story had on him, stating:

> I felt a fearful dread creep over me, that, ultimately, the mass of papers that lay before me, would record some frightful catastrophe as having happened to the beautiful and the gifted May Boyes. It was an exquisite relief to me to find that, after all, she suffered no more than I have

related. I certainly should have felt it keenly, had anything occurred to her to produce physical suffering, and, although I am far from underrating that which the beautiful girl endured, yet am I grateful to find that the truthful record from the old man's wallet has spared me a pang I almost anticipated it would have given me. (p. 125)

In the narrator taking on a dual role and anticipating the reactions of the reader, the narrative becomes a homage to traditional oral storytelling as well as illuminating how the written format, specifically through the faux-manuscript, can contain elements of reader interaction. The intimacy allegedly lost through oral storytelling is revived through the penny form. Moreover, Rymer draws attention to his own skill as a storyteller through his narrator in a way which once again points to the artificial nature of the supposed found manuscript.

The litany of voices used in *Newgate*, and in numerous other penny titles, emphasises the importance of a holistic range of sources for both accurately recording historical events and preserving a wider, more varied literary history. This is made apparent when the narrator and his companion are exploring underground Newgate and eavesdrop on two turnkeys, one of whom begins telling stories of his experiences with the supernatural. One of the turnkeys explains to his sceptical companion that he had been visited by the 'spectre of the iron room', a convicted murderer who was abandoned in the iron room of Newgate when his gaoler suddenly died; his dead body was found a week later (p. 416). For this portion of the narrative, the spectre narrates his own story – this additional level of removal away from the primary narrator further leads the reader to scrutinise the truthfulness of this story, and thereby the manuscript itself. While oral storytelling can provide intimacy between author and the reader community, it also decreases trust in the narrative whilst simultaneously evoking intrigue, mystery and romance.

The second, more sceptical or rational, turnkey admits that he too has heard voices from Newgate but dismisses this, commenting:

[i]f you were to disturb yourself about all the odd noises you might hear in Newgate, you would have enough to do. For my part, now,

when I do hear anything, I take it all quite easy and say nothing about it; and as nothing comes of it ever, that I know of, why I'm sure that is the best plan. (p. 416)

Rymer thereby reveals how an assemblage of different voices can give insight into the rich and complex tableau of city life. Rymer further emphasises that the contemporary reader has an appetite for fiction which engages with those from different classes, and places importance on the romance of experience rather than credibility and authority. The silence of the turnkeys not only adds to the cabalistic nature of Newgate, but also hints at the stories that are lost through the marginalisation of working-class voices and the privileging of only authoritative sources. Though the turnkeys disagree on whether there are ghosts that haunt Newgate, they both concur that working as a turnkey brings with it access to the secrets of criminals interred there, as '[t]hey knows as they can trust us, they does, and so we gets all the secrets as nobody else gets, and we keeps 'em as close as wax' (p. 422).

The disparate tastes of the reading public is reiterated in the conversation between the narrator and his friend who, upon hearing the turnkey's story, disagree on what they find more entertaining: while the narrator is fascinated by the contents of the manuscript, his friend finds the turnkey's 'brief but living chronicles of the times' to be of more interest than the manuscripts themselves (p. 422). However, both the narrator and his friend find the romance of these stories alluring despite their disagreement on whether historic or contemporary narratives are more entertaining. Rymer self-consciously bolsters not only the appeal of his own narrative, but penny dreadfuls more widely which featured a range of titles based on historic highwaymen such as Dick Turpin and Claude Duval and still included a range of urban Gothic narratives. Rymer appears to be suggesting that the penny form's incorporation of different styles, narratives and marginalised, often unheard voices was catering to a wider demographic who wanted to indulge in this new heterogeneous market.

By listening to these living chronicles in the space below Newgate, the characters are able to explore the secrets of the past and the present without fully participating in either. In determining to become participants rather than passive observers, and transform themselves into the characters they read about, the narrator decides to scare the turnkeys as a practical joke. The narrator states that 'it will be fine fun to hear, on another occasion, what they say about it' (p. 430). The narrator makes a 'diabolical noise' to startle the turnkeys into believing Newgate is haunted (p. 431). When the narrator becomes concerned that this jape may uncover them, his friend reassures him that it is unlikely that the guards will contact anyone in authority, saying:

> the turnkeys will keep this affair to themselves you may depend. It would be too good a thing not to be nursed up with care and attention for the long winter nights, and it will become such a stock anecdote that I'll be bound any new man that is employed at Newgate will have it related to him with so many additions, adaptations, and interlineations, that it will be quite a novelty for us to hear it. (p. 432)

Rymer here appears to embrace the recycling, repurposing and adapting narratives that both come from oral storytelling and were a key component of the penny publication market. While identifying the multitude of issues that can occur with documenting real events such as the memory of those who hear and retell the story as well as the narrator embellishing the narrative for entertainment purposes, Rymer thus promotes the recycling and adaptation of these stories for a new generation. All of these additional narrators – the criminals in the manuscripts, the turnkeys, the spectre – have their voices subsumed by the main narrator of the text. In ventriloquising their narratives, embellishing their stories with his own commentary, the reader becomes less certain over what is fact and what is fiction, what is serious documentary evidence and what is for entertainment.

Newgate's Continued Excavation

The combination of multiple styles, voices and frame narratives is typical of numerous penny texts, but few, if any, self-consciously deliberate on the nature of romantic Gothic fiction like Rymer's *Newgate*. Rymer's metafictional text revitalises the overused found manuscript trope, and uses it to comment on the adaptive style of the penny dreadful as well as addressing contemporary literary debates regarding fact and fancy in both fiction and journalism. This text is crucial in examining how working-class texts were actively encouraging their readers to scrutinise the accuracy of non-fictional sources whilst unapologetically celebrating reading imaginative, sensational literature for entertainment purposes.

Invoking the manuscript's fragmented form, *Newgate* ends with the story 'The Poisoner, or the Perils of Matrimony', and does not return to conclude the main frame narrative or explain to the reader what has become of the obsessive narrator. Admittedly, it is not clear whether this was intentional on Rymer's part as a way to continue the façade of the 'found manuscript', or issues with the publication that caused this abrupt conclusion. Whether intentional or not, by suddenly ending on the conclusion of a story from inside the manuscript, it is Rymer's reader who is left with the found manuscript as the narrator, the manuscript's owner, and our guide through the history of Newgate, abandons the reader in this fictitious space. It is significant that the reader's narrative journey ends in the past, rather than returning to the modern, above-ground metropolis as, like the narrator, the reader is left to linger in the past, suspended in this unfamiliar Gothic territory.

The text ends with the story of two lovers who, in their attempt to escape from the law, tunnel through the subterranean vaults of Newgate Prison and throw themselves down the well, plunging to their death. The manuscript states that 'to this day they lie two ghastly skeletons, locked in a horrible embrace of death' (p. 722). The text's main narrator does not, due to the finality of the manuscript, get the opportunity to try and find the remains of the two lovers, Marianna Wilmot and Edward Lancy, as he has done with other characters who have appeared in the manuscripts. It is left, then, for Rymer's reader to become the new obsessive owner of the manuscript, imagination incited by the story of Marianna and Edward, to continue the manuscript, picking up the threads from their previous guide and finally unearth Newgate's untold history.

Notes

1. Robert Mighall, *A Geography of Victorian Gothic Fiction: Mapping History's Nightmares* (Oxford: Oxford University Press, 2003), pp. 16–26.
2. Stephen Knight, *The Mysteries of the Cities: Urban Crime Fiction in the Nineteenth Century* (Jefferson, NC and London: McFarland and Co. Publishing, 2011), p. 9.
3. Rob Breton, *The Penny Politics of Victorian Popular Fiction* (Manchester: Manchester University Press, 2021), p. 47. While Breton attributes authorship of *Newgate* to Thomas Peckett Prest, work by Helen Smith in *New Light on Sweeney Todd, Thomas Peckett Prest, James Malcolm Rymer and Elizabeth Caroline Grey* (2002) makes a strong case for the likely author of the text being James Malcolm Rymer. Therefore, while authorship of penny serials is always uncertain, this chapter will attribute the text to James Malcolm Rymer in light of Smith's evidence.
4. Gary Kelly, *Newgate Narratives* (Abingdon: Routledge, 2016), p. xi.
5. See Ian Haywood, *The Revolution in Popular Literature: Print, Politics and the People, 1790–1860* (Cambridge: Cambridge University Press, 2004); Anne Humpherys, 'An Introduction to G. W. M. Reynolds's "Encyclopedia of Tales"', in *G. W. M. Reynolds: Nineteenth-Century Fiction, Politics, and the Press*, ed. Anne Humpherys and Louis James (Aldershot: Ashgate, 2008); Helen Hauser, 'Form and Reform in the "Miscellany Novel"', *Victorian Literature and Culture*, 41/1 (2013); and Anna Gasperini, *Nineteenth Century Popular Fiction, Medicine and Anatomy: The Victorian Penny Blood and the 1832 Anatomy Act* (Cham: Palgrave Macmillan, 2019).
6. L. Pykett, 'The Newgate Novel and Sensation Fiction, 1830–1868', in Martin Priestman (ed.), *The Cambridge Companion to Crime Fiction* (Cambridge: Cambridge University Press, 2003), pp. 19–40.
7. Diane Long Hoeveler, *Gothic Feminism: The Professionalization of Gender from Charlotte Smith to the Brontës* (University Park: Pennsylvania State University Press, 2010), p. 80.
8. Gasperini, *Nineteenth Century Popular Fiction, Medicine and Anatomy*, p. xi.
9. Timothy C. Baker, *Contemporary Scottish Gothic: Mourning, Authenticity, and Tradition*, (Basingstoke: Palgrave Macmillan, 2014), p. 55.
10. Helen R. Smith, *New Light on Sweeney Todd, Thomas Peckett Prest, James Malcolm Rymer and Elizabeth Caroline Grey* (London: Jarndyce, 2002), p. 20.

[11] James Malcolm Rymer, *Newgate: A Romance* (London: Edward Lloyd, 1846–7), p. 9.
[12] Dani Cavallaro, *Gothic Vision: Three Centuries of Horror, Terror and Fear* (London: Continuum, 2003), p. 115.
[13] Patricia Waugh, *Metafiction: The Theory and Practice of Self-Conscious Fiction* (London: Methuen, 1984), p. 4.
[14] 'From the Contemporary Press', *Globe* (12 October 1839), 4.
[15] Emma McEvoy, *Gothic Tourism* (London: Palgrave Macmillan, 2015), p. 92.
[16] Mikhail Bakhtin, *The Dialogic Imagination: Four Essays* (Austin: University of Texas Press, 1981), p. 84.
[17] Tales and sketches contributed by James M. Rymer to various periodicals (London: British Library, c. 1850). Variant vol. 2 title: 'Essays sketches &c, contributed by James M. Rymer to various periodicals'.
[18] Ivan Kreilkamp, *Voice and the Victorian Storyteller* (Cambridge: Cambridge University Press, 2005), p. 9.

List of Referenced Penny Titles, Organised by Date

෴

1. James Lindridge, *Jack Rann, Alias Sixteen-string Jack* (1840)
2. Timothy Portwine (pseud. Thomas Peckett Prest), *The Adventure of Valentine Vaux; or, The Tricks of a Ventriloquist* (1840)
3. Rip Rap, *The Monument; or, The Great Fire of London* (1841)
4. William Harrison Ainsworth, *Old St. Paul's* (1841)
5. Wizard, *The Wild Witch of the Heath; or, The Demon of the Glen, A Tale of the most Powerful Interest* (1841)
6. James Rymer, *Jane Brightwell* (1842–3)
7. James Malcolm Rymer, *Ada the Betrayed; or, The Murder at the Old Smithy. A Romance of Passion* (1842–3)
8. James Malcolm Rymer, *Manuscripts from the Diary of a Physician* (1844, 1847)
9. James Malcolm Rymer, *The Black Monk, or, The Secret of the Grey Turret* (1844–5)
10. James Malcolm Rymer, *Varney the Vampire* (1845–7)
11. George W. M. Reynolds, *Faust* (1845–6)
12. James Malcolm Rymer, *The Ordeal by Touch, a Romance* (1846)
13. Edward Bulwer-Lytton, *Lucretia, or the Poisoners* (1846)
14. James Malcolm Rymer, *The String of Pearls* (1846–7)

List of Referenced Penny Titles, Organised by Date

15. James Malcolm Rymer, *Newgate, A Romance* (1846–47)
16. George W. M. Reynolds, *Wagner, the Wehr-Wolf* (1846–7, 1857)
17. James Malcolm Rymer, *The Lady in Black, or, The Widow and the Wife* (1847)
18. George W. M. Reynolds, *The Mysteries of the Court of London* (1848–52)
19. Malcolm J. Errym (anagram of J. Malcom Rymer), *The Dark Woman, or Days of the Prince Regent* (1861)
20. Septimus R. Urban (pseudonym for James Malcolm Rymer), *The Vendetta; or A Lesson in Life* (1863), later known as *The Wronged Wife, or The Heart of Hate* (1870)
21. James Malcolm Rymer and Thomas Peckett Prest, *Varney the Vampire* (1845–7)
22. George W. M. Reynolds, *The Mysteries of London* (1844–8)
23. M. H. Ainsforth (pseudonym for Thomas Peckett Prest), *A Legend of Old St. Paul's* (1840–50)
24. James Malcolm Rymer, *The Sepoys, or, Highland Jessie: A Tale of the Present Indian Revolt* (1858)
25. Edward Ellis, *Ruth the Betrayer or The Female Spy* (1862–3)
26. Anonymous. *The Wild Boys of London, or The Children of the Night* (1864–6)
27. James Malcolm Rymer, *A Mystery in Scarlet* (1866)

Bibliography

'The 1848 Public Health Act', *UK Parliament* (n. d.), https://www.parliament.uk/about/living-heritage/transformingsociety/towncountry/towns/tyne-and-wear-case-study/about-the-group/public-administration/the-1848-public-health-act.

A'Beckett, Gilbert Abbott, *A Comic History of England*, 2nd edn, illustr. John Leech (London: John Dicks, 1880).

Adcock, John, 'Yesterday's Papers' (2008), http://john-adcock.blogspot.com/.

Ainsworth, W. H., *Old St. Paul's* (London: Collins Clear-Type Press, n. d.).

Alaimo, Stacy, *Bodily Natures: Science, Environment, and the Material Self* (Bloomington: Indiana University Press, 2010).

———, *Undomesticated Ground: Reclaiming Nature as Feminist Space* (Ithaca: Cornell University Press, 2000).

Anderson, Vicki, *The Dime Novel in Children's Literature* (Jefferson: McFarland & Company, Inc, 2005).

Anglo, Michael, *Penny Dreadfuls and Other Victorian Horrors* (London: Jupiter Books, 1977).

Anonymous, *Mysteries of Old St. Paul's: A Tale of the Plague* (London: George Vickers, 1841).

Anonymous, *Sweeney Todd, or The String of Pearls* (London: Wordsworth Editions Ltd, 2007).

Arata, Stephen D., *Fictions of Loss in the Victorian Fin de Siècle: Identity and Empire* (Cambridge: Cambridge University Press, 1996).

———, 'The Occidental Tourist: *Dracula* and the Anxiety of Reverse Colonization', *Victorian Studies*, 33/4 (1990), 621–45.

Auerbach, Nina, *Our Vampires, Ourselves* (Chicago: University of Chicago Press, 1995).

Babcock-Abrahams, Barbara, '"A Tolerated Margin of Mess": The Trickster and His Tales Reconsidered', *Journal of the Folklore Institute*, 11/3 (1975), 147–86.

Bailey, Peter, 'Breaking the Sound Barrier: A Historian Listens to Noise', *Body and Society*, 2/2 (1996), 49–66.

Baker, Timothy C., *Contemporary Scottish Gothic: Mourning, Authenticity, and Tradition* (Basingstoke: Palgrave Macmillan, 2014).

Bakhtin, Mikhail, *The Dialogic Imagination: Four Essays* (Austin: University of Texas Press, 1981).

Barger, Andrew (ed.), The *Best Werewolf Short Stories 1800–1849: A Classic Werewolf Anthology* (Collierville, TN: Bottletree Books, 2010).

Barnes, David S., *The Making of a Social Disease: Tuberculosis in Nineteenth-Century France* (Berkeley: University of California Press, 1995).

Barrow, Logie, 'An Imponderable Liberator: J. J. Garth Wilkinson', in Roger Cooter (ed.), *Studies in the History of Alternative Medicine* (Basingstoke: Macmillan, 1988), pp. 89–117.

Barstow, Anne Llewellyn, *Witchcraze: A New History of the European Witch Hunts* (San Francisco: Pandora, 1994).

Belanger, Jacqueline, Peter Garside and Anthony Mandal, *British Fiction, 1800–1829: A Database of Production and Reception–Phase II Report (February–November 2000) & Circulating-Library Checklist*; Cardiff Corvey, *Reading the Romantic Text* (Cardiff: Centre for Editorial and Intertextual Research, 2000), http://sites.cardiff.ac.uk/romtextv2/files/2013/02/dbf2.pdf.

Bergson, Henri, *Laughter: An Essay on the Meaning of the Comic*, trans. Cloudesley Brereton and Fred Rothwell (London: Macmillan and Co., 1911).

Berthin, Christine, *Gothic Hauntings, Melancholy Crypts and Textual Ghosts* (London: Palgrave Macmillan).

Blakey, Dorothy, *The Minerva Press, 1790–1820* (London: Oxford University Press, 1939).

Blécourt, Willem de, 'The Werewolf, the Witch, and the Warlock: Aspects of Gender in the Early Modern Period', in Alison

Rowlands (ed.), *Witchcraft and Masculinities in Early Modern Europe* (Basingstoke: Palgrave Macmillan, 2009), pp. 191–213.

Bond, C. G., *Sweeney Todd: The Demon Barber of Fleet Street* (London: Samuel French, 1973).

Botting, Fred, *Gothic* (London and New York: Routledge, 1996).

———, 'Monstrosity', in M. Mulvey-Roberts (ed.), *The Handbook of the Gothic* (Basingstoke: Palgrave Macmillan, 2009), pp. 204–5.

Boucher, Abigail, '"Her Princes Within Her Are Like Wolves": The Werewolf as a Catholic Force in *Wagner, the Wehr-Wolf*, *Revenant*, 2 (2016), 22–41.

Bourgault Du Coudray, Chantal, *The Curse of the Werewolf: Fantasy, Horror and the Beast Within* (London and New York: I. B. Tauris, 2006).

Breton, Rob, *The Penny Politics of Victorian Popular Fiction* (Manchester: Manchester University Press, 2021).

Brown, Charles Brockden, *Wieland; or The Transformation, and Memoirs of Carwin, the Biloquist* (Oxford: Oxford University Press, 2009).

Brown, Homer Obed, *Institutions of the English Novel: From Defoe to Scott* (Philadelphia: University of Pennsylvania Press, 1998).

Brown, Isaac Baker, *On the Curability of Certain Forms of Insanity, Epilepsy, Catalepsy, and Hysteria in Females* (London: Robert Hardwicke, 1866).

Brown, Jessica, *Cannibalism in Literature and Film* (London: Palgrave Macmillan, 2013).

Brown, Michael, *Performing Medicine: Medical Culture and Identity in Provincial England, c. 1760–1850* (Manchester: Manchester University Press, 2014).

Brown, P. S., 'Social Context and Medical Theory in the Demarcation of Nineteenth-Century Boundaries', in W. F. Bynum and Roy Porter (eds), *Medical Fringe and Medical Orthodoxy 1750–1850* (London: Croom Helm, 1987), pp. 216–33.

Budge, Gavin, *Romanticism, Medicine, and the Natural Supernatural: Transcendent Vision and Bodily Spectres, 1789–1852* (Basingstoke: Palgrave Macmillan, 2012).

Buel, James William, *Sea and Land: An Illustrated History of the Wonderful and Curious Things of Nature Existing before and since the Deluge* (Toronto: J. S. Robertson and Bros., 1887).

Bulwer-Lytton, Edward, *Lucretia: or, The Children of the Night*, 2 vols (Leipzig: Bernhard Tauchnitz, 1846).

Burgan, Mary, 'Mapping Contagion in Victorian London: Disease in the East End', in D. N. Mancoff and D. J. Trela (eds), *Victorian Urban Settings: Essays on the Nineteenth-Century City and Its Contexts* (New York: Routledge, 2015), pp. 43–56.

Burton, Brian J., *Sweeney Todd the Barber* (London: Samuel French, 1984).

Burz-Labrande, Manon, '"Useful knowledge" versus "wastes of print": Working-Class Education and Edward Lloyd', *Victorian Popular Fictions Journal*, 3/1 (Spring 2021), 123–39.

Butcher, Daisy, 'Introduction', in D. Butcher (ed.), *Evil Roots: Killer Tales of the Botanical Gothic* (London: British Library, 2019), pp. 7–10.

Carter, Robert Brudenell, *On the Pathology and Treatment of Hysteria* (London: John Churchill, 1853).

Cavallaro, Dani, *Gothic Vision: Three Centuries of Horror, Terror and Fear* (London: Continuum, 2003).

Chase, Malcolm, '"Stokesley Books": John Slater Pratt and Early Victorian Publishing', *International Journal of Regional and Local History*, 13/1 (2018), 32–46.

Cheap Books Published by Milner & Sowerby, Paternoster Row, London, and Sold by All Booksellers (London: Milner & Sowerby, 1866), digitised by the British Library at *http://access.bl.uk/item/viewer/ark:/81055/vdc_100037382337.0x000001*.

Clark, Stuart, 'Inversion, Misrule and the Meaning of Witchcraft', *Past & Present*, 87 (1980), 98–127.

Clayton, Edward, 'Aristotle: *Politics*', *The Internet Encyclopedia of Philosophy*, ISSN 1260-a11.*https://iep.utm.edu/aris-pol/*, 27 July 2005.

Cogan, Lucy, 'Introduction', in Charlotte Dacre, *Confessions of the Nun of St Omer* (Oxford: Routledge, 2016).

Cohen, Jeffrey Jerome, *Monster Theory: Reading Culture* (Minneapolis: University of Minnesota Press, 1996).

Colclough, Stephen, *Consuming Texts: Readers and Reading Communities, 1695–1870* (New York: Palgrave Macmillan, 2007).

Connor, Steven, *Dumbstruck: A Cultural History of Ventriloquism* (Oxford: Oxford University Press, 2004).

Cooke, J., *The Newgate Calendar or the Malefactors Bloody Register* (London: 1773).

Crawford, Joseph, *Gothic Fiction and the Invention of Terrorism: The Politics and Aesthetics of Fear in the Age of the Reign of Terror* (London: Bloomsbury, 2013).

Crone, Rosalind, 'From Sawney Beane to Sweeney Todd: Murder machines in the mid-nineteenth century metropolis', *Culture and Social History*, 7/1 (2010), 59–85.

——————, *Violent Victorians: Popular Entertainment in Nineteenth-Century London* (Manchester: Manchester University Press, 2012).

Crossen, Carys, *The Nature of the Beast: Transformations of the Werewolf from the 1970s to the Twenty-first Century* (Cardiff: University of Wales Press, 2019).

Dacre, Charlotte, *Confessions of the Nun of St Omer* (Oxford: Routledge, 2016).

Darwin, Erasmus, 'The Botanic Garden', in A. Komisaruk and A. Dushane (eds), *The Botanic Garden by Erasmus Darwin, Volume II* (London and New York: Routledge, 2017).

Davis, Jessica Milner, *Farce* (London: Methuen & Co Ltd, 1978).

Del Principe, David, 'Introduction: The EcoGothic in the Long Nineteenth Century', *Gothic Studies*, 16/1 (May 2014), 1–8.

Denning, Michael, *Mechanic Accents: Dime Novels and Working-Class Culture in America*, The Haymarket Series, rev. edn (London: Verso, 1998).

Diamond, Michael, 'From Journalism and Fiction into Politics', in Anne Humpherys and Louis James (eds), *G. W. M. Reynolds: Nineteenth-Century Fiction, Politics, and the Press* (London and New York: Routledge, 2008), pp. 91–8.

Dickens, Charles, *Oliver Twist, or, The Parish Boy's Progress* (London: Penguin Books, 2003).

——————, *The Pickwick Papers* (London: Amalgamated Press, 1905).

Dittmer, Nicole, 'Malignancy of Goneril: Nature's Powerful Warrior', in Krishanu Maiti and Soumyadeep Chakraborty (eds), *Global Perspectives on Eco-Aesthetics and Eco-Ethics: A Green Critique* (New York and London: Lexington Books, 2020), pp. 195–202.

———, 'Review: Nineteenth Century Popular Fiction, Medicine and Anatomy: The Victorian Penny Blood and the 1832 Anatomy Act by Anna Gasperini', *Gothic Studies*, 23/1 (2020): 123–5.

Dixon, William Hepworth, 'The Literature of the Lower Orders. Batch the First', *Daily News*, 440 (26 October 1847).

Dunae, Patrick, 'New Grub Street for Boys', in Jeffrey Richards (ed.), *Imperialism and Juvenile Literature* (Manchester, 1989), pp. 12–33.

Durey, Michael, *The Return of the Plague: British Society and the Cholera 1831–2* (Dublin: Gill and Macmillan, 1979).

Dziemianowicz, Stefan, *Penny Dreadfuls: Sensational Tales of Terror* (New York: Fall River Press, 2014).

Edgeworth, Maria, *Tales of Fashionable Life: Vivian*, 6 vols (London: J. Johnson and Co., 1812), https://www.google.co.uk/books/edition/Tales_of_Fashionable_Life_Vivian/K-s0AAAAMAAJ?hl=en&gbpv=0.

Elferen, Isabella van, *Gothic Music: The Sounds of the Uncanny* (Cardiff: University of Wales Press, 2012).

Eliot, Simon, 'From Few and Expensive to Many and Cheap: The British Book Market 1800–90', in Simon Eliot and Margaret Rose (eds), *A Companion to The History of the Book*, 2nd edn (Hoboken, NJ: Blackwell Publishing, 2020), pp. 471–84.

Ellis, Edward, *Ruth the Betrayer, or The Female Spy* (London: John Dicks, 1863).

Ellis, Sarah Stickney, *The Daughters of England: Their Position in Society, Character, and Responsibilities* (New York: D. Appleton and Company, 1842).

———, *The Wives of England: Their Relative Duties, Domestic Influence, and Social Obligations* (New York: D. Appleton & Company, 1843).

———, *The Women of England, Their Social Duties, and Domestic Habits* (New York: D. Appleton and Company, 1839).

Estok, Simon, 'Theorising the EcoGothic,' *Gothic Nature*, 1 (September 2019), 34–53.

Faller, Lincoln B., *Turned to Account. The Forms and Functions of Criminal Biography in Late Seventeenth- and Early Eighteenth-Century England* (Cambridge: Cambridge University Press, 1987).

Fisher, Mark, *Capitalist Realism: Is there No Alternative?* (Alresford: Zero Books, 2009).

Foucault, Michel, 'The Confession of the Flesh' (interview, 1977), in C. Gordon (ed.), *Power/Knowledge: Selected Interviews and Other Writings 1972–1977* (New York: Pantheon Books, 1980), pp. 194–228.

———, 'The Order of Discourse', in R. Young (ed.), *Untying the Text: A Post-Structuralist Reader* (Boston, London and Henley: Routledge & Kegan Paul, 1981), pp. 48–78.

Fraser, Robert, *Victorian Quest Romance: Stevenson, Haggard, Kipling and Conan Doyle*, Writers and Their Work (Liverpool: Liverpool University Press, 1998).

'From the Contemporary Prese', *Globe* (12 October 1839).

Frost, Brian J., *The Essential Guide to Werewolf Literature* (Madison: The University of Wisconsin Press, 2003).

Gamer, Michael, 'Gothic Fictions and Romantic Writing in Britain', in Jerrold P. Hogle (ed.), *The Cambridge Companion to the Gothic* (Cambridge: Cambridge University Press, 2002), pp. 85–104.

———, *Romanticism and the Gothic: Genre, Reception, and Canon Formation* (Cambridge: Cambridge University Press, 2004).

Garside, Peter, 'J. F. Hughes and the Publication of Popular Fiction, 1803–1810' (1987), *https://academic.oup.com/library/article-pdf/s6IX/3/240/9871843/240.pdf*.

Gasperini, Anna, *Nineteenth Century Popular Fiction, Medicine, and Anatomy: The Victorian Penny Blood and the 1832 Anatomy Act* (Cham: Springer International, 2019).

Gatrell, V. A. C., *The Hanging Tree: Execution and the English People 1770–1868* (Oxford: Oxford University Press, 1994).

Geier, Ted, *Meat Markets: The Cultural History of Bloody London* (Edinburgh: Edinburgh University Press, 2017).

George, Sam, and Bill Hughes (eds), *In the Company of Wolves: Werewolves, Wolves, and Wild Children* (Manchester: Manchester University Press, 2020).

Gilbert, Pamela K., *Cholera and Nation: Doctoring the Social Body in Victorian England* (Albany: State University of New York Press, 2008).

——————, *Mapping the Victorian Social Body* (Albany: State University of New York Press, 2004).

Goethe, Johann Wolfgang von, *Faust, Part I*, trans. David Constantine (London: Penguin Classics, 2005).

——————, *Faust, Part II*, trans. David Constantine (London: Penguin Classics, 2009).

Goodare, J., 'The Scottish Witchcraft Act', *Church History*, 74/1 (2005), 39–67.

Grant, Mary A. (trans.), *The Myths of Hyginus* (Lawrence: University of Kansas Press, 1960).

Greenwood, James, 'Penny Awfuls', *The St. Paul's Magazine*, XII (February 1873), 161–8.

——————, *Seven Curses of London* (London: S. Rivers, 1869).

——————, *The Wilds of London* (London: Chatto & Windus, 1874).

Griffin, Susan M., *Anti-Catholicism and Nineteenth Century Fiction* (Cambridge: Cambridge University Press, 2004).

Hacklenberg, Sara, 'Vampires and Resurrection Men: The Perils and Pleasures of the Embodied Past in 1840s Sensational Fiction', *Victorian Studies*, 52/1 (Autumn 2009), 63–75.

Haining, Peter, *Sweeney Todd: The Demon Barber of Fleet Street* (London: W. H. Allen, 1980).

——————, *The Penny Dreadful, Or, Strange, Horrid & Sensational Tales!* (London: Victor Gollancz Ltd, 1975).

——————, *Sweeney Todd: The Real Story of the Demon Barber of Fleet Street* (London: Boxtree, 1993).

Halberstam, J., *Skin Shows: Gothic Horror and the Technology of Monsters* (Durham, NC and London: Duke University Press, 1995).

Harrison, J. F. C., 'Early Victorian Radicals and the Medical Fringe', in W. F. Bynum and Roy Porter (eds), *Medical Fringe and Medical Orthodoxy 1750–1850* (London: Croom Helm, 1987), pp. 198–215.

Hauser, Helen, 'Form and Reform in the "Miscellany Novel"', *Victorian Literature and Culture*, 41/1 (2013), 21–40.

Haywood, Ian, *The Revolution in Popular Literature: Print, Politics and the People, 1790–1860* (Cambridge: Cambridge University Press, 2004).

Hazlitt, William Carew, *Lectures on the English Comic Writers* (London: John Templeman (1841).

―――――, *The Hazlitts: An Account of Their Origin and Descent: with Autobiographical Particulars of William Hazlitt (1778–1830), Notices of His Relatives and Immediate Posterity, and a Series of Illustrative Letters (1772–1865)* (Edinburgh: Ballantyne, Hanson & Co., 1911).

Hedges, Inez, *Framing Faust: Twentieth-Century Cultural Struggles* (Carbondale: Southern Illinois University Press, 2005).

'Heroism in India', *Reynolds's Miscellany*, 20/505 (1858).

Herr, Curt (ed.), 'Introduction', in James Malcolm Rymer, *The Black Monk, or, The Secret of the Grey Turret* (London: Valancourt Books, 2014), pp. vii–xix.

Herringer, Carol Engelhardt, 'Roman Catholicism in Britain and Ireland: On the Margins and in the Majority', *Victorian Review*, 46/2 (2020), 156–8.

Hester, Marianne, *Lewd Women and Wicked Witches: A Study of the Dynamics of Male Domination* (Routledge, 2003).

Hillard, Tom J., 'Deep into That Darkness Peering: An Essay on Gothic Nature', *ISLE*, 16/4 (Autumn 2009), 685–9.

Hills, Matt, 'Cutting into Concepts of "Reflectionist" Cinema: The *Saw* Franchise and Puzzles of Post-9/11 Horror', in Aviva Briefel and Sam J. Miller (eds), *Horror After 9/11: World of Fear, Cinema of Terror* (Austin: University of Texas Press, 2011), pp. 107–23.

Hodinott, Emma, 'The Early Gothic Romances of Regina Maria Roche and the Jane Austen Connection', The Corvey Project at Sheffield Hallam University, *https://extra.shu.ac.uk/corvey/corinne/1Roche/Roche%20and%20Jane%20Austen.ht*.

Hodgson, John A., 'An Other Voice: Ventriloquism in the Romantic Period', *Romanticism on the Net*, 16 (1999).

Hoeveler, Diane Long, *Gothic Feminism: The Professionalization of Gender from Charlotte Smith to the Brontës* (University Park: Pennsylvania State University Press, 2010).

———, *The Gothic Ideology: Religious Hysteria and Anti-Catholicism in British Popular Fiction, 1780–1880* (Cardiff: University of Wales Press, 2014).

———, *Gothic Riffs: Secularizing the Uncanny in the European Imaginary, 1780–1820* (Columbus: Ohio State University Press, 2010).

Höing, Anja, 'A retreat on the "river bank": perpetuating patriarchal myths in animal stories', in Douglas A. Vakoch and Sam Mickey (eds), *Women and Nature? Beyond Dualism in Gender, Body, and Environment* (Abingdon and New York: Routledge, 2018), pp. 27–42.

Horner, Avril, 'Victorian Gothic and National Identity: Cross-Channel "Mysteries"', in Andrew Smith and William Hughes (eds), *The Victorian Gothic: An Edinburgh Companion* (Edinburgh: Edinburgh University Press, 2012), pp. 108–23.

Houston, Gail Turley, 'Insanity', in James Eli Adams, Tom Pendergast and Sara Pendergast (eds), *The Victorian Encyclopedia*, vol. 2 (Danbury, CT: Grolier Academic, 2004), pp. 270–3.

Humpherys, Anne, 'An Introduction to G. W. M. Reynolds's "Encyclopedia of Tales"', in Anne Humpherys and Louis James (eds), *G. W. M. Reynolds: Nineteenth-Century Fiction, Politics, and the Press* (Aldershot: Ashgate, 2008), pp. 122–33.

———, 'G. W. M. Reynolds: Popular Literature and Popular Politics', *Victorian Periodicals Review*, 16/3–4 (Fall–Winter 1983), 79–89.

———, 'The Geometry of the Modern City: G. W. M. Reynolds and "The Mysteries of London"', *Browning Institute Studies*, 11 (1983), 69–80.

Hurren, Elizabeth, *Dying for Victorian Medicine: English Anatomy and its Trade in the Dead Poor, c. 1834–1929* (Basingstoke: Palgrave Macmillan, 2011).

Jackson, William, *The New and Complete Newgate Calendar; or, Villany Displayed in All its Branches* (London: Alex Hogg, 1795).

James, Elizabeth, and Helen R. Smith, *Penny Dreadfuls and Boys' Adventures: The Barry Ono Collection of Victorian Popular Literature in the British Library* (London: The British Library, 1998).

James, Louis, *Fiction for the Working-Man, 1830–1850* (London: Oxford University Press, 1963).

Johns, B. G., 'The Literature of the Streets', *Edinburgh Review*, 164 (1887), 40–65.

Johnson, Claudia L., '"Let Me Make the Novels of a Country": Barbauld's *The British Novelists* (1810/1820)', *NOVEL: A Forum on Fiction*, 34/2 (2001), 163–79.

Johnson, Steven, *The Ghost Map: A Street, an Epidemic and the Hidden Power of Urban Networks* (London: Penguin, 2008).

Jones, John Bush, *John Bush Jones, Our Musicals, Ourselves: A Social History of the American Musical Theater* (Lebanon, NH: Brandeis University Press, 2003).

Kantorowicz, Ernst H., *The King's Two Bodies: A Study in Mediaeval Political Theology* (Princeton: Princeton University Press, 1957).

Kelly, Gary, *English Fiction of the Romantic Period, 1789–1830* (London: Routledge, 1989).

——————, *Newgate Narratives* (Abingdon: Routledge, 2016).

——————, 'Sixpenny State? Cheap Print and Cultural-Political Citizenship in the Onset of Modernity', *Lumen*, 36 (2017), 37–61.

——————, 'The Popular Novel, 1790–1820', in J. A. Downie (ed.), *The Oxford Handbook of the Eighteenth-Century Novel* (Oxford: Oxford University Press, 2016), pp. 505–20.

——————, *Varieties of Female Gothic: Historical Gothic*, 6 vols (London: Pickering & Chatto, 2002).

Killeen, Jarlath, *Gothic Literature, 1825–1914* (Cardiff: University of Wales Press, 2009).

——————, 'Victorian Gothic Pulp Fiction', in Andrew Smith and William Hughes (eds), *Victorian Gothic: An Edinburgh Companion* (Edinburgh: Edinburgh University Press, 2012), pp. 43–56.

Killen, Alice M., *Le roman terrifiant ou roman noir: de Walpole à Anne Radcliffe et son influence sur la littérature française jusqu'en 1840*, Bibliothèque de la Revue de littérature comparée, 4 (Paris: Champion, 1923), https://books.google.ca/books?id=dRvLGj3RqbEC&pg=PA220.

King, Andrew, '*Reynolds's Miscellany*, 1846–1849: Advertising Networks and Politics', in Anne Humpherys and Louis James (eds), *G. W. M. Reynolds: Nineteenth-Century Fiction, Politics, and the Press* (Aldershot and Burlington, VT: Ashgate, 2008), pp. 53–74.

Kirkpatrick, Robert J., 'The Purkess Family of Dean Street', *Pennies, Profits and Poverty: A Biographical Directory of Wealth and Want in Bohemian Fleet Street* (London: CreateSpace Independent Publishing, 2016), pp. 66–75.

Knapp, Andrew, and William Baldwin, *The Newgate Calendar* (London: J. Robins and Co., 1824, 1826).

Knight, Stephen, *The Mysteries of the Cities: Urban Crime Fiction in the Nineteenth Century* (Jefferson, NC and London: McFarland and Co. Publishing, 2011).

Koch, Angela, '"The Absolute Horror of Horrors" Revised: A Bibliographical Checklist of Early-Nineteenth-Century Gothic Bluebooks'; Cardiff Corvey, *Reading the Romantic Text*, 9 (2002), 45–111.

Kramer, Heinrich, and James Sprenger, *The Malleus Maleficarum* (New York: Dover Publications, 1971 [1486]).

Kreilkamp, Ivan, *Voice and the Victorian Storyteller* (Cambridge: Cambridge University Press, 2005).

Kröger, Lisa, and Melanie R. Anderson, *Monster She Wrote: The Women Who Pioneered Horror & Speculative Fiction* (Philadelphia: Quirk Books, 2019).

Kudlick, Catherine, *Cholera in Post-Revolutionary Paris: A Cultural History* (Berkeley: University of California Press, 1996).

Laget, Pierre-Louis, 'Les lazarets et l'émergence de nouvelles maladies pestilentielles au XIXe et au début du XXe siècle', *In Situ*, 2 (2002).

Lamarck, Jean Baptiste Pierre Antoine de Monet de, *Zoological Philosophy: An Exposition with Regard to the Natural History of Animals*, trans. Hugh Elliott (London: Macmillan and Co., 1809/1914/2012).

Laycock, Thomas, *A Treatise on the Nervous Diseases of Women: Comprising an Inquiry into the Nature, Causes, and Treatment of Spinal and Hysterical Disorders* (London: Longman, Orme, Brown, Green and Longmans, 1840).

Ledoux, Ellen, 'Was there ever a "Female Gothic"?', *Palgrave Communications*, 3 (2017).

Léger-St-Jean, Marie, 'Price One Penny: Cheap Literature, 1837–1860', http://www.priceonepenny.info/index.php.

——————, 'Reprinting of first-wave Gothic novels in the 19th century: method and dataset', *Price One Penny*, new series, 27 September 2021, *https://popnewseries.hypotheses.org/574*.

LeGette, Casie, 'Reanimating Caleb Williams; or, How to Keep the 1790s Alive', in *Remaking Romanticism: The Radical Politics of the Excerpt* (Cham: Springer International Publishing, 2017), pp. 19–63.

Leprince, Chloé, 'Quand le père de Marcel Proust inventait le "cordon sanitaire"', *France Culture: Histoire* (9 March 2020), *https://www.franceculture.fr/histoire/quand-le-pere-de-marcel-proust-inventait-le-cordon-sanitaire*.

Lindridge, James, *Jack Rann, Alias Sixteen-string Jack* (London: G. Purkess, 1840).

'The Literature of Vice', *The Bookseller*, 110 (1867), 121–3.

Lloyd, Edward, *Penny Sunday Times and People's Police Gazette* (London, 1841–3).

Lodge, Mary Jo, 'From Madness to Melodramas to Musicals: The Women of Lady Audley's Secret and Sweeney Todd', *Theatre Annual: A Journal of Performance Studies*, 56/1 (2003), 78–96.

Looser, Devoney, 'The Porter Sisters, Women's Writing, and Historical Fiction', in Jacqueline M. Labbe (ed.), *The History of British Women's Writing, 1750–1830* (London: Palgrave Macmillan, 2010), pp. 233–53.

Lopez Szwydky, Lissette, 'Nineteenth-Century Tie-Ins, Commercial Extensions, and Participatory Culture', in *Transmedia Adaptation in the Nineteenth Century* (Columbus: Ohio State University Press, 2020), pp. 175–208.

Mack, Robert, *The Wonderful and Surprising History of Sweeney Todd: The Life and Times of an Urban Legend* (London: Continuum, 2007).

Mackey, J. S., 'Penny Dreadfuls and Spring-heeled Jack', in Clive Bloom (ed.), *The Palgrave Handbook of Steam Age Gothic* (London: Palgrave Macmillan, 2021), pp. 39–60.

Mahawatte, Royce, 'Horror in the Nineteenth Century: Dreadful Sensations, 1820–80', in Xavier Aldana Reyes (ed.), *Horror: A Literary History* (London: The British Library, 2020), pp. 77–101.

Maran, Timo, *Ecosemiotics: The Study of Signs in Changing Ecologies* (Cambridge and New York: Cambridge University Press, 2020).

Marlowe, Christopher, *Doctor Faustus*, ed. David Scott Kastan (New York and London: W. W. Norton & Company, 2005).

Martineau, Harriet, *Deerbrook* (London: Smith, Elder, and Co., 1817 [1839]).

Maxwell, Jr, Richard C., 'G. M. Reynolds, Dictions and the Mysteries of London', *Nineteenth-Century Fiction*, 32/2 (September 1977), 188–213.

Mayne, Fanny, *The Perilous Nature of the Penny Periodical Press* (London: Oxford Printing Press for Private Circulation, 1852).

McCalman, Iain, *Radical Underworld: Prophets, Revolutionaries, and Pornographers in London, 1795–1840* (Oxford: Clarendon Paperbacks, 1993).

McClean, Thomas, 'Hero between Genres: Jane Porter's *Thaddeus of Warsaw*', in *The Other East and Nineteenth-Century British Literature: Imagining Poland and the Russian Empire* (London : Palgrave Macmillan, 2012), pp. 66–87.

McDowell, Stacey, 'Penny Dreadfuls', in William Hughes, David Punter and Andrew Smith (eds), *The Encyclopedia of the Gothic* (Hoboken, NJ: Wiley-Blackwell, 2016), pp. 489–90.

McEvoy, Emma, *Gothic Tourism* (London: Palgrave Macmillan, 2015).

McLean, Thomas, 'Hero between Genres: Jane Porter's *Thaddeus of Warsaw*', in *The Other East and Nineteenth-Century British Literature: Imagining Poland and the Russian Empire* (London: Palgrave Macmillan, 2012), pp. 66–87.

McNally, David, *Monsters of the Market: Zombies, Vampires and Global Capitalism* (Leiden: Brill, 2010).

McWilliam, Rohan, 'Sweeney Todd and the Chartist Gothic: Politics and Print Culture in Early Victorian Britain', in Sarah Louise Lill and Rohan McWilliam (eds), *Edward Lloyd and his World: Popular Fiction, Politics, and the Press in Victorian Britain* (London: Routledge, 2019), pp. 198–215.

Medcraft, John, *Bibliography of the Penny Bloods of Edward Lloyd* (London: J. A. Birkbeck, 1945).

Merchant, Carolyn, *The Death of Nature: Women, Ecology, and the Scientific Revolution* (New York: Harper Collins, 1980).

Mighall, Robert, *A Geography of Victorian Gothic Fiction: Mapping History's Nightmares* (Oxford: Oxford University Press, 1999).

———, 'Gothic cities', in C. Spooner and E. McAvoy (eds), *The Routledge Companion to Gothic* (Abingdon: Routledge, 2007), pp. 54–62.

Miles, Robert, *Ann Radcliffe: The Great Enchantress* (Manchester: Manchester University Press, 1995).

Miley, Ursula, and John Pickstone, 'Medical Botany around 1850: American Medicine in Industrial Britain', in Roger Cooter (ed.), *Studies in the History of Alternative Medicine* (Basingstoke: Macmillan, 1988), pp. 140–54.

Miller, Dean A., *The Epic Hero* (Baltimore: Johns Hopkins University Press, 2000).

Miller, Peter, and T. Fothergill, *William Milner of Halifax, Printer and Publisher: Checklist of a Collection of Books Printed by William Milner and His Successors and Imitators* (York: Ken Spelman, 1991).

Miller, Peter, and Randall Lewton, *The Sweeney Todd Shock 'n' Roll Show* (London: Samuel French, 1980).

Miller, William Ian, *The Anatomy of Disgust* (Cambridge: Harvard University Press, 1998).

Millingen, John, *The Passions; or, Mind and Matter* (London: John and Daniel A. Darling, 1848).

Millsap-Spears, Carey, '"How about a pie?": Mrs. Lovett, "Sweeney Todd" and the Double', *Studies in Popular Culture*, 35/2 (2013), 111–27.

Mollin, Alfred, 'Mayhem and Morality in Sweeney Todd', *American Music*, 9/4 (1991), 405–17.

Morris, R. J., *Cholera 1832: The Social Response to an Epidemic* (London: Croom Helm, 1976).

Moruzi, Kristine, and Michelle J. Smith, 'Introduction', in Kristine Moruzi and Michelle J. Smith (eds), *Young Adult Gothic Fiction: Monstrous Selves/Monstrous Others* (Cardiff: University of Wales Press, 2021), pp. 1–14.

Mulvey-Roberts, Marie, 'The Female Body', in Avril Horner and Sue Zlosnik (eds.), *Women and the Gothic: An Edinburgh Companion* (Edinburgh: Edinburgh University Press, (2016), pp. 106–19.

Munson Deats, Sara, *The Faust Legend: From Marlowe and Goethe to Contemporary Drama and Film* (Cambridge: Cambridge University Press, 2019).

Bibliography

Neiman, Elizabeth, *Minerva's Gothics: The Politics and Poetics of Romantic Exchange, 1780–1820* (Cardiff: University of Wales Press, 2019).

Nesvet, Rebecca, '1837: "Miss Whitehead, The Bank Nun"', in Dino Franco Felluga (ed.), *BRANCH* (2020), https://www.branchcollective.org/?ps_articles=rebecca-nesvet-miss-whitehead-the-bank-nun.

———, 'The Bank Nun's Tale: Financial Forgery, Gothic Imagery, and Economic Power', *Victorian Network*, 8 (2018), 83–7.

———, 'The Mystery of *Sweeney Todd*: G.A. Sala's Desperate Solution'. *Victorian Institute Journal*, 47 (2019–20), n. p.

———, '*The Spaniard* and Sweeney Todd', *Notes and Queries*, 64/1 (2017), 112–16.

———, 'Sweeney Todd's Indian Empire: Mapping the East India Company in The String of Pearls', *Victorian Popular Fictions Journal*, 1/2 (2019), 75–90.

Neuburg, Victor E., *Popular Literature: A History and Guide: From the Beginning of Printing to the Year 1897* (Harmondsworth: Penguin, 1977).

The New Newgate Calendar: Containing a Complete History of the Remarkable Lives and Trials of Notorious Criminals Past and Present (London: E. Harrison, 1863).

Nöth, Winfried, 'Ecosemiotics and the Semiotics of Nature', *Sign Systems Studies*, 29/1 (2001), 71–81.

Oliphant, Margaret, 'The Byways of Literature: Reading for the Million', *Blackwood's Edinburgh Magazine*, 84 (August 1858), 200–16.

Ortner, Sherry B., 'Is Female to Male as Nature is to Culture?', in M. Z. Rosaldo and L. Lamphere (eds), *Women, Culture, and Society* (Stanford: Stanford University Press, 1974), pp. 68–87.

Owen, Robert, *Lectures on the Marriages of the Priesthood of the Old Immoral World, Delivered in the Year 1835, Before the Passing of the New Marriage Act* (Leeds: J. Hobson, 1840).

Parker, Elizabeth, *The Forest and the EcoGothic: The Deep Dark Woods in the Popular Imagination* (London: Palgrave Macmillan, 2020).

Patmore, Coventry, *The Angel in the House* (London: John W. Parker and Son, 1858).

Pelham, Camden, *The Chronicles of Crime or The New Newgate Calendar* (London: Thomas Tegg, 1841).
Pelling, Margaret, *Cholera, Fever and English Medicine, 1825–1865* (Oxford: Oxford University Press, 1978).
The Penny Satirist (August 1838), 4.
Piatti-Farnell, Lorna, *Consuming Gothic: Food in Horror and Film* (London: Palgrave Macmillan, 2017).
Pitt, George Dibdin, *Sweeney Todd* (Cabin John, MD: Wildside Press, 2002).
Pittard, Christopher, *Purity and Contamination in Late Victorian Detective Fiction* (Farnham: Ashgate, 2011).
Poovey, Mary, *Making a Social Body: British Cultural Formation, 1830–1864* (Chicago: University of Chicago Press, 1995).
Pope, Anne-Marie, 'American Dime Novels, 1860–1915', *Historical Association: The Voice for History* (2020).
Porter, Dorothy, and Porter, Roy, *In Sickness and in Health: The British Experience 1650–1850* (London: Fourth Estate, 1988).
Portwine, Timothy, *The Adventure of Valentine Vaux; or, The Tricks of a Ventriloquist* (London: E. Lloyd, 1840).
Potter, Franz J., *Gothic Chapbooks, Bluebooks and Shilling Shockers, 1797–1830* (Cardiff: University of Wales Press, 2021).
——————, *The History of Gothic Publishing, 1800–1835: Exhuming the Trade* (Basingstoke: Palgrave Macmillan, 2005).
Powell, Sally, 'Black markets and cadaverous pies: the corpse, urban trader and industrial consumption in the penny blood', in A. Maunder and G. Moore (eds), *Victorian Crime, Madness and Sensation* (Aldershot: Ashgate, 2004), pp. 45–58.
Power, Albert, 'Regina Maria Roche (1764–1845)', *The Green Book: Writings on Irish Gothic, Supernatural and Fantastic Literature*, 11 (2018), 35–41.
Price, Cheryl Blake, 'Vegetable Monsters: Man-Eating Trees in Fin-de-Siècle Fiction', *Victorian Literature and Culture*, 41 (2013), 311–27.
Price, Fiona, 'Conserving Histories: Chivalry, Science and Liberty', in *Reinventing Liberty: Nation, Commerce and the British Historical Novel from Walpole to Scott* (Edinburgh: Edinburgh University Press, 2016), pp. 135–70.

Bibliography

Priest, Hannah, 'Black Weddings and Black Mirrors: Gothic as Transgeneric Mode', in Jolene Zigarovich (ed.), *TransGothic in Literature and Culture* (New York and Abingdon: Routledge, 2017), pp. 199–217.

———, 'Like Father Like Son: Wolf-Men, Paternity and the Male Gothic', in Robert McKay and John Miller (eds), *Werewolves, Wolves and the Gothic* (Cardiff: University of Wales Press, 2017), pp. 19–36.

'Printing and Other Companies', *The Printing Times and Lithographer* (London: Wyman & Sons, 15 March 1883).

Punter, David, *The Literature of Terror: A History of Gothic Fiction from 1765 to the Present Day* (London & New York: Longman, 1980).

Punter, David, and Glennis Byron, *The Gothic* (Carlton, Victoria: Blackwell Publishing, 2004).

Pykett, L., 'The Newgate Novel and Sensation Fiction, 1830–1868', in Martin Priestman (ed.), *The Cambridge Companion to Crime Fiction* (Cambridge: Cambridge University Press, 2003).

Radcliffe, Ann, *The Castles of Athlin and Dunbayne* (London: Simon Fisher, 1823), https://www.google.co.uk/books/edition/The_Castles_of_Athlin_and_Dunbayne/92Vc2TuApO8C?hl=en&gbpv=0.

Raine, Sophie, 'Subterranean Spaces in the Penny Dreadful', in Clive Bloom (ed.), *The Palgrave Handbook of Steam Age Gothic* (London: Palgrave Macmillan, 2021), pp. 61–76.

Rap, Rip, *The Monument; or, The Great Fire of London* (London: Samuel Haddon, 1841).

Rede, Leman, *Sixteen-string Jack* (London: G. H. Davidson, 1823).

Reeve, Clara, *The Old English Baron* (Oxford: Oxford University Press, 2003).

Reeves, John K., 'The Mother of *Fatherless Fanny*', *ELH*, 9/3 (1942), 224–33.

Reis, Elizabeth, *Damned Women: Sinners and Witches in Puritan New England* (Ithaca and London: Cornell University Press, 1997).

——— (ed.), *Spellbound: Women and Witchcraft in America* (Lanham and Oxford: SR Books, 1998).

A Retail Catalogue of Books (London: Milner & Co., n. d.), https://books.google.ca/books?id=v186ehMjXmYC&pg=RA8-PA1.

Bibliography

Reyes, Xavier Aldana, *Spanish Gothic: National Identity, Collaboration and Cultural Adaptation* (London: Palgrave Macmillan, 2017).

Reynolds, George W. M., *Faust* 1, 1845 (Manchester: Hic Dragones, 2016).

———, *Faust* 2, 1846 (Manchester: Hic Dragones, 2016).

———, *Faust* 3, 1846 (Manchester: Hic Dragones, 2016).

———, *Faust* 7, 1846 (Manchester: Hic Dragones, 2016).

———, *Faust* 11, 1846 (Manchester: Hic Dragones, 2017).

———, *Manuscripts from the Diary of a Physician*, 2 vols (London: E. Lloyd, 1844, 1847).

———, *The Mysteries of London*, 4 vols (London: George Vickers, 1846–8).

———, *The Mysteries of London*, 1846 (Manchester: Hic Dragones, 2016).

———, *Wagner, the Wehr-Wolf*, 1846 (Manchester: Hic Dragones, 2015).

Rezek, Joseph, 'Bentley's Standard Novelist: James Fenimore Cooper', in Paul Westover and Ann Wierda Rowland (eds), *Transatlantic Literature and Author Love in the Nineteenth Century* (Cham: Springer International Publishing, 2016), pp. 49–74.

Rogers, Deborah D., 'Primary Bibliography: Editions and Translations', in *Ann Radcliffe: A Bio-Bibliography* (London: Greenwood Press, 1996), pp. 23–34, http://hdl.handle.net/2027/mdp.39015037833285.

Roper, Lyndal, *Oedipus and the Devil: Witchcraft, Religion and Sexuality in Early Modern Europe* (London and New York: Routledge, 1994).

Rosser, Austin, *Sweeney Todd: The Demon Barber of Fleet Street* (London: Samuel French, 1971).

Ruskin, John, 'Lecture II, Lilies: Of Queens' Gardens', in *Sesame and Lilies*, Harvard Classics, 28 (London and New York, 1865).

Rymer, Gaven, 'Fawkes Guy, or the Fifth of November': plate no. 6 from *London Scenes*, 1834. Lithograph, *London Metropolitan Archives*, no. 1, 239–846.

Rymer, James Malcolm, *Ada the Betrayed; or, The Murder at the Old Smithy. A Romance of Passion* (Fairford: Echo Library, 2015).

———, *The Black Monk, or, The Secret of the Grey Turret*, ed. Curt Herr (London: Valancourt Books, 2014).

———, *A Mystery in Scarlet*, in *The London Miscellany*, 1/18 (1866).

———, *Newgate: A Romance* (London: Edward Lloyd, 1846–7).

———, *The Ordeal by Touch: A Romance* (London: Edward Lloyd, 1846).

———, *The Sepoys, or, Highland Jessie: A Tale of the Present Indian Revolt*, in *Reynolds's Miscellany*, 20–1/504–541 (1858).

———, *Sweeney Todd, the Demon Barber of Fleet Street*, ed. Robert L. Mack (Oxford: Oxford University Press, 2007).

Sadleir, Michael, *XIX Century Fiction: A Bibliographical Record Based on His Own Collection*, vol. 2 of 2 (London: Constable, 1951).

Schimmel, Annemarie, *The Mystery of Numbers* (New York: Oxford University Press, 1993).

Schmid, Susanne, 'Eighteenth-Century Travellers and the Country Inn', in S. Schmid and B. Schmidt-Haberkamp (eds), *Drink in the Eighteenth and Nineteenth Centuries* (London: Pickering & Chatto, 2014), pp. 59–70.

Schöberlein, Stefan, 'Speaking in Tongues, Speaking without Tongues: Transplanted Voices in Charles Brockden Brown's *Wieland*', *Journal of American Studies*, 51/2 (2017), 535–52.

Schulte, Rolf, '"She Transformed into a Werewolf, Devouring and Killing Two Children": Trials of She-Werewolves in Early Modern French Burgundy', in Hannah Priest (ed.), *She-Wolf: A Cultural History of Female Werewolves* (Manchester: Manchester University Press, 2015), pp. 41–58.

Schülting, Sabine, *Dirt in Victorian Literature and Culture: Writing Materiality* (New York: Routledge, 2016).

Scott, Sir Walter, 'Charlotte Smith', in *Miscellaneous Prose Works: Biographical Memoirs*, 6 vols (Edinburgh: Cadell and Co., 1827).

———, 'Prefatory Memoir to Mrs Ann Radcliffe', in *The Novels of Mrs Ann Radcliffe* (London: Hurst, Robinson, and Co., 1824), pp. i–xxxix.

Shea, Victor, 'Penny Dreadfuls', in James Eli Adams, Tom Pendergast and Sara Pendergast (eds), *Encyclopedia of the Victorian Era* (Danbury, CT: Grolier Academic Reference, 2004), pp. 185–6.

Shepard, Leslie, *The History of Street Literature: The Story of Broadside Ballads, Chapbooks, Proclamations, News-Sheets, Election Bills, Tracts,*

Pamphlets, Cocks, Catchpennies, and other Ephemera (Detroit: Singing Tree Press, 1973).

Shoemaker, Robert B., 'The Street Robber and the Gentleman Highwayman: Changing Representations and Perceptions of Robbery in London, 1690–1800', *Cultural and Social History*, 3 (2006), 381–405.

Showalter, Elaine, 'On Hysterical Narrative', *Narrative*, 1/1 (Winter 1993), 24–35.

Smart, Carol, *Regulating Womanhood* (London: Routledge, 2002).

Smith, Adam, *An Inquiry into the Nature and Causes of the Wealth of Nations* (MetaLibri, 2007).

Smith, Allan Lloyd, *American Gothic Fiction: An Introduction* (New York and London: Continuum, 2004).

Smith, Andrew, *Gothic Death 1740–1914: A Literary History* (Manchester: Manchester University Press, 2016).

Smith, Andrew, and William Hughes (eds), *EcoGothic* (Manchester: Manchester University Press, 2013).

Smith, Helen R., *New Light on Sweeney Todd, Thomas Peckett Prest, James Malcolm Rymer, and Elizabeth Caroline Grey* (London: Jarndyce, 2002).

Sondheim, Stephen, *Sweeney Todd: The Demon Barber of Fleet Street* (London: Nick Hern Books, 1980).

Sparks, Tabitha, *The Doctor in the Victorian Novel: Family Practices* (Farnham: Ashgate, 2009).

Speaight, George, *The History of the English Toy Theatre*, revised edn (London: Studio Vista, 1969).

Springhall, John, '"A Life Story for the People"? Edwin J. Brett and the London "Low-Life" Penny Dreadfuls of the 1860s', *Victorian Studies*, 33/2 (Winter 1990), 223–46.

——————, '"Pernicious Reading"? "The Penny Dreadful" as Scapegoat for Late-Victorian Juvenile Crime', *Victorian Periodicals Review*, 27/4 (Winter 1994), 326–49.

——————, *Youth, Popular Culture and Moral Panics: Penny Gaffs to Gansta-Rap, 1830–1996* (London: Palgrave, 1998).

St Clair, William, *The Reading Nation in the Romantic Period* (Cambridge: Cambridge University Press, 2004).

Steven, Mark, *Splatter Capital: The Political Economy of Gore Films* (London: Repeater Books, 2017).

Bibliography

Straight, Sheryl 'The Erotica Bibliophile' (2006), https://www.eroticabibliophile.com/publishers_dugdale_title.php.

Summers, Montague, *A Gothic Bibliography* (London: Fortune Press, 1940).

―――, *The Gothic Quest: A History of the Gothic Novel* (New York: Russel & Russel, 1964).

Summerscale, Kate, *The Wicked Boy: The History of a Victorian Child Murderer* (New York: Penguin Press, 2016).

Sweeney Todd: The Demon Barber of Fleet Street (2007), directed by Tim Burton. Paramount Pictures.

Sweet, Matthew, *Inventing the Victorians* (London: Faber and Faber, 2001).

Thackeray, William Makepeace, *Vanity Fair* (Oxford: Oxford University Press, 2008).

Thomas, Trefor, 'Introduction', in G. W. M. Reynolds, *The Mysteries of London* (Keele: Keele University, 1998).

Topham, Jonathan R., 'John Limbird, Thomas Byerley, and the Production of Cheap Periodicals in the 1820s', *Book History*, 8/1 (2005), 75–106.

Turner, E. S., *Boys will be Boys: The Story of Sweeney Todd, Deadwood Dick, Sexton Blake, Billy Bunter, Dick Barton, et al.* (London: Michael Joseph Ltd, 1975).

University of Bristol Library Catalogue, https://bris.on.worldcat.org/oclc/931266932.

Valera, Luca, 'Françoise d'Eaubonne and Ecofeminism: Rediscovering the Link between Women and nature', in Douglas A. Vakoch and Sam Mickey (eds), *Women and Nature? Beyond Dualism in Gender, Body, and Environment* (Abingtdon and New York: Routledge, 2018), pp. 10–24.

Vargo, Gregory, *An Underground History of Early Victorian Fiction: Chartism, Radical Print Culture, and the Social Problem Novel* (Cambridge: Cambridge University Press, 2018).

Vasconcelos, Sandra Guardini T., 'From the French or Not: Transatlantic Contributions to the Making of the Brazilian Novel', in Leslie Howsam and James Raven (eds), *Books Between Europe and the Americas: Connections and Communities, 1620–1860* (Basingstoke: Palgrave Macmillan, 2011), pp. 212–32.

'The Vegetable Kingdom. The Upas Tree', *The Student: A Magazine of Theology, Literature, and Science, Vol. I* (London: James Gilbert, 1844), pp. 37–40.

Voltmer, Rita, 'The Judge's Lore? The Politico-Religious Concept of Metamorphosis in the Peripheries of Western Europe', in Willem de Blécourt (ed.), *Werewolf Histories* (Basingstoke: Palgrave Macmillan, 2015), pp. 185–204.

Wahrman, Dror, *The Making of the Modern Self: Identity and Culture in Eighteenth-Century England* (New Haven: Yale University Press, 2006).

Walkowitz, Judith R., *Prostitution and Victorian Society: Women, Class, and the State* (Cambridge: Cambridge University Press, 1980).

Ward, Frederick Oldfield, 'Sanitary Consolidation', *Quarterly Review*, 88 (March 1851), 435–92.

Waugh, Patricia, *Metafiction: The Theory and Practice of Self-Conscious Fiction* (London: Methuen, 1984).

Weltman, Sharon A., 'Boz versus Bos in Sweeney Todd: Dickens, Sondheim, and Victorianness', *Dickens Studies Annual*, 42/1 (2011), 55–76.

White, John, *Some Account of the Proposed Improvements of the Western Part of London, by the Formation of the Regent's Park, the New Street, the New Sewer, &c. &c.* (London: W. & P. Reynolds, 1814).

Wicks, Ulrich, 'The Nature of Picaresque Narrative: A Modal Approach', *PMLA*, 89/2 (1974), pp. 240–9.

Williams, Anne, 'Wicked Women', in Avril Horner and Sue Zlosnik (eds), *Women and the Gothic: An Edinburgh Companion* (Edinburgh: Edinburgh University Press, 2016), pp. 91–105.

Williams, Selma R., and Pamela Williams Adelman, *Riding the Nightmare: Women and Witchcraft from the Old World to Colonial Salem* (New York: Perennial, 1992).

Winslow, Forbes, 'Woman in Her Psychological Relations', *Journal of Psychological Medicine and Mental Pathology*, 4/13 (January 1851).

Wizard, *The Wild Witch of the Heath; or. The Demon of the Glen, A Tale of the most Powerful Interest* (London: T. White, 1841).

Wroot, Herbert E., 'A Pioneer in Cheap Literature, William Milner of Halifax', *The Bookman* (London: Hodder and Stoughton, March 1897), 169–75.

Bibliography

Yeo, Eileen, 'Culture and Constraint in Working-Class Movements, 1830–55', in E. and S. Yeo (eds), *Popular Culture and Class Conflict 1590–1914* (Brighton: Harvester Press, 1981), pp. 154–86.

Index

A

A'Beckett, Gilbert Abbott 193
Ada, the Betrayed, or, the Murder in the Old Smithy 183–4
  see also James Malcolm Rymer
adaptation 14–16, 28, 48–56, 58, 60–2, 132, 209, 216
Adcock, John 13
  'Yesterday's Papers' 13
'Address' 181
affectation 141, 148, 150, 153
Age of Enlightenment 143
Ahib, Jeffur 194–7
Ainsworth, William Harrison, 17, 120, 128–32
Alaimo, Stacy 155
Aldana Reyes, Xavier 40–1
Allen, Benjamin 'Ben' 119
  Pickwick Papers 119
ambivalent heroism 164
American culture 34, 52
An Inquiry into the Nature and Causes of the Wealth of Nations 49
  Smith, Adam 49–50
anachronism 185
anaemia 101
anatomy/anatomist(s) 16, 57, 62, 103, 115–16, 118, 121, 124–5, 132, 187
Anatomy Act 16, 115, 118, 121, 124–5, 132

Anatomy Act (1832) 16, 115, 118, 121, 124–5, 132
Anderson, Vicki 7–8, 10
angel/whore 141, 150
Angela, the Orphan; or, the bandit monk of Italy 38
Anglican 188, 191–2, 196
Anglo, Michael 6
animal sexuality 141
animism/animality 151, 157
Anne of Geierstein, or The Maid of the Mist 72
anti-Catholicism 69, 181, 185, 189, 191, 197
anti-European 69, 80
anti-hero/anti-heroine/anti-heroism 76
Antiaris toxicaria 104–106
antigothic 203
Arata, Stephen D. 105
archives 204
aristocrats 130, 195
Asiatic cholera 116, 127
asylum incarceration 169, 173
atmosphere 95, 116–17, 146
audience 2, 5, 9–10, 12, 17–18, 32, 48, 52, 59, 61, 80, 120, 124, 128, 165, 175, 181, 188
  see also readership
authority 16, 96, 107, 125–6, 133, 168, 170, 176, 195, 203, 208, 212, 215–16

Index

authorship 13–14, 33, 93
auto da fé 79
autopsy 13

B

Bakhtin, Mikhail 210
Ballantyne's Novelist's Library 30–6, 39, 41
Barbauld, Anna Laetitia 30–1, 34–5, 40–1
Barger, Andrew 87
Barry Ono Collection 14
Beckford, William 34, 195
Beggar's Opera, The 168
Belanger, Jacqueline 32
Bentley's Standard Novels 34–5, 37, 39
Berger, George 37
Bergson, Henri 171
Berthin, Christine 4
biology 18, 138, 140, 144, 148
biopower 94, 96
Blècourt, Willem de 76
bluebooks 11
bodily health 101
Bodleian Library 32–3
body-snatchers/body-snatching 120, 122
body horror 66, 75, 79, 82
body politics 102, 145, 189
Bond, C. G. 47, 50–4, 56–7, 60–2
Botanic Garden, The 105–6
botanical Gothic 94, 104–6
botany/botanists 104
Black Forest, The, or The Solitary of the Hut 38, 74
Black Monk, or, the Secret of the Grey Turret, The 12, 184
Botting, Fred 92, 108, 143, 169
Boucher, Abigail 75, 86
Boyes, May 209, 213
Bramstone, Septimus 170–1
Bravo of Venice, The 34–5, 37
Brent, Sir Rupert 187–8
Breton, Rob 5, 201, 218
British Library, The 212

British Novelists, The 30–1, 33, 35, 39–40
broadsheets 76
broadsides 8, 10, 27
Brontë, Charlotte 1
Brontë, Emily 1
Brown, Charles Brocken 172
Brown, Homer Obed 30
Brown, Isaac Baker 166
Brown, Jessica 52–3, 62
Brown, Michael 116, 118
Brown, P. S. 118
Buel, James William 106
Bull, Sarah 57
Burgan, Mary 96, 103, 109
Burke, William 115–16, 123
Burke and Hare Murders of 1828 115
burkers; burking 18, 114–16
Burney, Fanny 30–1
Burton, Brian J. 50,
Burton, Tim 15, 52–3
Butcher, Daisy 105,
'Byways of Literature' 92

C

Caffyn, William 37
Caleb Williams 34–5
cannibalism 15, 53, 61–2, 157
capitalism 15–16, 47, 49, 55–6, 59–62, 81, 83
Captain Hawke; or, May Boyes; and the Shadow of Death 209
Captain Manby 167
Cardinal Wiseman 192
Carlile, Thomas Paine 37–8, 40–1
carnivalesque 129
Carter, Robert Brudenell 139
casier sanitaire 96
Castles of Athlin and Dunbayne, The 30
Castle of Lindenberg, The; or The History of Raymond and Agnes, A Romance 29
Castle of Otranto, The 27, 29, 31, 34, 41, 68, 203
Castle Rackrent 33
Catholic Bishop of London 192

248

Index

Catholicism 19–20, 180–1, 185, 187, 189, 192, 196–7
Caxton, William 181–2, 199
Cecilia 30
Central Board of Health 94
Chadwick, Edwin 94, 133–4
Champion of Virtue, The 32
chapbook 2, 8, 11, 29, 34, 36–7, 180–1, 197
Charing Cross 196
Chartism 189
Chartist 5, 119–21, 123, 189, 192, 194–6, 213
Chartist Gothic 192, 195–6
Chase, Malcolm 42
Cheap Books Published by Milner & Sowerby, Pasternow Row, London 39
Children of the Abbey, The 32–3, 36, 38, 40–1
Cholera and Nation 95
cholera outbreak (1854) 95
'cholera outbreak' 17, 97–8, 118
Chowles, Anselm 129
Christianity 75, 107
'Christian' 106–7, 132, 149, 152, 192
Church 69–70, 72, 183–5, 187–8, 190–2, 196
Church of England 189, 192
circulation(s) 7, 17, 42, 91–3, 95, 97, 99, 102–4, 108–9
Civil War 189
Clark, Stuart 152
class boundaries 174, 177
class politics 166
Clements, John 34
Cockton, Henry 162, 170, 172
Cogan, Lucy 37
comedy; comic 129, 132, 163–8, 171, 175, 193
Comic History of England 193
comic violence 129, 165
conduct guides 137, 154
'Confession of the Flesh, The' 96
Connor, Steven 172
consent 58, 60

consumption 48, 52, 55, 58, 61–2, 93, 107, 109, 153
contagion 17, 91–5, 97, 99–103, 107–9, 127, 132
'contagious disease(s)' 93–5, 97–8, 101, 103
Contagious Diseases Act 94
contamination 17, 28, 91–4, 96–102, 104, 107–9
Cooper, James Fenimore 34
cordon sanitaire 96, 100
Corvey Project, The 32, 42
Cottage Library 39
Counter-Reformation 185
Cousins, Benjamin Davy 37
creationism 152
Criminal Law Amendment Act 60
criminality 2, 9–10, 91, 123, 125
Crone, Rosalind 7, 127, 152
Crossen, Carys 68
Crusades, The 183–4
Cumberland, Richard 181
Cunningham, John 36

D

D'Arste, Pietro 149, 151
dangerous influence 92
Darwin, Charles 140, 144, 155
Darwin, Erasmus 105–6
Davis, Jessica Milner 172
Days of May 117
Deerbrook 128, 130
degeneration 145, 151, 153, 155, 158
Del Principe, David 142–3
Demon of Sicily, The 37, 41
Descent of Man, The 140, 155
detective fiction 10, 92, 109
Diamond, Michael 192
Dick Turpin 163, 215
Dickens, Charles 3, 6, 52, 67–8, 78, 119, 169
Dicks, John 67, 193
dime novels 7
Dirt in Victorian Literature and Culture 98

249

Index

disease(s) 17–18, 91, 94–104, 117, 119, 127–32, 140
  see also outbreak(s)
disembodied voices 173
Dittmer, Nicole C. 8, 146, 148, 152
Dixon, William Hepworth 92
Doctor Calder 131
Doctor Hodges 129–30
Doctor Orthodox 132
Doctor Stanley 130
Donalda; or, the witches of Glenshiel 37, 41
Dr Lascelles 122
Dublin University Magazine 109
Dugdale, William 37
Dunae, Patrick 138
Duval, Claude 215
Dziemianowicz, Stefan 3, 9

E
East India Company 194
ecoGothic 138, 142–4, 148
economics 48–9
ecophobia 18, 106, 145
ecosemiotic(s) 18, 145, 141–2, 147–9
Edwin and Lucy; or the Happy Orphans 33
Elliott, H. R. 141
Ellis, Edward 200
Ellis, Sarah Stickney 138
Emans, William 33, 44
Emma 32
Empire 77–8, 94, 104–5, 194
Engels, Friedrich 68
English legal system 69, 78
English Novel, The 30,
environment 103, 138, 140–4, 146–52
epidemiology 94, 96
epigenetic 140
episode; episodic 9–10, 19, 69, 75, 161–2, 194, 205, 208
Eucharist 191
Euripedes 209
Evangelical 91, 191
Eve 149
Evelina 30

Evil Roots 105
execution 99, 162–3, 169–70, 177, 189, 205–6, 212
Expression of Emotions in Man and Animals, The 155

F
Fabulae 106
Faller, Lincoln B. 170
fantasy 10, 172, 205
farce 163–4, 169–70
farcical tropes 163, 166–7, 169–70, 172, 174–5, 177
Farmer of Inglewood Forest, The; or, an affecting portrait of virtue and vice 29, 32–3, 38, 40–1
Farr, E. W. 10
Father Georges 187
Fatherless Fanny 29, 33, 39–40, 42
Faust: A Romance 3, 65–7, 70–84
Faust: A Romance of the Secret Tribunals 16
Faustian pact 16, 76, 82
feedback loop 16, 18, 153
female reading habits 21, 80, 188
femininity 17, 138
fertility 104, 106
Fielding, Henry 162
fin de siècle 14, 22, 96, 109, 140, 153
first wave of the Gothic 6, 15, 27–8, 30, 33–4, 37–8, 41, 138, 152
Fisher, Mark 56
Fisher, Simon 29–30, 32–3, 36
'Fisher's Library of Modern Amusement' 29
Flanders, Judith 3
Fleet Street 15, 47, 50, 53, 61, 103, 190
flesh 53, 55, 58, 60–1, 79, 210
folklore 138
Forest and the EcoGothic, The 143
Forster's Education Act of 1870 48
Fothergill, T. 38
Foucault, Michel 93–4, 96
found manuscripts 20, 202–4, 207, 214, 217

250

Index

Frankenstein/*Frankenstein* 34, 120
Fraser, Robert 10
Friar Hildargo, The 37–8, 41
frightful maladies 97–8
Frost, Brian J. 75

G

Gamer, Michael 31, 183
Garden of Eden 106, 149
Garside, Peter 29, 32
Gasperini, Anna 7–8, 18, 115–16, 119–21, 123, 127, 144, 203
Geier, Ted 162
genre 1, 3–8, 11–12, 18–19, 28, 30, 32, 36, 105–6, 110, 143, 168, 185, 204
George II 196
Ghost Map 96
ghost(s) 22, 28, 173, 196–7, 208, 210–11, 215
Gilbert, Pamela K. 95, 127
Gleave, Joseph 33, 40, 44
Godwin, William 34
Goethe, Johann Wolfgang von 71–2, 75, 82, 86
Gothic ideology, 19, 180–1, 184–5, 190–1, 193, 196–7
Gothic Quest, The 5, 40–1
Gothic Revival, The 4, 21, 196
Gothic tourism 210
Götz von Berlichingen 72
Grant, Mary A. 106
grave-robbing 12–13, 120, 132
'grave robber(s)' 12
Great Famine, The 196
Greenwood, James 3, 97–100, 102, 104–7
Grey, Elizabeth 218
gynophobia 18, 138, 142, 144–5, 156

H

Hackenberg, Sara 74
Haining, Peter 48–50, 62
Halberstam, J. 93, 108

Halfpenny Marvel 102, 112
Hammer of Witches, The 145
Malleus Maleficarum 145
Handbook of the Gothic, The 92
Happy Orphans, The 33
Edwin and Lucy; or the Happy Orphans 33
Harmsworth, Alfred 101–2
haunting(s) 61, 210–11,
Haunted Horn, The 188
Hawkins, Caesar 194–5
Hawkins, Captain Hannibal 194–5
Hawkins, Vernon 194–5
Haywood, Ian 5
Hazlitt, William 36, 172,
Heiress, or, The mysteries of Brandon Abbey, The 12
Helme, Elizabeth 28–9, 31–3, 35, 38–42
Hemmens, Alfred Joseph Towers 37
Henry VIII 185, 188–9
Henry, Earl of Surrey 188
Hensman, Alice 188
Hensman, Ranulph 187–8, 199
Herr, Curt 185
Herringer, Carol Engelhardt 196
Hester, Marianne 144
Higden, Ranulph 199
hidden manuscript(s) 80
highwayman; highwaymen 2, 162–3, 166–8, 200, 207, 210, 215
History of Nicolas Pedrosa, The 181
Hodgson, John A. 172
Hoeveler, Diane Long 20, 69, 73, 180–1, 197, 203
Höing, Ania 139, 155
Horner, Avril 67–9, 78
horror 9, 47, 61–2, 65, 67, 75, 145–6, 157, 168, 170
House of Lords 174
Houston, Gail Turley 140–1
Hughes, James Fletcher 29, 33, 36–8, 41
Hughes, T. F. 10
Hughes, William 142
Hugo, Victor 68
humour 19, 131, 161–3, 167, 170–1, 174–5, 177

Index

Humpherys, Anne 68, 70, 74–5, 79, 81
Hyginus 106
hysteria 17, 138, 141, 143, 146, 156

I

imperialism 16, 98
Indian Revolt 193
indigenous 99–100, 112, 195
industrialisation 98
industry 21, 36, 38, 48–9, 92, 140, 142, 145, 190
infection 94, 100, 103, 117, 127, 130
inheritance of acquired characteristics 140–1
Inquisition, The 69–70, 72, 75–83, 87, 181
institution(s) 4, 16, 30, 51, 61, 78, 124, 133, 191–3
'Ireland's Ann Radcliffe' 31–3, 35–6, 38, 40–2
see also Regina Maria Roche
Italian, The 36, 39,
Italian Marauders, The 38

J

Jack Rann, Alias Sixteen-String Jack 19, 162–3, 165–7, 169–70, 177
James, Elizabeth 14
James, Louis 4, 92, 115, 120, 151
Jane Austen 32
Jane Eyre 1
Jane Brightwell 183
John of Trevisa 188, 199
Johnson, Claudia L. 31
Johnson, Steven 96, 99
Jonathan Wild 162
Jones, John Bush 52

K

Kantorowicz, Ernst 102
Kelly, Gary 202
Kelly, Thomas 33, 44

Killeen, Jarlath 1, 28, 67–8, 75, 81, 138, 161
King, Andrew 67–8, 180
King's Two Bodies 102
Kirkpatrick, Robert J. 44–5
Knapp, Andrew 200
Knight, Charles 101
Knight, Stephen 201
Knox, Robert 116, 123
Koch, Robert 109
Kramer, Heinrich 145
see also James Sprenger
Kreilkamp, Ivan 213

L

labour conditions 48, 50, 58, 81
Lady in Black, or, the Widow and the Wife, The 20, 190–1
Lamarck, Jean-Baptiste 16, 18, 140–1, 144, 146
Lancy, Edward 217
landscape(s) 6–7, 56, 105–6, 142–3, 150–1
language 5, 8, 16, 92, 107, 137, 166, 203
Lane, William 32, 37
Laycock, Thomas 16, 18, 140–2, 144, 146, 150, 156, 158
Leaves from the Note-books of a Queen's Messenger 204
Ledoux, Anne 31
Lee, Sophia 32
Leech, John 193
legitimacy 8, 72, 180
Leprince, Chloé 96
Lenin, Vladimir 15, 61
Les Mystères de l'Inquisition 66
Les Mystères de Paris 66
Lewis, Matthew 12, 29, 32, 34, 36–7, 68, 184
Lewton, Randall 59
Life and Adventures of Valentine Vox, The 162
Life in London, A 12
Lill, Sarah Louise 5

Index

Limbird, John 30–3, 35
Lindridge, James 19, 112, 162–3, 168–70
'Literature of the Lower Orders' 91
Literature of Vice, The 91
Lloyd, Edward 5, 8, 14, 37, 40, 42, 48, 130–1, 183–5, 188, 190–2, 197, 209
Lloyd's Entertaining Journal 185
Lloyd's Penny Weekly Miscellany 8, 183–4
Lloyd's People's Periodical and Family Library 190
Lodge, Mary Jo 57
London Journal, The 66–7, 70, 75, 79, 85–6
London Magazine 105–6
London Miscellany 196
Louisa; or, the Cottage on the Moor 38
Love and Crime 37–8
Lucretia, or the Poisoners 120
lycanthrope/lycanthropic/lycanthropy 16, 65, 75–6

M

Macbeth 147
Mack, Robert 7, 53
madness 155
madwoman 11
Mahawatte, Royce 145, 157
Making a Social Body 98, 111
malady; maladies 97–8, 122
Malleus Maleficarum, The 145
Malmaynes, Judith 120, 128–9
Malthusian 118, 128–9
Manchester 33, 98, 111, 114–15, 121
Manfroné, or the one-handed monk 36
manuscript(s) 19–20, 76, 78, 80, 188, 201–8, 210–17
  see also hidden and found manuscripts
Manuscripts from the Diary of a Physician 120, 204
'Mapping Contagion in Victorian London' 94
Maran, Timo 147–8
marginalisation 8, 17, 92, 94, 96, 204, 212, 215

Markham, Captain Weed 196–7
Marlowe, Christopher 71, 75, 82, 86
market 4–5, 7, 11–13, 15, 27, 30, 36, 48, 58, 92–3, 109, 130, 163, 215–16
Marryat, Frederick 1
Martineau, Harriet 128, 130
mass entertainment 93, 108
Maturin, Charles Robert 27
Maxwell, Richard C. 69, 78–80
Mayne, Fannie 91–2, 102, 108–9
McDowell, Stacey 9–10
McEvoy, Emma 210–11
McNally, David 62
McWilliam, Rohan 5, 192
'Meaters' 121
Medcraft, John 14
medical treatises 137, 140, 154
Melmoth the Wanderer 27
melodrama 2, 9–10, 20, 27–8
men-culture 139
Menzies, James Sutherland 76
Mephistopheles 71
metafiction 20, 206, 217
metamorphosis 65, 87
Merchant, Carolyn 139, 146, 150, 152, 157
miasma theory 95, 99
Mighall, Robert 6–7, 51, 180, 201
Millingen, John 156
Miller, Dean A. 59
Miller, Peter 38, 59
Miller, William Ian 52
Milner & Co. 38–41
Milner, William 34–5, 38–41
Millsap-Spears, Carey 57, 60
Milton, John 185
Minerva Press, The 32, 36
'Miss Whitehead, the Bank Nun' 190
Mollin, Alfred 54, 56, 60
monism 139, 144
Monk, The 29, 31, 36–7, 68, 184, 191
Monk. A tale of the Inquisition!, The 37
monomania 141, 156
monster 52, 58, 62, 68, 76, 92–4, 101, 103, 108, 133, 142–4, 146, 151

253

Index

monstrosity 8, 93, 139–40, 143–5
Monument, The 132
Montague, Edward 5, 37, 40
morality/immorality 2, 10, 56, 59, 65, 75, 83, 92, 95, 97–9, 101, 104, 107–8, 122, 169
Moruzi, Kristine 144
Motherwell Times 103
'Mrs Edgeworth' 33
Mr Hope 128
Mrs Lovett 47–8, 52–3, 55–8, 60–1, 121, 157
Mulvey-Roberts, Marie 92
murder 9, 12, 47, 50, 53–4, 56–8, 60–1, 73–4, 76, 80–1, 114–16, 118–22, 125–8, 131–3, 169, 173, 187–8, 190–1, 195, 214
musical 15, 50, 52–3, 58, 60
Mystery of Numbers 107
Mysteries of the Court of London, The 65
Mysteries of London, The 3, 5, 12, 16, 27, 65–70, 74, 78, 81, 84–5, 121–2, 125–7, 129, 131, 200–1
Mysteries of Udolpho, The 30, 33, 39
Mystery in Scarlet, A 20, 196

N

narrative forms 202
Nash, John 95
national identity 65, 67
(N)ature 3, 5, 13, 17–18, 28, 49, 53, 68, 92–3, 122, 137–53, 156, 162–3, 175, 188, 201–5, 207, 212, 214–15, 217
Neiman, Elizabeth 36
nervous fluid 141
Nesvet, Rebecca 14, 57, 79
Newgate: A Romance 13–14, 20–1
Newgate calendar 9, 27–8, 200–2
Newgate prison 74, 78, 99, 163, 167–9, 200–2, 217
Newman, Anthony King 32, 34, 36–7, 40
Newman, Cardinal John Henry 196
Nicholson and Sons 38

Night Adventurer, or the palaces and dungeons of the heart, The 13
Northern Typographical Union 49
Nöth, Winifred, 142
Novel Newspaper, The 34–8
Nuisance Removal 94, 190–1

O

O'Connor, Feargus 194
'Occidental Tourist' 105
OED 96, 101, 109
Offences Against the Person Act (1875) 60
Old English Baron, The 29, 31, 33–4, 41
Old Manor House, The 30, 40
Old St. Paul's 120, 128–32
Oliphant, Margaret 92
Oliver Twist 169
On the Mode of Communication of Cholera 95
ontology 139
oral storytelling 20, 202, 213–14, 216
Ordeal by Touch, The 20, 185–9, 197
'Order of Discourse' 93
Orientalist Gothic 195
Origin of Species, The 140, 155
Ortner, Sherry B. 155
outbreak(s) 17, 81, 94–8, 103, 111, 118
 see also diseases(s)
outlaws 9–10
Owen, Robert 175
'Ozymandias' 184

P

Paine's Popular Reprints of Novels 40–1
'Panther Bill' 97
Parke, Walter 109
Parker, Elizabeth 144, 150, 152, 157
parody 32
Pasteur, Louis 109
pastoral 187
Paternoster Row 39, 106
Patmore, Coventry 138

Index

Peirce, George 38
penny-issue novels 92
'penny packets of poison' 91, 102, 104, 107
Penny Satirist, The 37
Perilous Nature of the Penny Periodical Press 102
pernicious reading 2, 4, 17, 92, 101–2, 104, 137, 205
Peterloo 189
Phantom Ship, The 1
Philosophie zoologique 141
physiology 109
'Physiology of Penny Awfuls' 109
Piatti-Farnell, Lorna 55
Picaresque 19, 33, 162–3, 167, 176
picaro 162
Pickwick Papers, The 119
Pilot, The 34
Pitt, George Dibdin 50, 53, 55
Pittard, Christopher 91, 109
plague(s) 91, 97–101, 104, 106–7, 120, 126–32, 157
plagiarism 6, 21, 40, 130, 137, 139, 162, 170, 181, 203
Pliny, the Elder 209
Plowden, Edmund 102
poison 11, 17, 73, 78, 92–4, 100–2, 104–7, 117, 119–20, 128, 131
politics of humour 163
Polychronicon 199
polyphony 20, 202, 212
Poor Law (1843) 94, 115, 118, 124–5, 128
Poovey, Mary 98, 134
pornography 37, 70
Porter, Jane 40
Portwine, Timothy 178
    see also Thomas Peckett Prest
Potter, Franz J. 11, 29, 38, 180
Pratt, John Slater 38, 40
Prest, Thomas Peckett 4, 14, 19–20, 40, 42, 120, 130–2, 162, 170, 172, 174–5
    see also Timothy Portwine
Price One Penny 15, 27–8, 45

Priest, Hannah 3, 68
printing press 48, 207, 213
prison(s) 20, 69, 74, 78, 81, 124–5, 167, 177, 191, 200, 202, 204, 217
propaganda 69, 180
Protestantism 69, 180–3, 185, 187–9, 191–2, 197, 199
proto-Gothic 188
Proust, Doctor Adrien 96
public health 16, 94, 96–7, 117, 127, 132–4
    Public Health Act (1848) 16, 94, 133
Pulp 67–8, 85, 138
Punter, David 11
Purkess, George 37
Purkess, Henry Hemmens 37
Purity and Contamination 91, 109
Pythagoras 150

Q

quest romance(s) 10–11

R

Radcliffe, Ann 12, 28–36, 38–9, 41, 184
'Radcliffe, Mary Anne' 36
Raine, Sophie 67, 81
Rann, Jack/John 19, 162–3, 165–70, 177
Raymond and Agnes; or, The Bleeding Nun 29, 36
readership 2, 4, 7, 12, 17–19, 66, 70, 93, 98, 109, 177, 180, 213
    see also audience
Recess, The, or, A Tale of Other Times 32
'Red Library' 34, 39–40
'Red and Blue Library' 34, 39
Rede, William Leman 163, 168
reductionism 58, 60, 140
Reeve, Clara 29, 31–4, 41, 36
Reeves, John K. 33
reflex theory 138, 141
Reformation, The 181, 185–90, 196
Regency 181

Index

Regent Street 95
Reis, Elizabeth 145, 157
religion 19, 72, 82, 106–7, 144, 180–1, 184, 189–97
repetition 19, 162, 171, 173
reprint(s) 15, 27–42, 209
Report on the Sanitary Conditions of the Labouring Population of Great Britain 94
reproduction 15, 139–42, 146, 153, 155–6
resurrectionists 18, 37, 115–16, 122, 123–5, 127, 188, 196, 213
'Resurrection Man' 122, 124–5, 127, 74, 82
 see also Anthony Tidkins
Reynolds, George William MacArthur 3–6, 12, 16–17, 27, 65–86, 88, 121–4, 130–1, 157, 192–5, 197, 200–1, 213
Reynolds's Miscellany 66, 70, 85, 192–3
Rezek, Joseph 34
rhetorical devices 94
Richard I 184
Ritchie, Leitch 76
rituals 58, 76, 117, 187
Robert, Francis 39
Robin Hood 9, 165
Robinson Crusoe 9
Roche, Regina Maria 31–3, 35–6, 38, 40–2
 see also 'Ireland's Ann Radcliffe'
Rogers, Deborah D. 28
romance(s) 6, 10–11, 28, 32, 35, 38, 40–1, 43, 67–70, 72, 78, 80–1, 87, 162, 183–5, 187–8, 196, 203–4, 211, 214–15
Romanticism; Romantic 11, 31, 34, 55, 73, 93, 180, 186, 194, 197, 210–11, 217
Romance of the Forest, The 30, 32, 39
Romancist, The 34–8
Ross, Kathryn 40
Rosser, Austin 53
Ruskin, John 139

Ruth the Betrayer 200
Rymer, James Malcolm 3–4, 7, 12–14, 16–17, 19–20, 27, 47–9, 53, 120, 152, 157, 181, 183–5, 187–91, 193–7, 201–7, 209, 211–17
Rymer, Malcolm 181–2
Rymer, Gaven 182–3, 198

S

Sadleir, Michael 34–5
Sahib, Nana 195
Sala, George Augustus 14
Sallust 209
sanitary conditions 94
'Sanitary Consolidation' 103
Satan 71, 73, 76, 79, 82
Sawyer, Bob 119
Schimmel, Annemarie 107
Schmid, Susanne 163
Schulte, Rolf 76
Schülting, Sabine 98
Scotland 114, 137, 145
Scott, Sir Walter 30–2, 35, 37, 41, 72, 183
Scottish Chiefs, The 40
Scottish Witchcraft Act (1563) 138
Sea and Land 105
secularisation 72
sensationalism 2, 6, 70
Sepoys, or, Highland Jessie: A Tale of the Present Indian Revolt, The 20, 193–6
serial fiction 1–5, 8–9, 11–17, 19–21, 28–9, 31, 50, 65–7, 69–71, 84, 121, 130, 138–40, 158, 162–3, 183, 185, 190, 193–6, 201, 203, 207, 209, 212–13, 218
Seven Curses of London 97, 107
Severs, Dennis 210–11
Shakespeare, William 105, 147
Shakespearean witches 105
Shannon, Mary L. 5, 213
Shea, Victor 2, 3, 7, 10
Shelley, Mary 34

256

Index

Shelley, Percy Bysshe 184
Sheppard, Jack 163
shilling shocker 11
Shoemaker, Robert B. 168
'Short Way to Newgate, A' 99
Showalter, Elaine 153
Sir John 163, 168, 209
Sixteen-String Jack 19, 162–3, 167, 178
Skin Shows 93
Skultans, Vieda 141
Smith, Adam 49–50
Smith, Andrew 142–3
Smith, Allan Lloyd 143
Smith, Charlotte 30–2, 40
Smith, Helen R. 6, 13–14, 204, 218
Smith, Michelle J. 144
Snow, Doctor John 95
Socialists 19, 174–7
Society for the Diffusion of Useful Knowledge 109
Sondheim, Stephen 15, 47, 50–8, 60–2
Southey, Robert 195
Southwell, Robert 196
Sowerby, John Edwin 39
Spaniard, or, the Pride of Birth, The 181, 197
Species 108, 141–3, 147–8
Splatter Capital 62
Sprenger, James 145
   see also Heinrich Kramer
Springhall, John 2–3, 98, 101
Spring-heel'd Jack, The Terror of London 3
St Clair, William 28
St Clair of the Isles 28–9, 32–3, 38, 40
St Dunstan's Church 127, 190
St Leon 34
Stereotype 11, 146, 163, 190
Steven, Mark 47, 55, 61–2
'Story of the Crusades' 183
Straight, Sheryl 37, 45
String of Pearls, The 3, 7, 12, 14–16, 20, 27, 47–56, 58, 60–2, 121, 127–8, 152, 157, 190–1, 194
String of Pearls, or, the Sailor's Gift, The 190
String of Pearls, or, the Barber of Fleet-Street, a Domestic Romance, The 190

Student, The: A Magazine of Theology, Literature, and Science 106
subterranean space(s) 71, 74, 81, 86, 123, 202, 217
Sue, Eugène 12, 66–7, 69
Summers, Montague 5–6, 40–2
Summerscale, Kate 103
supernatural 1, 5, 9, 68, 142–3, 145–7, 151, 214
Sweeney Todd the Barber 50, 53
Sweeney Todd: The Demon Barber of Fleet Street 15, 48, 50, 53
Sweeney Todd Shock 'n' Roll Show, The 53, 59
Swing Riots of 1830 117

T

Tales of my Landlady 37
'tales of terror' 152
Tales of Wonder 31
Tempest, The 147
Thackeray, William Makepeace 40, 52, 86, 169
Thalaba the Destroyer 195
theatre 114–15
theology 20, 149, 184, 192
Third Chartist Petition 192
Thomas Richardson and Son 38
Thomas, Trefor 12
Thompson, Charles and William 33
Thornley, Herbert 12
Tidkins, Anthony 74, 82
   see also 'Resurrection Man'
Todd, Sweeney 7, 47, 53, 56, 62, 121, 127, 181, 190
Topham, Jonathan 30
torture 62, 69–70, 75–6, 79, 82–3, 161, 164, 181
Tractarians 196
transgression 57, 108, 138, 141, 143–4
trauma 61, 76, 82, 126, 132
Treatise on the Nervous Diseases of Women, The 140
Tribunal 16, 71–3, 79

Index

True Briton, The 91
Tudor era 187–9
Turner, E. S. 4, 50, 55
Turpin, Dick 54, 61, 163, 215
Tyburn 99
Tyburn Tree: Or, The Mysteries of the Past 98–9

U

University of Bristol 40
urban fiction 68
urban Gothic 7, 51, 215
urban mysteries 12, 67, 81
urban planning 94
urbanisation 98, 103
upas 104–6
'useful knowledge' 92, 110

V

Valentine Vaux 19, 161–2, 166–7, 170–1, 174, 177
vampire 11, 47, 127
Vanity Fair 40, 86
Varney, the Vampire 3, 27, 120
Vasconcelos, Sandra Guardini T. 40
Vathek 34, 195
vault(s) 127, 202, 204–5, 208, 210, 217
'Vegetable Monsters' 106
Vehmgericht 72–3, 78–9, 86
Vehmic courts 72
Ventriloquism 162, 170–3
Vickers, George 37, 131
Victorian Gothic, The 67–8, 138
Victorian horror fiction 67
villains 1, 5, 9–11, 120–3, 126, 130–1, 133, 138, 147, 151, 153, 190, 195
violence 2, 7, 10, 19, 53, 56, 65–6, 68, 72, 123–4, 138–9, 150–2, 161–2, 165–6, 172, 176–7, 184, 195
Virtue, George 33, 40, 44
Viscount Dunbardon 147, 151, 153
Vitriol Bob 124
Voltmer, Rita 76, 87

W, Y

Wagner, the Wehr-Wolf 3, 16, 65–9, 74–7, 83–5, 157
Wahrman, Dror 168
Walker, J. 31
Walpole, Horace 27, 29, 31–3, 36, 41, 68, 203
Ward, Frederick Oldfield 103
Watson, Sharon 42
Waugh, Patricia 206–7
Weller, Sam 119
Weltman, Sharon 52, 58, 60–1
werewolf; werewolves 11, 16, 47, 67–8, 74–6, 79–80, 84–5, 87
Whigs 187, 190
White, William Job 37
Whitehead, Reverend Henry 95, 190
Wicks, Ulrich 162, 167
Wicked Boy 150
Wide, Wide World Library, The 39
Wieland; or, The Transformation 172–3
Wild Boys of London; or, the Children of Night, The 13, 200
Wild Witch of the Heath, The 18, 138, 146–8, 153
wilderness 92, 147, 150
William Tell, the Hero of Switzerland 38
Wilmot, Marianna 217
Winslow, Forbes 140, 156
witch; witchcraft 17–18, 76, 87, 105, 138–9, 141–57
witchcraft treatises 76
Wizard 18, 137–8, 142–54
womanhood 18, 58, 139, 188
women-nature 139–40, 150–1
working-class 1–3, 5, 7–10, 20–1, 48, 57, 62, 80–1, 96, 120, 126, 131, 133, 166, 170, 177, 182, 202, 212, 215, 217
WorldCat 32
Wroot, Herbert E. 41
Wuthering Heights 1

Young Adult Gothic Fiction 144
Young, Mary Julia 37